PRAISE FOR *MEDI(*

"A twenty-five-year-old former consultant walks into a monastery in a forest in Thailand carrying delusions of spiritual grandeur, unspeakable grief, and a diary where he relentlessly logs his 'extraction of insight.' Fortunately, among his first lessons [he learns] a sense of humor is considered, by many senior monks, to be 'the single most important virtue.' Grant Lindsley's bildungsroman about his six months of monastic life is as funny as it is self-lacerating and perceptive, bringing a classic story—the pursuit of 'certainty, a calling, a mission I never doubted,' as Lindsley puts it—into the present day. I loved—and to a slightly uncomfortable degree related to—this book." —Charles Bethea, staff writer at the *New Yorker*

"If you start reading this book, you are very likely to finish it. If you like rolling your eyes at earnest autobiographies, you won't get much chance to do that here. You will smile a lot, and probably laugh. And you'll come to understand and appreciate what a stealth insight looks like: the small 'OK, got it, moving on' followed, hours later, by the 'Ohhhh, OK.' Read the first page; you'll see." —Allan Filipowicz, clinical professor of management and organizations at Cornell University's Samuel Curtis Johnson Graduate School of Management

"Honest and intimate, Lindsley's arresting account of his time in the forests of Thailand speaks to struggles at once deeply personal yet universal: love, grief, desire, self-doubt, and the ever-urgent question of how to live this one precious life." —Megan Molteni, STAT

"Grant Lindsley's *Mediocre Monk* is a page-turning true story of [a] spiritual quest as riveting and thought-provoking as any you will ever read. It is funny and serious and searching and heartbreaking and unforgettable in every way, with crisp prose and a voice that rings out from the darkness of human misunderstanding and tries its level best to brighten the path for us. Lindsley has created *The Razor's Edge* for our time in *Mediocre Monk*, a work of great intelligence, honesty, humility, and literary value, and it will change your life as much as Lindsley's experiences in Thailand have changed him." —Mike Magnuson, author of *Lummox: The Evolution of a Man*

"Brimming with self-deprecating humor and understated insight, *Mediocre Monk* is an immensely readable story about the most important challenge we all face: how to live in our minds and with each other. Lindsley's writing is sharp, and his curiosity is infectious." —Maya Dusenbery, author of *Doing Harm: The Truth About How Bad Medicine and Lazy Science Leave Women Dismissed, Misdiagnosed, and Sick*

"Grant Lindsley's lived a life unlike anyone I know, but while reading this book, I couldn't help see[ing] myself in his story. There are lessons here for anyone who's searched for answers within and found connection with others. Plus, it's very funny. I'm glad Lindsley's vow of silence is over and he's chosen to share this with us." —Jody Avirgan, *30 for 30*, "Good Sport" (TED), *FiveThirtyEight*

"*Mediocre Monk* is a brutally honest and self-aware telling of a story familiar to us all: the shock of an unexpected loss, a search for meaning in its wake, and the wanting of validation from your peers. Lindsley knows who he is, and his memoir knows what it should be. It's a fascinating look behind the curtain of Buddhism in far-off places many of us will never traverse, viewed with the critical eye of a millennial Westerner. But it's also a funny, self-deprecating mockery of who Lindsley thought he was as a young man and an honest reckoning of what you can learn from months in solitary meditation." —Isaac Saul, founder of *Tangle News*

"It doesn't seem fair that a world-class athlete can also be such a gifted writer, but Grant Lindsley's extraordinary story is simultaneously gripping and masterfully crafted. In his painfully personal journey, you'll feel transported into the mysterious world of a remote monastery, a place that seems both beautiful and excruciating. An enjoyable and thought-provoking read, *Mediocre Monk* is powerful, fascinating, and deeply honest." —Evan Lepler, ESPN

"Grant Lindsley's must-read book, *Mediocre Monk*, isn't just a humorous, honest tale about his quest for enlightenment. Lindsley learns to see himself in everyone from hard-core monks to those who embrace the materialistic world he leaves behind. Most importantly, Lindsley's fabulous book serves as a mirror through which you can see yourself." —Andrew Hallam, international bestselling author of *Balance* and *Millionaire Teacher*

MEDIOCRE
MONK

MEDIOCRE
MONK

*A Stumbling Search for Answers
in a Forest Monastery*

GRANT LINDSLEY

GIRL FRIDAY BOOKS

 GIRL FRIDAY BOOKS

Published by Girl Friday Books™, Seattle
www.girlfridaybooks.com

Produced by Girl Friday Productions

Cover design: Pablo Rochat
Production editorial: Katherine Richards
Project management: Sara Addicott

ISBN (paperback): 978-1-954854-98-7
ISBN (ebook): 978-1-954854-99-4

Library of Congress Control Number: 2022946625

First edition

For James, Pax, and Goodgame

CONTENTS

Leaf 1
Cinnabon 17
Vacation 27
Diplomat 42
Gecko 62
Poo Jom Gom 85
Chill 117
Sauna 136
Cave 151
Zen 168
Viper 178
LinkedIn .191
U-Turn 209

Epilogue 221
Acknowledgments 225
About the Author 229

LEAF

We eyed each other from across the airport tram. For two people in Bangkok, we had a lot in common: white, early twenties, backpacks with hip straps. It would be easy to talk to her.

Ever since my first visit to a monastery, I'd made a habit of waxing poetic to pretty women about mindfulness. Maybe I'd start by asking if she had ever meditated. When she finished talking, I'd wait for her to return the question.

"Actually," I might yell over the bar music, "I spent a month in a remote forest monastery once . . . eight-day silent retreat, one meal a day, the whole thing. Yeah . . . I know, kinda wild, right?"

Sometimes it would work, meaning the pretty woman would sleep with me, or at least make out on the dance floor, or at least think I was *complex* and *psychological*. Other times it would backfire. She'd light up and shout back, "Oh my God, have you read *Eat Pray Love*?"

I'd grit my teeth. "Yeah! Well, no—I mean, parts of it. I know the story, at least. Anyway, what I did was *way* more intense."

The tram wobbled around a turn. The blonde backpacker and I steadied ourselves on a yellow handrail overhead. We both looked up. Our eyes connected.

I jerked my head away, trying to look intrigued by the view out the window, even though there wasn't one. It was dark, and I was tired of reciting my sensitive-guy guru script. It went nowhere. Or in circles. In the three years following that month-long first foray into monastic life,

I'd been genuinely disappointed to discover that talking about meditation yielded none of the benefits of practicing it, no matter how attractive my listener. That was partly why I was going back to monastic
life now—to return to practice, to escape my insufferable impulse to
preach.

And this time, I was going big: venturing into the heart of the Thai
Forest Tradition, home of the strictest Buddhist monks in the world. I
hadn't requested a couple of measly weeks of PTO for this trip. No, I'd
quit my fancy health-care consulting job outright. I'd booked a one-
way flight. No return for at least half a year. Maybe no return at all. I'd
shunned romance, moved out of my apartment, cut ties with civilization. I repeated that phrase often in my head, *cut ties with civilization*.
It felt glorious. Staring at my reflection in the tram window, I drew in a
long breath and offered small nods of approval.

The tram banked around another bend. I glanced at the backpacker. She was looking right at me.

"Hey," she said.

I swallowed. "Hey."

"Where you from?"

"Uh, Minnesota. You?"

"Alabama. Here for ten days to meet some girlfriends in Phuket,
take cooking classes. What about you?"

"Um." I hesitated. "I'll be here a few months."

She raised her eyebrows.

I realized I'd have to say more. "I'm heading to a monastery . . .
out in the . . . eastern part." I spoke cautiously, for I could feel my old
mating call, Mindful Man on a Grand Adventure, rising in my throat
like the jingle of a TV ad, perpetually promoting the product of *Me*.
I'd already undersold the length of my trip to downplay her interest. It
hadn't worked. Her eyebrows remained lifted like invitations.

Had I paused at that moment to notice what transpired in my own
body, I might've registered a small flare of pride in my chest, an impulse
to glance back at my reflection with a smoldering look that said, "Still
got it." I might've also glimpsed the conflict between my urge to dwell
in total supreme solitude and my need to be *seen* and *lauded* as such
a person. But I didn't pause, and it never occurred to me that I didn't
actually want to temper her curiosity at all, that in fact, I sought the

pleasure of feeling modest *and* the conceit from her interest. Restraint felt good. Attention felt better. I wanted both.

In ditching one script, I'd unwittingly picked up another. This new one congratulated me for being exhausted with my old self. It claimed my ego was already in the process of rapid dissolution thanks to this adventure—and by virtue of grief. See, a young friend had died in a car accident earlier that year. Drinking and sex and professional prestige— three of the most important things to me—had all lost their allure. I mistook the ensuing numbness for an accelerated transcendence of all earthly pleasure. It was in this period of grieving that I'd quit my job and cut my ties and flown halfway around the world to get away from everyone and everything I felt was holding me back. Grief and adventure, I was certain, were transforming me into a venerable sage before I'd even shaved my head and donned robes.

The girl's expression had lowered into confusion. I realized I had drifted off in thought.

I stammered, "You know, um, I actually grew up in Atlanta. It's nice to hear a southern accent all the way out here."

We got off the tram and walked toward a line of waiting taxis, agreeing on the importance of the word *y'all*.

She opened the back door of a cab at the front of the line. Then she paused at the curb, turned, and looked back at me as if she had something to say.

The street was quiet. Past midnight. I held my breath. I knew what came next. I had spent the whole walk from the tram to the cabs fearing this moment.

She was going to invite me in. And if I accepted, we would hook up. And if that happened, I'd feel like I was betraying another woman, a woman named MJ, whom I'd met over a weekend in New York a few months earlier. See, even though I'd shunned romance after the car accident, and even though I was about to take an oath of celibacy for six months, if not the rest of my life, I had still, well, fallen completely in love.

MJ and I had video-chatted every day for weeks. I'd visited her for another weekend right before I left. We'd gone to *Les Mis* on Broadway and held hands—both pairs of hands—the entire show. The day before my flight to Thailand, I'd mailed her a box containing six letters sealed in individual envelopes, labeled for each of the months I knew I'd be off the grid. If I stayed longer or ordained, I had recorded her address in a diary buried in my backpack so that I could write to her again from the monastery. In my final moments of phone service, I'd called her from my gate at the Dallas/Fort Worth International Airport and told her I loved her. Which, in the moment, felt courageous and liberated on my part. It didn't occur to me that professing my love on my way out of the country may have in fact been cowardly, offering such a connection while simultaneously severing it.

For MJ's part, she had simply chuckled and replied, "I was afraid you were going to say that." We had already agreed we wouldn't commit to each other. She wasn't going to wait for me, and I wasn't sure I was ever coming back.

In other words, I was single. Still, some small part of me understood that sleeping with a stranger after saying I loved someone else a mere twenty-six hours earlier would make it difficult to maintain my self-image as a precocious spiritual practitioner. It would feel disloyal—to MJ and to myself. I'd come to Thailand for cross-legged contemplation in the forest, not canoodling in the back of a cab in Bangkok.

And yet I hesitated. Flat-footed on the curb, I gaped at her, listening for once. If pressed to explain my stupor, I might've claimed I was doing something vaguely Buddhist-y, like *impartially observing the situation* or *letting things be as they were*. I couldn't see the trap I'd laid for myself, alternately craving austerity and indulgence, unable to see why neither one worked. Nor could I see that if I couldn't have both, then I wanted someone else to choose for me.

"Well," she said, "have a good trip. Sounds kinda crazy."

She ducked and closed the door behind her. The cab drove off and disappeared into the night.

I shook my head and scoffed at myself. Her invitation had seemed so inevitable that I'd skipped ahead to fearing I would accept it. This was exactly why I needed the severe isolation of the wilderness, I thought. I didn't trust myself. I was the type of person who was drawn to extremes. Extremes made me feel like a warrior, which was great when so much had come easily in my life—praise, stability, exceptions. Maybe too easily. I'd become slippery. A weasel, close friends joked.

An imp, my father warned. They were right, and I knew it, but I still couldn't help it. That was why I was diving into the most intense monastic tradition I could find on planet Earth—because extremes also held me accountable. I needed from the outside what I couldn't muster from within: discipline, insight, and self-reliance, all of which I thought I had gained the *first* time I went to a monastery. But they'd worn off. I had come to Thailand to get them back, to shove myself once and for all into enlightenment.

Clearly, I wasn't there yet. I sighed and turned toward the second taxi in line.

From the back seat, I asked how much it would cost to get to the Bangkok bus station.

"Five hundred bucks," he said.

I laughed out loud. A joke the driver probably told every American tourist.

"OK, OK, three hundred," he said.

I realized he wasn't saying *bucks* but *baht*, the Thai currency. I'd accidentally bargained.

We skimmed through a dark, wet city. After a while, the driver pulled over beneath a pedestrian bridge. He turned back to me, pointed up, and held out his hand for payment. I'd have to walk from here.

On top of the bridge were gray puddles, exposed rods of rebar, and a view of a building the size of a stadium. The bus terminal. On the other side of the freeway, I ducked between canvas tents on metal stilts with greasy stoves and men seated on plastic crates. I crossed a parking lot and entered the terminal, a single cavernous room. Small ticket windows lined the walls, which were painted pink and lime green and smattered with dense, curly Thai text. Zero English.

I walked the perimeter, searching for a red-eye trip east. But every ticket window was empty. I tried not to groan. I'd have to sleep in the station. Aluminum chairs littered the center. I lined up four and lay across them. Overhead, industrial-strength floodlights hung from rafters and buzzed like the drill of a dentist. I draped one arm over my eyes and looped the other through a backpack strap and tried to sleep.

In the morning, I relocated to a wall of tall windows on the far side of the station. The street below bustled in the blue light of dawn. Parked buses grumbled and lifted to life. Pedestrians jostled through an intersection. Moto drivers waddled on their small bikes through foot traffic, dangling plastic bags from either end of their handlebars. Short honks. Black hair. Greetings in cheerful tones. A flash of orange in the crowd.

A monk! I leaned forward to get a closer look. But then, upon closer inspection, I slumped.

This was not a *forest* monk. His robes were not deep ocher—not dyed in the traditional method of stirring cloth in a boiling cauldron filled with woodchips from the jackfruit tree. No, his was a robe one might find at a big-box store—mass-produced, starchy material; garish color. He flailed his legs carelessly ahead of him. He smoked a cigarette.

This was a city monk. An imposter monk, I thought, pursing my lips, not a disciplined jungle dweller like the ones I would study under, like the one I hoped to become.

I turned from the street view to find my ride. Without Wi-Fi or English, all I could do was visit ticket windows one by one and repeat the name of the region I was headed to, Ubon Ratchathani, a rural province tucked in the far corner of northeast Thailand on the border of Laos.

Eventually, I found a bus and climbed aboard and settled into a seat near the front. I assumed, with no concrete information, that the trip east would last around five hours—a solid chunk to get some real sleep.

I reached under the armrest for a button to recline. Nothing. I patted along the edges of the suede seat but found only a sticky residue that remained on my hands. No button. No lever. No exit row with extra legroom. My knees pressed against the back of the plastic seat ahead of me. I'm not large. I'm a lean 5'10" guy who quit basketball in junior high because the sleeveless jerseys revealed the horrific fact that my elbows were the biggest part of my skinny arms.

In this bus, though, I felt like a giant. My breathing grew short. We sped down a highway pointing directly into the rising sun. No tint in the windows. No shades to pull for relief from the glare. Within twenty minutes, I was sweating like a pack of ham in a VCR. I tried resting my head on the window, but my skull vibrated against the glass. Strip malls lined the road. Behind them, flat, sun-bleached grasslands stretched toward a horizon blurred by heat.

This irritated me. Dry fields were not the misty mountains I had envisioned. I prayed for civilization to dissipate. Two hours later, though, we were still in the suburbs. I noticed an outlet store with an English sign in all caps: "TIMBERLAND." Later, we passed the entrance to a golf course with a brick-wall entrance and a sign that read, "PINEHURST."

That was it. I couldn't look out the window anymore. Fuming, I turned my attention back inside the bus. A small TV hung above the aisle. As if it had heard my thoughts, it fritzed on.

A commercial played. The volume was so loud as to seem accidental, but I checked my attitude. Maybe this ad was an *opportunity*. A chance to pick up some Thai. A cultural learning experience, perhaps. The ad showed a young guy with a gelled bouffant hosting a block party. He grinned and yelled and thrust something toward the camera—a pack of mints? A SIM card? I couldn't tell.

The ad ended, then started over from the beginning. A little annoying, but hey, I thought, a second chance to pick up some vocab.

Still, I could not decipher a single word or even where words began or ended. I took a breath, pushing away the creeping thought that it might've been wise to learn some Thai before moving to Thailand. Instead, I'd spent the months leading up to this trip telling myself *immersion was the best classroom.* That was my advice—unsolicited—to other travelers, too, as if the single summer I'd spent as a high schooler binge-drinking in Madrid had minted me an expert in language acquisition. That was also my approach to meditation. Rather than slowly building a meditation practice over the previous months, I'd gotten stoned and read books and fantasized about meditating in the woods. I trusted the magic of immersion, the power of the extreme.

The ad drew to a close. My shoulders softened. I decided it was fine that I hadn't learned any Thai. After all, I would dwell mostly in solitary sylvan silence. Maybe I wouldn't need Thai. Maybe I wouldn't need any language—English, even—ever again.

When the ad began playing for the third time in a row, I straightened and sought the gaze of fellow passengers. All appeared twenty years older and twelve inches shorter than me, and none seemed to notice or care about the unfolding travesty.

I still couldn't figure out what the ad was even peddling, so I directed my anger at the producers. They should've known to commu-nicate the core message visually, without sound, because didn't they know people mute commercials? In our living room growing up, my dad would hover his trigger finger over the mute button with a sniper's focus, and I'd come to appreciate the quiet breaks. But I was too shy to stand up and ask how to turn the volume down. I didn't want to be *that* American tourist. It didn't occur to me that, having landed in Thailand with no language preparation whatsoever, no address for the rural monastery where I planned to live, yet total confidence that it would all work out, I already was that American tourist.

More than that, trying to mute the TV would amount to an ad-mission that it bothered me, which in my mind indicated a failure of spiritual strength. I was on a mission to train myself to withstand any-thing. Besides, I thought, the ad was almost over. After three times, some show was sure to resume. I let out a simmering exhale and tried to think a good Buddhist thought. *Just let it be. Let the ad be.*

When it played again, I turned my ire upon the story. It was unre-alistic! No teenagers would dance with such abandon unless they were wasted! The fifth time the ad played, it dawned on me: creating the ad must have been worse than viewing it. The main actor with the gelled hair must have bared his teeth in that desperate smile shape through dozens of takes. By the seventh repetition of the commercial, I grew sympathetic to the young man. I pictured him at home, practicing his smiles in front of a mirror. Maybe he would shut his bathroom door like I had done, listening for the creak of approaching footsteps from my parents or sister, rehearsing a whole suite of suave expressions and clever lines in a whisper only I could hear. As I remembered this, the actor suddenly disgusted me again, and I crumpled into a kind of full-body pout in my undersize seat.

The ad played again, and soon I lost count.

Samsara. The word popped into my head—the Buddhist idea of life as an endless cycle of wanting, getting, and wanting more. This ad was a *metaphor*, I realized, for the endless cycle of pursuing shallow pleasure. That was it! The ad might have been on a samsaric loop, but I didn't have to be.

I sat up and smiled and nodded. *I get it! Lesson learned, universe! We can get on with the show now, thanks!*

But there was no show. Only this ad. Over the first hour of repetition, I initially tried to adopt the ear of an anthropologist, straining to glean insight into cultural norms or unique Southeast Asian advertising practices. Something. Anything. Cinematography. Soundtrack. But the frenetic pace and nasal tones precluded such study. In fact, I was horrified to register a budding aversion to the sound of the Thai language.

Next, I began limiting my focus, on each repetition, to single parts of the main actor's face. In isolation, his mouth opened and shut like a machine, revealing rows of straight white stones that, to my eyes, betrayed some deeper truth—underneath all the enthusiasm of the actor's face was a sphere of bone with open sockets and a fixed grimace that would long outlast the flesh.

On the next run-through, I zeroed in on his eyes. They looked desperate. I felt I could see behind the scenes. I imagined his story. He was about my age, twenty-five. He'd shouted his way through this script fifteen times that day. The muscles of his mouth were sore. Perhaps professionally feigning excitement had begun to inspire a brooding skepticism of joy itself. That had been my experience as a consultant, at least. Perhaps he'd been complimented all his life and encouraged to become what he'd become. Boy wonder. He'd grown to like the idea of a lead part with the cameras rolling. And now his bright eyes cried for help, trapped inside his beaming face. He'd gotten exactly what he thought he wanted. He didn't know what else to do.

Six hours later, the bus groaned onto the road shoulder and exhaled into dust under the midday sun. Passengers rose and filed into the aisle, leaving their bags behind. We'd been on the road an hour longer than I expected, but I still saw nothing but dry grassland in every direction. I rose and approached the driver and said, "Is this . . . ?"

He made quick small bows and said in English, "Half."

I gaped. "Half . . . halfway?"

He nodded and grinned and bowed some more.

I melted. Hobbled down the stairs. Squinted in the shrieking sun. Looked both ways and crossed toward a gravel lot, where a lone cinder-block structure stood crumbling by the roadside. From a few open windows, the other passengers took trays of food.

These lunches looked nothing like the dishes I thought I knew from Thai restaurants in the US. These had bird feet, gristle, tufts of hair. In theory, I craved cultural immersion. I fancied myself as one who would relish the novelty of every unknown dish. Maybe I'd banter with the cooks, and they would take a liking to me and share a couple of anecdotes of their family histories through the lens of food, and we'd all part ways feeling as if we'd briefly grasped some paradox about how the world was both so big and so small, or how we were all at once so different and yet the same. Basically, I wished I was the host of a cooking show, which I wouldn't have admitted because it felt uncool and like cultural appropriation—and because I couldn't bring myself to be adventurous in practice.

Alone, disgusted with my fantasies and my inability to act on them, I ate white rice off a disposable plate and took in the dreary scene before me. Clouds of flies hovered above emaciated feral cats that slept as flat as puddles in scant spots of shade. I brushed flies from my own face, put the plate aside, and lowered my head to my knees.

This was nothing like my first trip to a monastery three years ago. I'd been personally greeted at the airport in Auckland, New Zealand, by the head monk himself. His nephew had come along—because monks aren't allowed to drive—and we'd cruised through rolling hills of green farmland and pine forest until arriving at a bucolic hermitage, one of the many branches of the Thai Forest Tradition that had spread around the world since the 1990s. The head monk had escorted me down a grassy path to my own private lodging—a rustic 8'-by-10' hut with cedar shakes that smelled inside of sandalwood.

Instead, I was now bent over at a bus stop, covered in sweat and dust, getting a sunburn. When I heard the bus wheeze to life, I was the first back on board.

Over the next six hours, I slid into a clammy, claustrophobic fog. The commercial resumed on the small TV. The sun eventually gave up and left us in darkness. I slouched into the mark of a question and, for a moment, began to wonder what the hell I was doing here. But I pushed the thought away. I *had* to be here. This was what I wanted. I didn't know what else to do.

Finally, the bus halted. Ubon Ratchathani. End of the line.

No sooner had I limped down the steps than a small crowd of men surrounded me. They shouted in tones of accusation. For a moment I gripped my backpack straps and thought to run, but then I realized they were moto drivers, offering me a ride.

Despite my twelve-hour language immersion course, courtesy of the ad, I understood nothing.

"Wat Pah Nanachat," I said—the name of the monastery where I was headed.

They stopped talking. Looked at each other. Shrugged.

I tried again. "Wat Pah Nanachat?"

Still, no go.

I said the three words slowly, pausing in between. *Wat*, I did know, meant "monastery." *Pah*—"forest." And *Nanachat*—"international." The international forest monastery. I gesticulated, tracing a roof over my head, clasping my hands, and closing my eyes as if in meditation.

At this, one driver exclaimed, exactly as I thought I had said it, "Ah, Wat Pah Nanachat!"

Yes. That.

I followed the man to his moto, basically a dirt bike, and perched on the back tip. He shook his head and beckoned me closer. I scooted up an inch and placed a tentative hand on his waist, feeling transported back to the awkwardness of a junior high dance. The bike accelerated, and I nearly flew off. By the time we reached the road, I was clutching him like a koala.

From over the driver's shoulder, I saw a surprising midnight rush hour. At a stoplight, vendors on foot weaved in between idling vehicles, peddling snacks in plastic bags. Suddenly, as if a sack had broken from above, it started to pour. Vendors scattered. Traffic slowed. The driver and I ducked, but we sped onward, our view reduced to blurry bulbs of light.

I grew scared. The road was slick, and we were top-heavy. The thin bike tires could easily slip and send us skidding into one of the oncoming trucks stacked with chicken cages. *This is how it happens,* I thought. *This is how it happened.* Ice had sent my friend's car into the path of a semi.

I began planning how to survive a crash. Maybe, after impact, while my body flew through the air, I could curl into a ball and land on my backpack and slide along the asphalt to safety. I found myself rehearsing this twisting acrobatic maneuver in small twitching movements. The driver must've felt my quivering because he soon pulled off the road and under the canopy of a car-repair shop. We dismounted, stood on either side of his bike, and waited for the storm to subside. I let my shoulders relax, but when I looked around, my relief for safety soured to a new frustration. The repair shop had a soaring glass roof supported by shiny steel columns, signs of modernity that didn't mesh with my ideal of a rural wilderness where every eye was virgin to smartphone screens and every roof was thatched and handmade from palm fronds that also possessed healing properties when brewed into a tea. I neglected to think how grateful I would've been for the Ubon hospital had we actually gotten into an accident.

I pouted next to the driver. He lit a cigarette and turned to the three mechanics in the back. He pointed down the road and said, "Wat Pah Nanachat." They pointed in three different directions and shared what sounded like competing ideas about how to get there.

The driver nodded and turned back, and we resettled into silence. I was soaked, steaming, and all of a sudden, grateful for the stillness. I'd been churning for weeks—packing my stuff, saying goodbyes—and now there was nothing I could do but be where I was.

Minutes passed. The driver and I occasionally smiled at each other and repeated our one shared phrase back and forth—"Wat Pah Nanachat." I felt we used tone to communicate.

He said it first, in a small-talk way I took to mean, "So, you're heading to the temple, huh?" Wat Pah Nanachat.

I said it back in a solemn way that meant, "Yep, I'm headed there all right. It's exciting and, I'll admit, a little intimidating." Wat Pah Nanachat.

The driver tilted back and exhaled a column of smoke out into the rain. He said it again, this time with an air of wistful reverence that I was pretty sure meant, "I'm impressed. It's a tough monastery. Rigorous. There's a saying, you know, that three months at an Ajahn Chah forest monastery is like twenty years at any other monastery. So good for you for coming here and dedicating yourself, boy of great promise. Good for you." Wat Pah Nanachat.

I nodded in humble acceptance of this praise.

The rain soon subsided. We returned to the highway, which, to my satisfaction, had begun to feel remote and undeveloped: a few lanes wide, no shoulder, no guardrails, and no painted lines to separate fast, slow, or oncoming traffic. The driver swerved off the road; I uttered an involuntary yelp. I hadn't noticed the narrow, unlit side street until we were speeding along it. This one-lane track was rough and deepened the hum of the moto tires. The back wheel dipped in and out of potholes, sending me briefly airborne. Away from the lights and rush of the main road, I could make out a landscape. In every direction lay horizon, a flat silhouette of fields. Agriculture, I guessed.

It seemed my driver was also guessing. At each sign-less crossroads, he decelerated and squinted up and down the street. Eventually, he made a U-turn. He didn't need to say it for me to know: we were lost.

I noticed small structures every couple hundred yards, just off the road: tin roofs on knobby stilts made from thin tree trunks—roadside shade for field-workers, I decided. I wondered if I might sleep under one if we couldn't find the monastery.

I savored the idea. "Yeah, it was intense," I imagined telling people later. "Not even the local driver could find the monastery, it being so remote and all, so eventually I was just like, 'You know what? Just drop me here,' and he was like, 'No way,' in Thai, of course, and then I was just like, 'Dude, I got this.'" I grew increasingly giddy at the prospect of having no choice but to complete the final leg of my journey on foot and in darkness. A true pilgrim to destiny's doorstep.

At an intersection we had passed earlier, the driver gasped. He braked and pointed to some trees that were partially obstructing a wooden sign. He pulled close and read the Thai text while I read the English transliteration beneath it.

We shouted in unison, "Wat Pah Nanachat!"

But there was no apparent entrance. To our right spread more fields. To our left, as we crept on, rose a tall, dense forest. The driver seemed to spot something; he stopped in the middle of the road and waddled us toward a small break in the trees.

There was a gate. Total darkness beyond.

The driver motioned for me to dismount, as if our trip were complete. I motioned for him to continue through the gate. I wasn't going to just hop off and walk through some unmarked gate into pitch-black woods, even if that was exactly what I had just imagined bragging about.

He shook his head. He wouldn't budge. He jerked his hands and began to look frightened, which frightened me, which made me want him to stay even more. But his agitation also activated my southern-mannered instinct to pacify at all costs. I relented and paid. He stuffed the bills in his jacket pocket, quickly bowed three times, and buzzed off the way we'd come.

I stood alone in the middle of the wet street. A thousand pothole puddles reflected the moonlight. I regarded the gate. It was maybe ten feet wide, metal, and curiously open. For a moment, I considered digging my phone out of my backpack for the flashlight but thought better of it. I might disturb monks who were sleeping on the ground. I didn't want *that* to be my first impression—*loud American disrupts wise men's sleep with iPhone.*

The whine of the moto faded, replaced by a chorus of nocturnal insects. Stalling my entrance, I peed in the grass, then dug out my toiletries bag. I brushed my teeth and crossed the street to spit at the base of a fence post, then gagged and jumped at the sight of a snake, which turned out to be a curled line of barbed wire.

If I wouldn't use light, I realized I might lose track of the path. So I devised a gait that dragged my soles along the ground, a short shuffle to maintain contact with the path at all times. As for my arms, I'd wave them like windshield wipers to prevent branches I couldn't see from poking my eyes.

And so I proceeded through the gate, shuffling blindly ahead and flailing my arms like a madman. If this was a metaphor, I missed it.

Soon I was immersed in black. I paused and held my hands up to my eyes. Seeing nothing of them, I felt dizzy. Then, headlights appeared. Through the dense forest, an SUV wound toward me and stopped. A window rolled down, and a man's voice said in English, "You are arriving?"

"Yes," I said.

"Now? Hmm." He didn't seem pleased. "Go up path. Building on right. Sleep upstairs."

The window rolled up, and the SUV moved past. Red taillights blinked on the street. The driver got out and swung the gate's two metal wings shut behind him, locking me inside.

I shuffled forward. Having seen the contour of the SUV's path, I had an idea of the route ahead. Sure enough, a clearing opened after a while, allowing the moon to illuminate the outline of a building.

Two stories. The first was open to the air, supported by thin columns. I crept closer. At the edge, something cracked underfoot, and I jumped: a dried leaf the size of a dinner plate lay next to a row of shoes.

Kneeling, I removed my running shoes and picked up the cracked leaf to consider it. Monks' orange-brown robes mimic the color of fallen leaves, representing detachment—the leaf from the tree, the monk from the desires that lead to suffering. I twirled the stem in my fingers and pondered if the appearance of such a symbol on the threshold of my journey was the universe's way of confirming that I was indeed endowed with special potential. I did not reflect on the significance of having stepped on that symbol.

I heard something and froze. From inside the open building, two shadows emerged. One short and slim, the other tall and round. They headed straight toward me.

"Welcome, mate," the short one said in a cheerful English accent. "Just arriving, are you? C'mon, then. We'll show you upstairs. We've only been here a couple of days ourselves. Staying just a few more."

I trudged behind them up a central staircase and into an enclosed room. A dozen people lay sleeping on the floor like sardines. My jolly guide pointed to an open corner. I whispered an obligatory thank-you, but once I had slipped into my sleeping bag, I simmered. This wasn't a private hut that smelled of sandalwood but a crowded second-story dormitory that smelled of body odor. And my roommates weren't monks but rather visitors, laypeople with their own backpacks and toiletry bags and electronics. The sight of them repulsed me, and I had no idea that my reaction might've had something to do with seeing myself in them. I wanted the extreme of sleeping on a rock on the edge of a cliff, not beside some random person who, good God, was texting. Never mind that I had quietly inflated my $119 Exped camping pad, which looked plush compared with the thin plastic mats everyone else was sleeping on. I wasn't pampered, I thought reflexively, in response to no one. I was *prepared*. Besides, *these* were surely transient visitors. The two Brits, despite their warmth, were simple tourists, passing by for less than a week. No one seemed to understand that I was in this for the *long haul*. I wouldn't have admitted it, but I registered a deep disappointment. No one had been stunned by the gravity of My Arrival.

CINNABON

I awoke to the sound of creaking floorboards. My dozen roommates grumbled and stretched around me. They rolled up their sleeping mats and flocked to stack them along one wall, jockeying for position like subway commuters impatient to get to work.

I sat up and blinked, confused. My watch read 6:00 a.m. The Wat Pah Nanachat website had promised wake-up would be three and a half hours earlier, at 2:30 a.m. That there had been a website at all for this monastery had been upsetting—a blemish on my ideal of a tech-free sanctuary. That it had also apparently misinformed me added to my consternation. Instead of rising hours before dawn to the solemn reverberations of a gong, I was wincing to the clang of pots and pans downstairs.

As the room emptied, I approached an older man. He was white, in his fifties, I guessed, and unlike the rushing throng who had fled downstairs, the man lingered by the stack of mats with a slowness I interpreted as patience. Maybe he could explain what was going on.

Before I could formulate my question, though, he snapped. "There's no time for meditation," he said. "It's nothing but chores. No teaching. Just work, work, work."

My mouth dropped open. "Really? Why?"

His face twisted. "*Kathina*," he spat. "That's why."

"What's that again?"

"Some holiday. It's only gonna get worse here, more crowded. But I'm not staying for it. I'll be long gone by then."

I turned away from the scowling man. I hoped he would be long gone by then, too. His manner broke an unwritten social code of my upbringing: you can experience negative feelings, just don't express them. I didn't realize it at the time, but he also scared me. His foul mood was contagious, and I was at risk of catching it.

Downstairs, the commotion was intense. So much that I paused halfway down the steps to take it all in. Swarms of people—women, mostly forty and older—bustled between a kitchen on one side and an open serving area on the other. They marched around stove tops and stainless-steel sinks. Some crouched on plastic crates along the outside of the building, where additional makeshift stoves burned on the ground. They hauled thirty-pound bags of produce and beat blackened woks the size of battle shields.

Another unit ferried trays of finished food to the serving area—fresh fruit, hard-boiled eggs drenched in soy sauce, mountains of sticky rice in blue plastic bins the size of kiddie pools. Because the first floor had no walls, I could see outside beyond the serving area. There, more people—men, mostly forty and older—hovered around the perimeter with brooms, sweeping leaves from the dirt trails that extended into the forest. It didn't occur to me that the women were the engines of the whole operation, with their soot-stained arms and athletic efficiency. I preferred to imagine monks existing in supreme self-reliance, like Thoreau at Walden Pond, although I'd later learn that Thoreau's mother had brought him food. I would also learn that these women who cooked and men who swept were residents of the surrounding towns, not overnight guests of the monastery like me, and that their routine was so tight because many of them had been supporting the monastery like this every day for years.

The women also directed the overnight residents, my roommates who had stumbled downstairs. The overnighters were easy to spot: all-white clothing and awkward attempts to insert themselves into what was an already well-choreographed dance.

All the while, I waited for someone to notice me, the new guy, lingering halfway down the stairs like a prom-goer awaiting an ovation.

No one looked up.

I didn't dare step into the churn of the kitchen, and I didn't know where the brooms were to sweep outside. The only task for which overnight guests seemed qualified was sitting in the serving area and waving fans over trays of food to keep away flies.

But then I noticed another contingent of overnighters. They stood huddled off to one side, fidgeting on the fringe, looking both shy and angry. The scowling man was among them, and I realized that his slowness, which I had taken to indicate patience earlier, may have been procrastination. Not one of them was helping. I sensed these were not the people to emulate. Then, watching everyone work, feeling timid and a bit miffed about my lack of reception, I realized I already was.

I hopped down, found a spare fan on the floor, and swung it back and forth over an unattended bowl of curry. From there, I continued to survey the room. I wasn't seeing what I wanted. Lots of people. No monks. A fly landed on the edge of my bowl, and I swiped at it with a little too much force.

Someone shouted at me.

I stooped, raising both hands, preparing my apology. First day, and I'd already violated rule number one, the first precept of Buddhism: nonharm.

But then I noticed the fly buzz off unhurt, and when I turned to the voice of my accuser, I saw the shout wasn't aimed at me. There was another shout, and the tempo of scampering feet picked up between the kitchen and serving area. Other voices hushed the shouts, as if in the moments before a surprise party. My fellow flyswatters stood up from the floor to look in the direction everyone else was nervously glancing, into the woods.

There was a glimmer of orange through the brush. Emerging through the trees in a single-file line were ten, twenty, thirty bald men in umber robes. I stopped fanning and stared. The men sweeping the perimeter dropped to their knees and began bowing in the dirt.

The train of monks curved closer. Their pace was smooth and efficient, their spacing tight, and their barefoot gait so fluid as to create the impression that they formed a single organism. When the end of the line came into view, I counted forty monks altogether.

A few men rose and rolled wooden tables on casters across the tiles, aligning them end to end at the edge of the building nearest the monks. Serving bowls were lifted from the floor and passed in a fire line to the tables. One monk materialized ahead of the pack to participate in a ritual I remembered—the offering of food. This monk stood across the tables from a male volunteer, and the two walked down either side of the buffet line in tandem, the layman briefly lifting each dish an inch off the table, the monk receiving the offered dish and setting it right back down. This procedure designated the food as officially "offered" to all the monks. It was a formality but a critical one, I knew, because monks in the Thai Forest Tradition are prohibited from eating food that has not been offered to them. They also are prohibited from storing offered food overnight, so this step would be a daily requirement.

Meanwhile, the rest of the monks came to a halt at the front of the first table. My eyes ran along their robes. I knew the line was organized by seniority, and I lingered on the most junior of them in back. Unlike the ordained monks, this handful of monks-in-training wore white skirts and T-shirts that were missing the right sleeve. They looked like kids. As my eyes adjusted, I realized they were closer to my age, but their shaved heads, faces, and eyebrows made them look like shorn sheep.

I studied their expressions, which seemed intentionally set to offer little. They had an audience, after all. At least a hundred laypeople knelt on the tile floor, silent now, staring up at them. Each junior held his eyes downcast. Some looked resolute, others forlorn, but all seemed stern. It rubbed me wrong. If the British guests from last night hadn't taken monastic life seriously enough, then these juniors seemed overly grim. I didn't realize that I felt only *I* had struck the appropriate balance.

Ahead of the juniors were the novices, monks who had recently undergone full ordination—the lifelong commitment I was considering—and whose new robes shone with the richness of freshly dyed fabric. The monks' outer robes were roughly the shape and size of a bedsheet. A coil of fabric at the left sleeve joined the two ends to wrap each monk's body in a kind of full-length dress. The novices tugged at their twists of cloth as if to make sure they weren't unraveling behind them, which some were.

At the front of the line, the coils were tight. Here were the senior monks. The big-timers. I strained to examine their faces, hoping to glean some insight I might carry with me forevermore. Perhaps one might catch my eye and offer a subtle solemn nod of acknowledgment, validating my place among them, real recognizing real. But I was dismayed to see not majesty but indifference. They seemed accustomed to the fawning ceremony around them, even resigned to it. Just another day at the office.

Despite the forty men all being bald, I was struck by how different they looked from one another. Some wrinkled. Some tall. Some Asian. Some white. One Black. Some wore glasses, which gave me pause. Such a dainty accessory with an otherwise restricted wardrobe seemed indulgent. A forest monk's possessions basically amounted to three pieces of cloth, a pair of sandals, and a single bowl. A pair of glasses carried some inherent sense of design in their shape and material, so wearing them inevitably made a statement of personal style and preference, which seemed contradictory, in my mind, to the seventh precept, prohibiting adornment and beautification, as well as games and entertainment. I found myself resolving that if *I* were a senior monk, I would not wear glasses. If my vision deteriorated, then I imagined *accepting it for what it was.* The expression sounded decisive and wise and Buddhist-y. Perhaps I had never noticed that the phrase was also a kind of brutish club because I so enjoyed swinging it.

At the front of the line, the two senior monks seemed distracted. They chatted quietly, ignoring their bowls and creating a traffic jam. Beneath them, ten pots of sticky rice sat at different heights, brought from different homes, some covered, some steaming, all waiting. I glanced around for someone to meet my eyes and endorse my impatience with a shrug, headshake, and upturned palm. But most people knelt in apparent tranquility, with heads bowed and eyes closed. Of the few who peeked at the monks over their prayer hands, none looked my way.

Finally, the two monks lifted the sticky rice base into their bowls, then moved down the tables, selecting from appetizers—vegetables, hard-boiled eggs; then main dishes—green and yellow and red curries, lentils; and lastly to desserts and drinks—fresh fruit, wrapped candy, juice boxes filled with soy milk.

The rest of the monks followed behind, and soon, nearly all had filled their bowls and carried them off into the woods until only the most junior monk-in-training remained: a thin white boy with erect posture, bony shoulders, and an especially grim demeanor. At the dessert section, he reached for a wrapped candy, then paused. Glancing up, he seemed to remember he had an audience. His hand hovered in midair. His eyes darted across the other sweets, and his stoic posture, seemingly designed to hide tension, had the effect of magnifying it. He was caught, I decided, between taking a treat and being *seen* taking a treat. It was a conflict with which I was familiar—indulgence versus austerity—and that was as uncomfortable to experience as it was riveting to watch.

The junior retracted his empty hand and turned red, as if he'd been caught sneaking from the cookie jar. But then, in one swift motion, his hand shot back out. He grabbed a treat. He turned to flee. Rotating to shield his body from our view, he crawled his hand along another bowl of treats *and snatched a second one.*

I gasped. I grinned. I gloated. He was a fraud, I thought. I didn't think about how I wouldn't have paid him any mind if he had confidently taken two treats and been on his way, as other monks before him likely had. His attempt to hide the indulgence struck a familiar chord in me that I found loathsome.

With the monks all gone, the laypeople around me rose. I was famished after forty-eight hours of travel with only a plate of rice the day before and stood and reached for a bowl. An overnight resident behind me whispered, "No, no, not yet. To the sala."

Empty-handed, we followed the monks into the forest.

The sala stood about forty yards away. Compared with the kitchen/dormitory, it was a cathedral. Thick marble columns supported a roof that was easily three stories high. Inside, the floor was polished stone, and people sat directly on it. At the far end, on a raised step reminiscent of a stage, the forty monks sat cross-legged in evenly spaced rows, facing us, with their untouched meals before them on place mats.

If we were an audience of a hundred, the sala's capacity was over a thousand. For some reason, we all sat in the back, leaving a gulf of open floor between us and the monks onstage. A layman crawled forward on his hands and knees to set a microphone beside one of the head monks. While a mic offended my rustic ideal, it also meant I was finally going to hear a monk speak. I took a deep breath and leaned in.

The monk closed his eyes, cleared his throat, and began chanting:

"Namo tassa bagavatto arahato samma sambuddhassa."

He repeated it twice more, and I remembered. It was customary for monks to pay homage to the Buddha in Pali before speaking in a public setting. To my mind, these were the previews before the movie, and I was happy to sit through them.

After the third run-through, the monk cleared his throat again. He was slender and prim and carried his frame with the poise of someone accustomed to formality. Opening his eyes, he gazed upon his congregants and began to speak. In Thai.

For the first minute, I tried, really tried, to open myself to the universe so that one word, just one, might suddenly make sense and I might snag a glimpse of something divine. But I came up empty, just like I had on the bus across the country.

By the second minute, I tuned out. The monk didn't seem particularly inspired anyway. In fact, I got the sense he was running through a housekeeping checklist. The Thai audience gave no signs of absorbing profundity, either, and a minute later, the spiel concluded, which the monk signaled by shifting on his cushion and raising his hands in prayer. He cleared his throat a third time, and all the other monks clasped their hands and cleared their throats, which prompted the audience to do the same.

One layperson dished out booklets with laminated covers. The head monk muttered another thing in Thai, and then he leaned close to the mic and raised his gaze to address the overnight residents huddled in a corner.

I straightened and inhaled, preparing myself to receive, at last, my first words of monastic instruction.

"Page seven," he said.

While the audience scrambled, the forty monks on the stage, who knew the chant by heart, fell into a monotonous mumbling. On the page, I saw that the chants were again in Thai with phonetic spellings in English—helpful for participation, useless for comprehension. It shouldn't have frustrated me so much to encounter Thai in Thailand, but Wat Pah Nanachat, the *international* forest monastery, was supposedly designed for English speakers. And I was after immediate insights.

My eyes wandered to the monks on the stage. A few of their heads were cocked back, and while their mouths were chanting, their eyes glared at the ceiling. Was one of them rolling his eyes? A horrible suspicion crept over me. Most of these monks looked grumpy.

No, no, no, I thought and pulled my eyes back to the chanting booklet. I couldn't entertain these thoughts. This was supposed to be a *happy* place. *Maybe,* I thought, *yeah, probably, I'm just hungry.*

The chanting ended. We were dismissed without a word. Once we'd made our way back to the buffet tables, I took a soup spoon, filled a large enamel bowl, and followed the resident laypeople around a lone dividing wall to our dining room, a sectioned-off corner on the far side of the building. The Thai day visitors served themselves last. Which might've seemed strange because they had prepared all the food. But I knew nearly everything in Thai forest monasteries followed a hierarchy of tenure. The monks ate first in the sala. The overnight residents ate second on one side of the dividing wall. The Thai visitors from the surrounding towns ate last in the serving area.

The overnight guests themselves were also organized on the floor by seniority, like the monks on the stage. Residents who had been at the monastery longer sat toward the front, facing a Buddha statue. No one had started eating. I was the last to arrive, and once I'd taken my seat in the back, someone at the front tapped a bell, which prompted everyone to pick up a laminated card that had been set on each place mat beforehand. This contained our own chant, in English, and together we read aloud in a robotic tone: "Wisely reflecting, I use alms food: not for fun, not for pleasure, not for fattening, not for beautification. Only for the maintenance and nourishment of this body. For keeping it healthy, for helping with the holy life. Thinking thus: I will allay hunger without overeating so that I may continue to live blamelessly and at ease."

The bell rang again. Everyone descended upon their bowls with ravenous quiet. Although my legs were already sore from sitting on the floor all morning, I lost all sense of discomfort. This was my one bowl of food for the day. I didn't hear the songbirds chirping in the woods behind us. All I could do was gather rice and sauce and vegetables onto my spoon, shovel them into my face, and immediately begin assembling the next bite.

I like to save the best for last, so rather than eating the fresh cinnamon bun I'd selected and placed like a crown atop layers of fruit, curries, and sticky rice, I maneuvered my spoon around the pastry, allowing it to gradually sink and settle on the bottom of the bowl as I ate. Normally, I didn't even eat dessert—long-distance running for ten years had whittled away my sweet tooth—but I had seen the bun glistening at the end of the buffet table, noticed I still had room in my bowl, and remembered I wouldn't get to eat again for twenty-four hours. The absence of an inspirational talk on mindfulness in the sala had also left me with a residue of bitterness, so when I passed the dessert tray, I thought, *Fuck it—I'm taking something sweet.*

I took a huge bite and instantly gagged. The brown wisps I had taken to be cinnamon crisps were, in fact, hair. The shiny glaze was not melted sugar but a smothering of lard. I succeeded in swallowing without making a noise, but my mouth remained coated in a thick layer of fat. I had eaten everything else. No drink to wash it down. No sticky rice with which to scrub my mouth. Second helpings were forbidden, so I couldn't run to the tables and grab some fruit. I was stranded in an ocean of grease.

I gulped, which forced me to taste the bun all over again, and I felt the entire meal lift into my throat. If I had felt frustrated at the lack of philosophical instruction thus far, here was a rare clean lesson in karma that I missed entirely. Clenching my mouth shut, I swallowed again, and this time the slippery film dissipated—and with it, the flavor. My stomach resettled, and I lifted my shirt to mop sweat from my brow. Residents who had finished eating walked their empty bowls to the kitchen to clean and dry them. I quietly rose, tilting my bowl to my chest to hide the uneaten bun, grateful to find an open garbage can by a sink where I could quickly dump the hairy remains.

For the rest of the day, we did chores. The scowling man had been right. We didn't meditate once. Still without a formal greeting or orientation, I learned what to do simply by following after others who knew where to find the brooms and brushes and shovels and what to do with them. Everyone seemed keen on *not* interacting with each other. No small talk. No eye contact. We were like strangers in an overcrowded elevator.

"I didn't come all this way to do chores," I wrote in my diary that night, then launched into a fantasy of escape: my story, I thought, was one of a kid prodigy getting *discovered* and brought to his rightful place at the top, an unrecognized genius waiting to catch the eye of a mentor. That it hadn't happened already was concerning. I gripped the pen and scrawled a string of commands. "Stay open-minded. Reserve judgment. Relax." If I couldn't get spiritual advice from others, at least I could give it to myself.

I closed the diary and rolled over on my sleeping pad to face the wall. I imagined myself deep in the forest, alone in my own hut. With my eyes shut, I could almost feel a sense of solitude. I remembered a saying from a legendary Thai forest monk: "If you have time to breathe, you have time to meditate." Well, I had time to breathe. I sighed, listening to the thrum of nocturnal insects, allowing my forehead to soften and my chest to expand for what felt like the first time all day.

I heard something in the distance. Car engines, revving. Distant bass thumped—the swell of a Friday night in a town some miles away. I pictured people my age in tank tops hanging out of car windows, flirting and shouting and carrying on. I pictured a young driver turning up the volume, pressing the accelerator, taking his eyes off the road.

I glared up at the ceiling, forehead crumpled again. I was supposed to have left everything behind—three flights around the world, twelve hours on a bus, and a moto drive through a thunderstorm to a place so far-flung even the locals weren't sure how to find it. I'd abandoned everything to live in the wilderness and reconfigure my life from scratch. But instead of allowing the sounds of the night wind to carry me off to peace, all I could hear was the thump of techno music, and all I could think about was the car accident.

This shit's not supposed to happen. That was the first thing I had said the night it did happen. People younger than me weren't supposed to die. And that was what I thought now, sulking in my sleeping bag, surrounded by laypeople, one of whom had begun to snore. It wasn't supposed to be like this. I fought with that idea more often than I knew. As if promises had been made. As if the phrase I'd heard someone back home use to describe what I was going through, a quarter-life crisis, could somehow guarantee that three-quarters remained. My grief was too much to bear, so I hated the village kids and their music, and I bent into a ball in the corner, scowling like the man I was trying to avoid.

VACATION

Day two. I beat the other guests up and out the door, congratulating myself for being the first to leave the dorm. Such initiative, I believed, suggested a certain spiritual superiority to the other overnighters.

I felt no competitiveness with the Thai cooks and sweepers. For one, I would've lost to them in this contest of my own devising. They had clearly awakened much earlier than I had. The kitchen was already abuzz with meal prep. Many had brought covered platters that appeared to have been partially prepared even earlier in the morning. For two, the Thai volunteers exhibited a comfort with the routine and a respect for the place that, in my mind, accentuated my position as their *guest*. Even though they were technically on the bottom of the monastic hierarchy—eating last, going home after the meal, free from our strict rules of conduct—I felt deference toward the Thai volunteers akin to what I felt for the monks. This was *their* monastery. They were not rivals. They were judges.

To my chagrin, I noticed a new layperson sitting on the tile. I wasn't the first downstairs.

"Josh," he said, grinning with tense lips that made his mouth look like a bird beak. He had arrived overnight, he told me, and he paused with eyes wide, as if expecting congratulations.

Repulsed, I broke his gaze. "Nice," I muttered and swatted at a fly that had landed on a platter on the tile floor. "You can grab a fan if you want."

Josh grabbed two.

Whoa, I thought, *overachiever. Cool.*

Other overnight guests hobbled downstairs, rubbing their eyes. As platters arrived from the Thai cooks in the kitchen, Josh flapped his two fans and chirped his spiel to anyone unlucky enough to approach.

In an accent that was part Malay, part Australian, he told me that he was "almost twenty." Then he proudly repeated this to another acquaintance.

When he said it a third time to another guest, I blurted, "So you're nineteen."

"Well," he said. "Right now. But I won't be much longer."

He also told everyone within earshot that he was going to ordain for life.

"Really?" I said.

"For sure," he said, "yeah. For sure. Life is meaningless on the outside."

He suggested we get permission sometime to leave the monastery and go to the internet café in town. He could show me the manifesto he'd posted on Facebook, plus the video of him burning all his stuff, bidding the world farewell.

"Hmm, yeah, maybe sometime," I said, but I could barely look at him. Something about his certainty and melodrama and desperation for praise disgusted me. I made no connection between his manifesto and the lengthy email I had written to all my colleagues on my last day of work, announcing not only my departure from the consulting firm but also my leap from the corporate treadmill, once and for all, I thought, to pursue a higher plane of existence.

A woman sat across from us. Named Autumn, she was in her forties—tall, white, from Berkeley, California. When Josh had mentioned Facebook, she had lowered her head to hide a smirk.

"Do you know why monks can't be alone wiff women?" Josh said to no one in particular.

I lowered my eyes, too.

"Wanna know why?" Josh said again.

With an audible inhale, Autumn raised her head, met Josh's eyes straight on, and said, "Why's that?"

"Because," Josh said, "women try to seduce monks and get 'em to disrobe and then marry 'em. Yeah. So that's why monks aren't even allowed to touch women. And that's why another man has to be wiff a monk if a woman's there, and it's why women aren't even allowed back in the forest. That's why there's the rules."

"Wow," she said, smiling. "I had *no idea* women were such a threat."

Josh nodded earnestly, as if he had taught Autumn something important about herself.

Autumn glanced at me. We raised eyebrows at each other as if to say, "This guy."

I smiled and fanned the food. It was a relief to know someone else thought Josh was an idiot. *I* knew better. Josh's juvenile drivel was as old as the idea that Eve had corrupted Adam. I knew the story—*conniving female has way with blameless man*—and I saw right through it. What I didn't see was that I had cherished this narrative myself countless times. See, a version of it also turned out to be my most frequent fantasy—*busty MILF dominates unsuspecting boy*, a premise whose appeal I'd never really paused to unpack. It offered two things I craved: sex and receiving sex without having to ask for it or even admit that I wanted it. The image of innocence but the experience of decadence. Austerity *and* indulgence. I wanted both, again, and I didn't see it. I only felt a vague sense of shame, so I couldn't understand that what most irritated me about Josh was that, in broadcasting his witlessness, I felt he was airing mine.

One thing he said was true: there were rules. Women weren't allowed in the forest beyond the sala where we chanted before the meal. Women didn't sleep above the kitchen, either. I realized I didn't know where they slept. I asked Autumn.

"Back there"—she pointed from the serving area toward the exit—"in a little henhouse closer to the gate. Definitely heard the party in the village last night. Loud and clear. Could you?"

I rolled my eyes and nodded.

She told me she'd arrived a couple of weeks earlier on a foldable bike she was riding all over the country.

"How's it going here so far?"

"Actually," she said, "I know people are complaining about Kathina and not having time to meditate, but for us, we're getting to participate in the work and actually interact with the monks a little. Once

Kathina's over and the normal schedule resumes, you'll see. Women can hardly join anything."

"Jesus," I said.

"Yeah, well, you know, it's a *lot* of responsibility," she said gravely, "keeping all these monks celibate."

During a work break that afternoon, I took a walk in the woods. I needed distance from the crowd. Also, I was hunting for face time with a monk. Nearly two days had passed, and I still hadn't gotten a single word of greeting, much less instruction. Behind the sala, single-room huts called *kutis* were spread throughout the forest. This was monk territory, and I hoped to run into one.

And I did. A few times. I'd spot a man in orange walking down the path. I'd slow down and hold my breath and smile brightly. Each time, the monk averted his eyes and rushed by like a celebrity hoping not to be stopped by a fan.

It hurt. But I only felt anger. My jaw tightened as I walked, and my arms clamped to my sides. If these monks didn't recognize my potential, I thought, then they must not be so special after all. Their silence was too precious. Their rules were archaic. It was dumb that women weren't allowed back on these trails, that they were confined to one structure in the smallest area receiving the highest foot traffic. Not that they were missing anything back here, I thought, besides being snubbed.

After a third missed connection, I began daydreaming of hiding off-trail to ambush passing monks with screamed salutations. Imagining the scene, I stopped walking and stood in the path, frowning at the ground. I didn't notice someone approaching.

"Hello!" a voice said.

I looked up, then immediately wished I hadn't. It was Josh, the almost twenty-year-old, heading straight toward me. I made a move to avert my gaze and rush off, but it was too late.

He stepped directly in front of me and shoved his grinning face in front of mine.

"Hey," I said.

"Where you goin'?" he said.

"Just walking," I said and made a move in the opposite direction.

He turned with me. "Great," he said.

I sighed. Monks we encountered would now associate me with Josh's insufferable exuberance. They'd be even less likely to stop and talk.

Josh said, "What do you fink of the monastery so far?"

I shrugged. But then I remembered something. Before the meal, I'd overheard him telling another guest about other monasteries in Thailand. "Hey," I said, "did I hear you say you'd visited other monasteries around here?"

"Oh, yeah," he said. "I stopped at Wat Pah Ratanawan on my way."

"What's that?"

"'Nother monastery. Beautiful. Deep jungle. Wild elephants. The abbot's also from Australia. He's coming for Kathina, I fink."

"The abbot is coming here?" I said. "How do you spell it? Ratanawan?"

The thought of a different monastery felt hopeful. But as we continued along the sandy trails, the feeling transformed to dread. To have asked about another place was to admit my doubts about this one. Fantasizing about another monastery while living at a monastery was the opposite of what one was supposed to do in a monastery.

But it was too late. I'd spoken, and now I recalled the response from the head monk in New Zealand when I had sent him a message unveiling my plan to spend at least half a year at Wat Pah Nanachat, where he himself had ordained twenty years before. "In the heart of the tradition," I wrote, as if he might have forgotten. I had awaited his compliments.

Instead, he had simply written, "Nanachat is a good place to start."

I'd disregarded the tepid reply at the time, but now I thought, *A good place* to start? That was consultant-speak for *bad idea*.

Josh prattled on beside me. He had his grand plan to ordain as a monk for life. I made occasional humming sounds to make it seem like I was listening, but I was lost in my own vision of a new, better monastery. It would be quiet and secluded, with fewer harried visitors and more welcoming monks. Maybe this Ratanawan was the place. There, I pictured becoming a renowned teacher in record time. In the evenings, I'd speak to visitors about the nature of the mind. When I grew tired, I'd say, "Well, that'll be all for today," and make a clicking sound with my tongue. This would summon a wild elephant, which would amble out from the jungle and bow down for me to climb aboard. The guests would gasp, and a volunteer would remind them photography was not permitted.

Over the next couple of days, more visitors crammed into Nanachat. The day before Kathina, a middle-aged Thai man showed up. At the meal, he literally jogged around the kitchen building, snapping photos like a tourist, waving and yelling, "Ooh!" to get the attention of the monks, who tried like librarians to keep him quiet. While we fanned away flies and refrained from eating the food before us, he stood and, in plain violation of the norm, munched on snacks. He wiped his hands on his pants. The other Thai villagers shot him glances but said nothing.

When it came time for us to serve ourselves, the unruly man cut in front of the other Thai day visitors, directly behind me. While I lifted one of the blue-rimmed enamel bowls from the stack and lined the bottom with sticky rice, the man bounced on his heels and drummed his soup spoon against his forearm. When I took a second scoop of rice, the man pressed the edge of his bowl into my lower back.

I was raised in a culture that discouraged confrontation. It might've been healthy to calmly request that the man not enter my personal space, but I conflated confrontation with aggression. Outside of sports, the only aggression with which I felt comfortable was passive. Finally, this man had given me an outlet. If I wasn't receiving any mindfulness instruction, then at least I could give some.

At the curries, I relished a prolonged pause to consider my options.

The man elbowed me in the ribs. He said something terse under his breath.

At this, I slightly rotated back toward him so that he could glimpse the serenity of my smile. Languorously, I stretched an arm across the table to a pot of lentils, took a spoonful, and softly bounced it in the air, draining the liquid. I drew in a long, peaceful breath. I exhaled a sigh of contentment just loud enough for him to hear.

The man kicked my ankle.

I gently deposited the spoonful along one edge of my bowl, knowing I was being a dick but also savoring what I told myself was an opportunity to teach someone a lesson in patience. Trying, again, to have it both ways. I returned the serving spoon to the pot, then hesitated, hovering my hand in midair, offering the man one last moment of mindfulness, before reaching back out for another half scoop.

Word spread after the meal that we were to gather at the office, which I learned by following others to it was a small building beside the sala with a porch. There, monks milled about at the foot of a few stairs. The two head monks sat side by side on the tile porch, facing out as if preparing to speak. Two village men positioned another microphone before them. All of a sudden, the monks and overnight guests got onto all fours, then bowed three times to a Buddha statue. The two head monks faced us again, and we all bowed three more times to them. Then we sat, cross-legged, knee to knee, some on the porch, others on the stairs, and the rest scattered on the gravel below.

One of the head monks cleared his throat. Not the prim one who led the chanting on the first day, but the other, who was burly—probably 6'3" and 220 pounds.

"So," he said, "today is the day before Kathina." He was German, wore rimless glasses, and spoke at a volume that was better suited to a concert than a monastery. "It seems to be a good time to give everyone a brief dhamma talk."

Dhamma, in this context, meant "teaching." The word comes from Pali, a language similar to Sanskrit (*dharma*) and in which the original Buddhist teachings, called the Pali Canon, were recorded. A dhamma talk is like a sermon, something I'd sat through during childhood as a reluctant Episcopalian. During those sermons, I had only worshipped the girls from public school who sat in the front pew. But dhamma talks I'd heard were truly inspirational. *Finally,* I thought.

The monk pointed in the direction of the entrance gate behind us. One thousand visitors were expected to come through it tomorrow, he said, but we shouldn't let the outside world intrude upon our thoughts. He casually remarked that life "out there" was mostly meaningless, and people "out there" were riddled with defilements.

I shifted. I understood the rhetoric—in a way, it was easier to endure the discomforts of monastic life if you believed that the alternative was a cesspool. I'd made the same argument to myself when considering ordination. But when I heard *him* say it out loud, I squirmed and found myself taking the other side. How would he explain acts of kindness and grace? Wasn't he sacrificing the truth of ambiguity for the false comfort of certainty? And why was he yelling?

I glanced around. Luckily, no one else seemed particularly impressed. Normally, I'd seen dhamma talks last an hour. The German's lasted less than five minutes. Then he bent the mic toward his partner, the tan, slender monk who had guided our chanting and who I'd since learned was from Malaysia.

If the beefy monk tripped on simplistic thinking, his prim co-abbot shielded himself with sophistication. His English accent suggested aristocracy. He was handsome. His head was shaved, but his hairline was tightly edged.

"Right, then," he said and proceeded to assign tasks to us in the audience. After giving an order, he peppered in brief bits of gratitude and flashed a suave smile that disappeared the moment he moved on. "Excellent, perfect, and now for you . . ."

His efficient warmth emitted something corporate. He reminded me of a senior director from my old consulting firm, a rising star who wore tailored suits and once gathered our team in a conference room in the East Texas medical facility we flew to and from each week. "We got a nine-million-dollar bogey here," he had said, "so we're gonna really need to manage perception from the C-suite on down." I didn't understand any of what he'd said, but I found myself nodding emphatically and repeating his phrases later under my breath.

The refined monk managed us in a similar fashion. I was aware of his charm and skeptical of it—but not immune. When he looked at me, I froze like a dog told to sit. When he suggested I help with the shoveling, I found myself nodding as if he'd asked if I wanted a treat.

"Wonderful," he said and then looked at Josh, "and why don't you help out with that, too, yes? Right. Excellent."

The group split. We set to work. Chores, I'd learned, were called "working meditation." This struck me as spin, the way an Ultimate Frisbee coach had once called sprints "fitness rewards." In my case, at least, there was nothing meditative about listening to Josh's half-baked theories on Buddhism while hauling wheelbarrows of dirt to a path that was eroding even faster than my optimism. Although it did feel good to work up a sweat.

The sound of an engine interrupted our labor. Turning, I gaped. A spotless black Mercedes-Benz glided up the entrance. Glossy reflections of the forest canopy washed over its polished hood, and it parked in the center of the roundabout at the end of the entrance driveway, front wheels angled like a showroom display. A man wearing a short-billed chauffeur cap hopped out and scampered around to open each of the back doors.

Ocher robes billowed from the back seat like smoke from a hotbox. Gasps and titters rippled throughout the villagers who had gathered and recognized the two celebrities.

"Ajahn Jayasaro!"

"Ajahn Amaro!"

In slow motion, two senior monks rose from either side of the Benz like Big Boi and André 3000. The driver might as well have turned up "SpottieOttieDopaliscious" to give them a soundtrack of smooth bass and a horn section fit for royalty. As if the two sages were allowing time for a low-angle arc shot, they stood tall, squinting in a survey of their former domain.

They were both white. Brits. Despite their fame, and despite my prior experience seeing Caucasian monks, some small voice in my head whispered that they looked like posers. Perhaps this feeling was a relic of growing up a white hip-hop fan in Atlanta. I'd felt a combination of joy and terror when a buddy in junior high had given me a pair of his old FUBU jeans, a brand expressly for Black people by Black people (For Us, By Us: FUBU). I was honored by the gift, although my progressive liberal training had instilled a healthy fear of cultural appropriation. And yet, I had worn those jeans with a shy and furious pride, even though they weren't for me or by me. Now I was a white guy wearing the garb of a monastic postulant in Southeast Asia. Maybe I worried I was the poser.

Despite my allegedly deep mindfulness practice, I couldn't see the simple fact that I was also jealous. Perhaps because they were white, I could see myself in them, so I was keenly aware of what they had that I didn't.

For one, they had experience. Each had spent over forty years in robes and studied under Ajahn Chah himself, the legendary late Thai monk who was a father of the modern Thai Forest Tradition.

For two, they got respect. At the sight of these two monks, people in every direction stopped what they were doing and dropped to
the ground and began frantically bowing—not once, not the standard
three times, but continuously—heaving forward and back like students
in a CorePower workout class.

I remained standing. I knew who they were, but I wasn't so sure
about throwing myself into the dirt. Beside me, Josh lowered himself
to his knees but didn't bow.

Having nailed the arrival, the monks sauntered among the masses
as if a red carpet unfurled beneath their every step. Each threw a casual wave off the side of his hip, partly in greeting, partly to dampen
the fandom, as if to say, "Hey, thanks, we know we're a big deal, but try
to be cool about it."

I propped an elbow on my shovel, crossed one leg over the other,
and spat. This was the entrance *I* had wanted. *I* wanted to be the guru
hoppin' out of the Benz. And if that wasn't going to happen, I wanted
one of the gurus to sense my presence in the crowd, wave me over,
take me under his wing. Offer me solitude punctuated by one-on-one
consultations in a cedar-scented cabin. Ask me questions in low tones:
How was I doing after what had happened to those boys on the icy
road, what had I learned about death and purpose, and would I be interested in maybe doing an opening act on their global speaking tour?

If that wasn't going to happen, I wanted someone to at least notice
that I wasn't bowing and chastise me for it.

But no one saw me. It dawned on me that I might not get to know
any of these monks, ever. I might be doomed to the role of disgruntled
fanboy whose only companion was nineteen-year-old Josh.

I watched the two monks disappear into the office, said, "Pfft," and
went back to shoveling.

That afternoon, the monks and residents gathered in a new building on the other side of the sala for tea. More of a covered porch, the
structure had two walls at a right angle and a supporting stilt in the
other corner to hold up the roof. By the time I arrived, rows of plastic
mats had been rolled out lengthwise. Sandals lined the foot of the open
sides—mostly orange flip-flops but a few brown Tevas and black Crocs.
Monks sat on the mats in rows according to the hierarchy and selected
a drink—or two—from a couple of coolers on wheels.

Besides the morning meal around 10:00 a.m., this was the only time we could consume anything besides water. Peering over heads and between shoulders, I glimpsed the menu: bottles of aloe vera, green and black tea. Aloe vera sounded perfect after a half day of manual labor. Cool, sweet chunks of pulp.

But by the time the cooler wound its way to me, I lifted the lid and saw red. Mtn Dew Code Red—a neon-colored syrup drink with enough sugar to give a small mammal a seizure. But it was the only option left. When I cracked mine open, red fizz shot out the sides, staining my white shirt. I chuckled, took a sip, then downed the bottle without thinking. I hadn't had a calorie in hours. I glanced at Josh, who had done the same thing and grinned at me with a stained-red mouth. If I looked anything like him, it struck me that I looked like I had a blood-splattered shirt from having been punched in the mouth. That, in other words, I looked the way I felt. Which made me feel better for a moment.

Every row faced the wall, except for the front row of the most senior monks. They faced us, and the prim Malaysian cleared his throat to get everyone's attention. One thing I had learned so far: monks were always clearing their throats. They did it even in brief group meditations when they didn't need to speak. Another thing I was learning: the more senior the monk, the longer and louder the throat-clearing.

This time, though, he had a real announcement. To celebrate Kathina, another distinguished visitor was among us—the abbot of Wat Pah Ratanawan.

I perked up. Here? The head honcho of the place with wild elephants? I leaned left to get a look at him. I'd need to remember his face if I wanted to make an inroad later.

And there he was: a portly white man beside the Malaysian, raising his head and a hand in greeting. He coughed once, then sank back into a slouch. He cleared his throat.

Then he spoke in an Australian accent. With the dutiful drone of someone tasked with reading a legal disclaimer aloud, he reminded us that Kathina was a celebration. I might've found the irony funny if I hadn't been so disappointed. He looked and sounded like a sad frog. He croaked about savoring the tradition, and I noticed monks ahead of me looking at their laps and twiddling their thumbs.

This wasn't my guy. Cross Ratanawan off the list. I was back at square one.

He concluded, we responded with obligatory bows, and pockets of conversation resumed. Josh, unable to monitor his volume, often grew so animated beside me that one monk—a Sri Lankan with a massive forehead—glared back at us from a few rows ahead and said, "Shh!"

Everyone hushed. I scoffed under my breath. This was not a *senior* monk, I thought, not even an *Ajahn*, which is Thai for "teacher," a title every monk has added to their names after ten years in robes. So then, who did he think he was, this middle-management monk, this self-appointed arbiter of noise?

At the same time, a small part of me rejoiced, because someone had shut Josh up.

Hushing monk aside, the atmosphere at tea felt almost collegial. Only the residents of the monastery attended tea. No Thai volunteers were present because they all went home each day after the meal. Drinking and fraternizing felt refreshing and earned after the chaos of the morning and the sweat of the work period. It was a truly international group. I had a running list of nationalities represented at the monastery in my diary, and I'd already recorded over ten: Thailand, India, Sri Lanka, England, Italy, Australia, Canada, the Netherlands, Malaysia, Germany, and the US. The diversity was impressive, I thought, forgetting that half the population—women—was excluded.

Up front, the senior monks yukked it up, the German being almost as loud as Josh. My lips curled. Of course, the Sri Lankan would never shush him.

I considered the third precept of monastic life, which concerned speech: *No lying* was the main thrust. *No harshness* was a second bullet, and lastly, as if in fine print, *no idle chatter.* Teatime discussions, it seemed to me, were the definition of idle chatter. I glared at the first row and thought, *Hypocrites. Give me profound discourse or give me silence.* Or at least an invitation to come hang out up front. Anything to get me away from Josh.

To my left, I noticed a junior in white. I'd since learned that they weren't called *juniors* but *pakaos*, in Thai, or *anagarikas*, in Pali, and they were indeed monks-in-training. One would wear white as a pakao for six months, then become a novice in orange for a year, and then, after eighteen more months, one could ordain as a full-on monk for life. The pakao beside me was a short, thin Thai boy. He detected my sideways glance, said hello, and introduced himself as Ben.

I'd noticed him before. During brief group meditations, I'd peek at the other monks to judge how enlightened they looked. Many didn't look calm at all—eyes scrunching in an excess of determination or noggins toppling with fatigue. But Ben seemed quietly comfortable in his own skin, his face relaxed but not sleepy, his posture alert but not strained, even when he didn't seem to think others were watching.

Through a new set of braces, he mumbled that he was nineteen years old.

I liked him already. He hadn't said "almost twenty." If he was Thai, I asked, why had he chosen Nanachat, the international monastery?

"Um, my parents," he muttered. "They want me to practice my English." He grinned and then stifled it as if to hide the sight of his braces.

In Thailand, many young men spend three months in a monastery as a rite of passage to be considered fit for marriage. That Ben was encouraged to hit two birds with one stone—rite of passage, language immersion—suggested a backdrop of supportive pressure that felt familiar to my own. I told him I'd be happy to help him practice.

He nodded in genuine appreciation, then hesitated. "Could I ask you for one favor?"

"Sure."

"I must move out of my kuti this evening. To make room for senior monks coming for Kathina. Could you help me with my things?"

After tea, I followed Ben along a narrow trail at dusk. He veered down a faint pathway that led to a sandy clearing. In the center stood an 8'-by-10' wooden kuti on stilts. I waited outside while he climbed the stairs and packed his belongings, which were few. We'd need only one trip. I stuffed his bug net under one arm and his rolled sleeping mat under the other. When his hands were full, I turned to leave but noticed him waver.

"I have a question," he said. "What do your parents think of you coming here?"

"Mine? They're . . . supportive, I guess. I worked a job for a few years after college, so I think that helped them trust what I'm doing."

"You are lucky," Ben said.

"Yeah . . ." I shrugged and trailed off. I wasn't in the habit of considering myself fortunate recently, nor was I sure if my parents were truly all that supportive. All my life, I had absorbed subtle, persistent nudges toward conventional respectability, from my mother's side at least. Never explicit, lessons were imparted through vigilant but mild-mannered osmosis. "To whom much is given," my mother had once said, "much is also expected." I didn't know what that meant but took it to mean something about not being a disappointment. I wanted to buck those expectations and be alone for long enough to figure out what I wanted. I didn't realize that grief had given me the perfect cover to do just that.

I realized Ben was staring at me.

"I guess I am lucky," I said. And I remembered that, in the end, my parents had given their blessings, in their own ways, from their separate homes on opposite sides of Atlanta.

My dad understood. He hadn't come from money or the South. He'd given me his tattered, dog-eared copy of a book filled with quotes by Jack Kornfield and watercolor paintings of bamboo beside ponds. "Remember to nourish your spirit," he had written inside the cover. My sister also got it. "Well," she'd said, "don't let a scorpion crawl on your face," a reference to our shared fear on a family trip to southern Utah when we were kids. And my mom, too, had nodded her approval and smiled through tears before I'd left. "Having children is like this," she'd said, pulling an imaginary arrow back on a bow, then releasing it. Maybe my whole family was totally supportive. Maybe it was me who wasn't so sure.

Ben tilted his head. "So how has it been here so far?"

"Challenging," I said. I'd been trained to use this word often as a consultant. The word *challenge* avoided emotion. It confined hardship to that which could be met with analysis and action.

But Ben wasn't a consultant. He wrinkled his face. "Challenging?" he said. He bit his lips to conceal a smile.

I turned red. His amusement was so genuine, his curiosity so free of judgment, that I couldn't help but wonder if he was onto something. The truth was, my mother had told me that line about much being expected *after* she had told me I was the beneficiary of an inheritance.

Upon learning of the gift, I'd said at one point that I felt like I was somehow in debt to the world, and my mother had chuckled and firmly corrected me: "Actually," she said, "you are literally in the opposite of debt." Growing up, I'd laughed with scorn when entitled kids were called *trustafarians*, but now I glimpsed myself in a different light—a young man with a safety net who had abandoned a secure job with good pay to go starve himself in Southeast Asia and nurture an inner monologue that largely consisted of whining.

And what Ben said next struck me as so painfully accurate that, for a moment, I understood a new set of truths: that I was here of my own volition, that I could leave anytime, and that I reeked of self-pity.

"But," he said, "isn't this your vacation?"

DIPLOMAT

Today was Kathina.

By now I'd learned what the holiday was all about. It celebrated the end of the rains retreat, an annual three-month period of intensive meditation practice. Buddhist monks were originally wandering mendicants, so this season of hunkering down was practical, corresponding with the monsoon season. Today, Theravada monks stop traveling and reaffirm their commitment to the practice. The number of completed rains retreats determines a monk's "age" and, therefore, seniority. After five rains retreats, for example, you graduate from the mentorship of a preceptor. After ten, you become an Ajahn. If the end of the rains retreat was a birthday, then Kathina was the party—a chance for the lay community to shower appreciation on the monks, who, at Wat Pah Nanachat, at least, seemed to want the attention as much as a cat wants a bath.

Over a thousand visitors descended upon the monastery. People scurried about, clicking cameras and taking selfies. A couple of women strutted up and down the entrance path in platform heels, full makeup, and elaborate satin dresses. I thought the precept was clear: no adornment, beautification, revealing clothes, or fragrances. It was like they had worn lingerie to a funeral. I threw up my hands and huffed and followed after them to continue hating the sight.

And yet, there was also an air of festivity even I couldn't ignore. Perhaps my conversation with Ben the day before had softened me, for the collective excitement of the visitors nearly overwhelmed the dreariness of the residents.

The morning sun smiled through the forest above the frown of the horizon. Visitors began organizing themselves along the sides of the driveway, lining it shoulder to shoulder like fans at the finish of a road race. The human corridor stretched all the way down to the entrance gate.

I joined a line. Everyone was holding a bowl full of sticky rice. A Thai man in a green polo and baggy nylon pants handed me one. He bowed and smiled so big that I couldn't help but do the same. He filled me in on what to do: when the monks arrived, I'd place a pinch of rice in each bowl—no more, or else I'd run out early.

He bowed again and left me to stand regarding the rice in my bowl. I knew from experience that the monks wouldn't actually eat what I offered them. They'd march down the line, fill their bowls with ten pounds of sticky rice, and dump it all right back into the plastic tubs where we'd gathered it in the first place. They'd serve themselves at the buffet line an hour later, after this ceremony, which, despite the general enthusiasm, struck me as a paltry imitation of the ancient tradition of gathering alms, where monks were truly nomadic ramblers who didn't have hordes of people doting on them and cooking for them in an on-site kitchen. I shifted my weight in line. Pursed my lips. Tapped my foot.

But then I saw someone I recognized ambling around the curve of visitors. A hush fell over the crowd. Another celebrity monk.

I'd seen him in pictures but never in person: a broad man with a large head and rimless glasses that tinted in the sunlight. He wore an expression of such unflappable ease that I later wondered if he'd somehow retrained his facial muscles to rest in a smile. Fifty years in robes and counting. His name: Ajahn Sumedho. One of the first Western disciples of the Thai Forest Tradition, an American who had woken up from the American Dream, he had founded Wat Pah Nanachat himself with Ajahn Chah back in the 1970s. He walked toward me on bare feet whose arches had long ago collapsed.

I was barefoot, too. That was customary for anyone making an offering. Every layperson in line had parked their shoes in the dirt behind where they stood. And suddenly I was fumbling with my bowl, rolling a ball of rice between my sweaty fingers to prevent it from sticking to my hand. Before I knew it, the great man was in front of me, pausing for my offering. I bent, reached out, and deposited the rice into his alms bowl. He nodded slightly and passed on like a breeze. I bowed and remained so, not out of obligation but reverence. My chest flushed with an unfamiliar expansion, and I heard myself think, *This is an honor to be here,* again and again, *an honor to be here,* and for the first time, I actually believed I was doing a small part to help sustain a group of men who had cumulatively dedicated hundreds of years to the patient study of the mind. I felt like the Grinch at the end of the book.

After the meal, Ajahn Sumedho gave a short talk at the office. He sat cross-legged on a bench elevated above the porch for all to see. His voice was deep and unhurried and put me in mind of a steam train traveling at low speed. Monks leaned forward and stifled their coughs so as not to miss a word. I forgot all about the pain in my knees.

He only spoke for a couple of minutes but communicated years of understanding. He discussed wisdom, different levels of enlightenment, transcendent states of meditation called *jhana*—in other words, everything I wanted to achieve. Then he paused and surveyed all the hungry eyes in the audience.

"But you know," he said, "*attainment* really isn't a suitable word for what we're doing here. *Release* is much more appropriate."

This shocked me into a dazed sense of calm for the rest of the day. So much of what I wanted had to do with accumulation—a private hut, a better monastery, an attentive audience. My vision of monastic training was that of an extreme expedition to scale the mountain of the mind, fight bitter wind, and eventually stab a flag on the summit. Ajahn Sumedho had even dangled these ideas before us, only to flip the script at the last moment and suggest the opposite was the best path forward: don't grip tighter; let go.

Now *this* was the kind of profound dhamma talk I had come for. I basked in its wisdom, hoping to be irreversibly altered. I had no way of knowing that the lesson wouldn't stick, that lessons required continuous learning no matter how well crafted the mantra. Nonetheless, Ajahn Sumedho had cracked a window in my mind, and I felt a fresh air of possibility.

The day after Kathina felt like the Monday after the Super Bowl.

The visitors were gone, and the residents had to clean everything up. Some overnight guests, like the scowling old man, had left. So had a number of monks, including most of the celebrities. Although I had briefly reveled in the idea of settling into life at Nanachat, I wondered where those monks had gone and whether I might join them.

At the office again after the meal, the prim Malaysian co-abbot assigned work tasks and then announced that there would be a question-and-answer dhamma talk in the evening. I already knew my question.

When we broke for the work period, a monk with a square head approached me and said hello.

For a moment, I was speechless. No monk had directly addressed me yet.

He said he wanted to officially welcome me to the monastery.

Before I could say anything, Josh appeared by my side and shouted, "I wanna ordain."

The monk laughed. "Ordain? You just got here!"

Josh looked down.

I liked this guy.

The three of us walked and talked on our way to work. A path had eroded. We were to fill wheelbarrows with dirt, roll them over, and even out the surface.

"I am the guest monk," he told us, which meant he was in charge of orienting newcomers. "It's busy right now. Normally, it's not like this."

I tried to play it cool. I committed myself to keeping the conversation to small talk. I asked where he was from—the Czech Republic—and opened my mouth for a follow-up but then doubted myself. Maybe asking about a monk's former life and homeland was like asking someone newly sober about their favorite cocktail. And so as we reached the pile of dirt, I heard myself blurt, "What made you decide to become a monk?"

"The lifestyle," he said and started shoveling.

That was it. He'd said it like it was no big deal. I straightened, stunned that someone had dodged such a golden opportunity to expound upon their Grand Life Mission.

I examined the guest monk from behind. Dark spots of sweat had spread across his orange underrobe while he worked. I'd heard once that monks weren't allowed to dig in the dirt—they'd risk killing a worm, which would violate the first precept of nonharm. That application of the rule had struck me as a bit excessive, even as a sneaky loophole for monks to shirk labor under the guise of maintaining purity of mind. But here was this guy with a square head, hunched and huffing and digging away. I realized *I* was the one who had stopped working in order to think.

I dug in. A frog the size of a dinner plate squatted on top of a dirt pile, camouflaged in the red soil. The monk drove his shovel in midway up the mound. The frog didn't budge. It was much bigger than a worm, and I wondered if the karmic consequences of hurting it would be proportionally worse.

I didn't want to find out, so I pointed at it and said lamely, "There lotsa frogs like that around here?"

"Yep," he said, hardly looking, and pushed his spade back in.

Again, I was shocked. He was so casual. No profound discourse, no existential concern. I felt my wiring move toward the extreme short-circuit. I couldn't tell whether the guest monk was onto something or missing the point entirely.

That evening, we gathered for the Q&A at a new structure. Tucked into the woods off the entrance path, the dome-shaped concrete construction put me in mind of a spacecraft—fitting, I thought as I approached, for blasting me off into new galaxies of insight. Rumor had it that our host was a monk from Israel who lived in a secluded hermitage nearby.

Inside the dome, a handful of pakaos and residents grabbed cushions, bowed three times on their own, and sat facing a Buddha statue at the front. No monk. I brought a cushion to the front row, bowed, and waited.

I glanced at the others. Josh, who seemed to have already been staring at me, grinned. Ben sat still with his eyes closed, looking tranquil as ever. A few other pakaos sat stoically with squeezed eyes and strained postures. When a throat cleared from the entrance behind us, everyone straightened.

The tall monk from Israel strode in. His long face gave nothing as he passed. No smile, no nod, no greeting. He knelt before the Buddha statue, bowed to it, then turned to sit and face us.

We had risen to our knees and simultaneously bowed again to the statue. When he turned to us, we bowed to him. That was the custom: three bows every time you sat in a place of meditation, six bows every time someone spoke—three to the Buddha in unison, three more to the speaker. At the top of my bows, I stole glances at his face, hoping to read him, to see how he reacted to people bowing before him. His expression was stone.

After the requisite introductory chant, he allowed silence to refill the room.

Finally, after half a minute, he said, "So."

He waited again, as if letting us adjust to the sound of his voice. Then he said, "What questions do we have?"

No one spoke. No raised hands. I jiggled my knees.

"I have a question," I said. I had prepared a zinger after hearing the German co-abbot say everything was meaningless on the outside. "The first noble truth is that life is suffering, right? But I don't know if I agree that all life is—"

"No."

My face grew hot, and I shrunk between my shoulders.

"The first noble truth isn't that *all* life is suffering," he said. "It's that life *involves* suffering." He let this sink in a moment. "But even that's beside the point. The Four Noble Truths, when taken together, simply say this: things arise, and things pass away."

This was a head-scratcher. The historical Buddha had based his teachings on the concept of the Four Noble Truths: (1) that life involves suffering, which I apparently misunderstood; (2) that craving causes suffering; (3) that the cessation of craving will end suffering; and (4) that following an eight-step program called the Eightfold Path would help kick the craving habit. But this monk was saying that the Four Noble Truths said something else: things arise and pass away. I hadn't thought about it like that.

Finished, the monk cast his solemn gaze around the room like a bird of prey. Another resident began a question, but I didn't hear it, nor the Israeli's answer. I was still reeling from how firmly he'd put me in my place. He hadn't beaten around the bush like a consultant, no "Great question, glad to clear this one up because it's actually a

common misperception that leads people to think Buddhism is pessi-
mistic." No, he was direct. He let me wallow in the shame of showing
my ignorance. I kinda liked it.

For the rest of the Q&A, I found the Israeli monk to be the most
somber, deliberate, and focused person I had ever seen. His merciless
candor was the opposite of my hardwired bend toward nervous equiv-
ocation. He rejected all conventions associated with putting his audience at ease. When someone spoke, he watched as if they weren't
watching back. No murmurs, no movement. He paid complete attention to *you*.

It was unnerving. And not just for me. Under his stare, people
trailed off and simply stopped talking. Some swallowed midsentence
and started apologizing. Some began chuckling, perhaps fishing for re-
ciprocation, but he did not rescue them. He let each syllable of their
laughter fade, like pebbles dropped into an abyss.

This was my guy.

An hour later, when the Q&A was done and we rose from our
cushions, I whispered to the nearest pakao, "Where does he live?"

"Ajahn Sukhito? He's at Poo Jom Gom."

I made a beeline to the place where he stood, wrapping himself in
his outer robe.

I hesitated as if approaching a wild animal. But he turned and
began walking away. This might be my only chance. Without thinking,
I stepped into his path.

"Um, Ajahn Sukhito?"

He stared at me. Up close, he was taller than I thought. His eyes
sunk into an elongated head, which perched between angular shoulders. He resembled a vulture. He said nothing. Blinked once.

I took that to mean that I should start talking. I introduced myself, outlined my plan to live in a monastery for six months, and wondered if, after some time to adjust at Nanachat, maybe I could visit Poo
Jom Gom?

"Are you considering ordination?" he said.

"I don't know," I said. "I'm here to try and see," which was true, and
which I also knew was the right way to frame it after having witnessed
the guest monk laugh at Josh's eagerness. I needed to thread the needle
between zealot and tourist.

He nodded once and said, "That's the way to do it."

I sensed an opening. "Maybe after a month or so at Nanachat," I said, "if things are going well, I could visit?"

He nodded once more. "We'll see in a month," he said and strode off.

I could've done a pirouette. Another pakao later confirmed that his monastery, Wat Pah Poo Jom Gom, was a secluded hermitage farther east, near the border of Laos, surrounded by miles of wilderness. Apparently, there were caves.

Back at the dorm, I grabbed my diary, bounded downstairs, and began writing on the edge of the porch under the light of the moon, recording everything I could remember from his talk. Remembering my question, I smiled at my past ignorance, which already seemed so distant to me now. I had raised a finger in semantic protest like a good liberal-arts student and *really* thought I had caught the first noble truth flat-footed. *The first noble truth!* And Ajahn Sukhito hadn't even let me finish.

I drew a graph to visualize his answer:

THE FOUR NOBLE TRUTHS

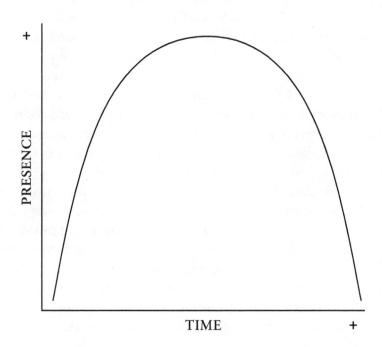

My caption: "Things arise, things pass away. Everything follows the curve. Suffering happens when we crave otherwise."

That is good shit, I thought, admiring my rendition of a universal truth, hardly registering the blossom of pride that came from writing the word *we*.

As the guest monk had promised, the standard daily schedule resumed. At 2:30 a.m. each morning, the sound of a large, distant bell filled the forest. I didn't know where it was or who had rung it, and I cherished the mystery.

By 3:00 a.m., the monks, pakaos, and overnight residents were seated in rows of cushions in a second sala, this one deeper in the woods. Dark forest surrounded us. Orange candlelight flickered on stone columns and the curves of a golden Buddha statue at the front of the room. Off to one side, in a glass case, hung a human skeleton, an object for the contemplation of death. Beside it was a smaller, sturdier case that rose to the skeleton's knees. It was filled with formaldehyde and the preserved body of a dead child. I'd examine this box later, on my own, noting how almost everything was preserved, pale skin, delicate closed eyelids, wisps of orange hair that floated in the liquid. It was also a tool for the contemplation of death, but it was too effective. If I looked at the child for too long, I felt my throat choke.

I had heard that funerals at the monastery involved burning a body in a charnel ground and letting it decompose in plain view. Another tool. I'd quietly hoped to view such a ceremony for its unique intensity and the lessons it might offer. But when faced with an actual dead body, I recoiled. It was easy to draw a graph in my diary and claim acceptance of everything passing away, or to study a skeleton that might as well have been a Halloween decoration. Not so much when it came to an actual boy whose real future had been cut short.

We would chant for thirty minutes in the forest sala each morning and evening. Despite my initial aversion, I found one particular chant compelling. Others must have, too, for over the course of this chant, our volume swelled. Individual voices blended into a collective incantation, rising and falling and turning between each of the three notes with the swift unity of a school of fish. Immediately afterward, the air felt charged. In the ringing moments before we closed our eyes and began sixty minutes of meditation, I found myself absorbing the sight of our group and feeling awe, understanding for a fleeting moment that I was surrounded by decent, disciplined people, people committed to harmlessness and who woke in the middle of the night to gather in the forest and sing.

After a couple of days of the standard routine had passed, Autumn, the woman from Berkeley, protested. It was bullshit, she said, that female residents weren't allowed to go to morning or evening chanting. She had warned me that this would happen. I agreed. It *was* bullshit. Also, I didn't want to look like I had forgotten entirely about the female residents, which I had, which was embarrassing. I also wasn't aware that while I genuinely agreed with her, at the same time, I was hunting for opportunities to criticize Nanachat under the cover of a righteous cause. Despite a handful of positive moments and a nascent sense that I was responsible for my own experience, monastic life still had not met my expectations, and I blamed Nanachat.

At first, I tried suggesting to Autumn that she wasn't really missing much, that chanting mostly sucked, and that I kind of wished I could miss it, too.

She patiently explained that that was completely beside the point. "What do they think is gonna happen?" she said. "Like, people are gonna sneak off and make out in the bushes? Is this a junior high dance?"

I laughed. She was right. But nodding in agreement was the extent of my support. It didn't occur to me to take any action. That would involve confrontation, and I was uncomfortable standing up for people, including myself.

Autumn spoke to the German abbot, who, after a couple of meetings, finally relented. While she was at the monastery, he said, evening chanting would move to the main sala, where women were allowed.

I noted that the abbot had accommodated her request only for the duration of her visit.

"Oh yeah," she said, shaking her head and shrugging. "Very aware they're just greasing the squeaky wheel. I mean, I'll take it, but . . ."

The next day, after the first evening of coed chanting, I asked what she thought.

"So, it was great," she said, then laughed. "*And*, I have to say, I get why the abbots don't want us there."

"Wait, what?"

"I don't expect you to have noticed, but did you watch any of the younger monks?"

I shook my head.

"Yeah." She grinned. "I haven't been looked at like that since I was twenty-five."

Hearing about the young monks put me in mind of how the kids with the strictest parents often went the wildest once they left for college. They'd had no chance to learn moderation. I was all for extremes, but the cons of barring women seemed to outweigh the pros, for women, certainly, but also for men, who were essentially trained to view all women as sex threats to be feared, avoided, and perhaps, craved even more.

Autumn's perspective helped plant a small seed of suspicion, even if I remained oblivious in other areas. For example, I didn't extend my suspicion of the Thai Forest Tradition any further, didn't pick up on the contradiction between excluding half of humanity while also claiming to cultivate generosity, spread unconditional love, and realize universal truth. I also didn't remember how the fear and craving I was projecting onto the young monks was, in fact, what I myself had felt back when I'd landed in Bangkok and met the woman from Alabama. I drew no parallel between my own misguided extreme and the monastery's.

Instead, I did what I usually did when I felt uncomfortable. I ignored it. I hoped, without admitting it, that the issue would simply disappear with time. Which might've also been what the German co-abbot hoped, that Autumn would eventually go back to Berkeley and take all her risky ideas with her.

Throughout the forest, there were signs with sayings nailed to the trunks of trees. Brown panels with white hand-painted messages in English hung beside trails like billboards along a highway.

"Who is the mind?" read one.

"Do not be arahant," read another, referring to an enlightened being. "Do not be anything at all. If you are anything at all, you will suffer."

Most quoted Ajahn Chah, the Thai master who was also known for cheekiness. The sign I reflected on the most stood near the office and had a translated quote from him that read, "Looking for peace is like looking for a turtle with a mustache. You won't be able to find it. But when your heart is ready, peace will come looking for you."

I didn't get it. What I *did* get was that I wanted to write little aphorisms like that myself. In my diary, I made earnest attempts at wisdom, writing abstractions with the inclusive *we* to give my words an air of the universal. Doing so felt majestic, and after filling a few pages, I reclined to imagine a future in which explorers discovered my precious text, brushed dust from the tattered pages, and painted the words onto signs.

When I wasn't writing truth, I read it. I devoured the titles on the small bookshelf in the dorm. Most were dhamma books by monks, but a few had been donated by visitors from the outside. In two ravenous sittings, I read *The Power of Now* by Eckhart Tolle, prying myself from the pages only to experience how it felt to rewrite his own words verbatim in my diary. His story was the one I craved—hit rock bottom, wake up enlightened, sit for days on a park bench in awe. Instant, irreversible growth, then a book about it.

Another book I picked up was called *Way of the Peaceful Warrior*. I transcribed an early quote fit for a tree sign:

"Stress happens when the mind resists what is."

Perfect, I thought. *Exactly.*

But as I read on, I felt duped. The main character's initial flaws were too obvious to be believable. Then, his transformation was too immediate and total. I flipped back a page in my diary and scratched out the quote about stress until the pen ripped the paper. It was nothing but a book of bumper-sticker wisdom. Worst of all, I'd fallen for it.

Somehow, my disgust for his story didn't taint my own hopes for metamorphosis. It didn't occur to me that the premise—*mysterious sage teaches white kid the meaning of life*—might have inspired some jealousy, especially because the writer seemed so sure of his own growth, nor did it strike me that as a white kid who had traveled to Southeast Asia in search of answers, I might not have been as original as I felt.

Having grown up around Black hip-hop culture in Atlanta, as both a fan and an outsider, I carried the fear that being white automatically rendered me unoriginal. Which made it hard to do anything without feeling like I was stealing from someone else. Self-loathing, then, seemed like the only appropriate option, but because I occupied the position of oppressor, not victim, my style of self-loathing would need to be preemptive and performative. But even that could morph into self-absorption. No one wants to hear the owner of a yacht lament the injustice of it.

Silence, then, was ideal. Annihilation. Simply ceasing to pollute the world with my existence. In a way, that was what the historical Buddha had initially tried when he set off in search of enlightenment. He'd left his family, starved himself, and brought his body to the brink of death. That was more or less what I was trying to do. Fasting, bowing, gone from everyone I had ever known. I was spurred by acute grief from my friend's death but also motivated by a general uncertainty of whether I mattered in the slightest. I'd flown to a country I knew nothing about to see if I could disappear.

But the thing was, I couldn't commit to the act. I wanted to exist; I just didn't know how. And I was furiously jealous of this other guy who had done something sort of similar and then felt confident enough to write a crappy book about it.

For a full day, I sulked. I longed for a place like Vimutti, the monastery I'd first visited in New Zealand a few years before. Back then, we had discovered a helpless baby goat in a pine forest, named it Lucky, and nursed it back to health until a Kiwi family on a farm nearby adopted it. Here at Nanachat, the wildlife I'd encountered so far included a centipede the size of a hot dog, which charged me with pincers bared.

At Vimutti, we awoke at sunrise and made fresh-fruit smoothies together around a communal blender in the kitchen. In the afternoon, there'd been free access to a pantry to partake of hunks of cheese, spoonfuls of honey, and swigs of ginger beer. Although the sixth precept prohibited eating after noon, a select few snacks and drinks were technically allowed. These were officially called "allowables," and the Buddha himself had apparently outlined the list so that monks could keep their energy from flagging in the afternoon.

But allowable didn't mean available. At Nanachat, there was no morning smoothie and no cheese and no public pantry. At tea the next afternoon, the sight of a food bowl trailing behind the drink coolers momentarily lifted my spirits. This was a first in Thailand—an actual afternoon snack!—but then I saw that the bowl was tiny, and its contents worse than nothing. Betel nuts. One per person. Bitter. Chalky. Joyless.

Vimutti, I remembered, was Pali for "freedom." Little did I know how much I had. There had been plentiful kutis, all stunning and positioned out of sight from one another to offer each resident a sense of solitude in nature. Mine had an incense holder and a large window overlooking a soft hillside of tall grass. I had been allowed to lace up my sneakers during free time—free time!—and go on long runs through the rolling farmland. There, I could picture ordaining as a monk. Not so at Nanachat. I was no longer asking monks why they ordained. I wanted to leave, but I had nowhere else to go.

One morning, something was wrong. I returned from a walk in the woods to find the Malaysian abbot with his arm draped around Ben, the young Thai pakao, whose eyes were red. He hid his face in his arm and sniffled through his braces.

I met the eyes of another witness, a skinny, somber pakao from Italy I had come to know as the one I had watched take two treats from the buffet tables on my first morning. He was named Giorgio, and he smiled at me sadly.

I asked in a low voice what was going on. Was Ben hurt? Had someone died?

"Ah. No, Grant," Giorgio said. "Everyone is healthy. He is leaving."

"Like, leaving the monastery?"

Giorgio closed his eyes, lifted his chin, and lowered his head in a single nod like the gavel of a judge.

"Why?"

"His parents. They are not allowing him to stay." Giorgio placed a commiserating hand on my shoulder. "They want him to have a job, to become a—how do you say?—*dentista.*"

"A dentist?"

"Yes, Grant. They want him to become a dentist."

I found Ben later, on a trail behind the sala. Unsure of what to say, I offered a hug. He allowed it, but he kept his arms by his sides and hardly looked up from the ground. The following morning, he was gone.

I'd fantasized about leaving, but not like that. I pictured going further into obscurity, not back toward technology and a career and parental pressure. Still, I thought of my own family. It had been almost two weeks since I'd arrived, and they were probably wondering if I was all right.

At the daily meeting after the meal, I asked the Czech guest monk for permission to walk to the internet café in town. I half hoped he'd say no. That way, I could relish and despise my severe living conditions.

But he shrugged and said, "Yeah, of course. Go now if you want."

"Oh, um, OK," I said. "I promise I won't be gone for too long."

But he wouldn't play along. "Take your time," he said.

I was frustrated by his flippant response, but I forgot about it the moment I stepped foot outside the entrance gate. Squinting, I surveyed the bright surrounding landscape for the first time in daylight. Out from under the forest canopy, the temperature was easily fifteen degrees hotter. I turned right on the pitted road, passing the fence where I'd brushed my teeth and stalled on the night of my arrival. On the other side stretched a dry field. A single water buffalo with a nose ring was lying in cracked mud.

Oddly enough, it had taken leaving the monastery to get some time alone. The sun warmed the white robes I'd taken from a communal bin at the dorm. I felt like I was thawing in spring. I swung my arms and hummed the tune that had been stuck in my head the last four days—the Game's "Too Much." I'd been amazed at how my mind, without all the distracting influences of urban life, could reproduce full songs I hadn't realized I knew, complete with lyrics and harmonies and instrumentation. I let my knees wobble into a dance on the side of the road as I replayed the track. Nate Dogg sang background. I *missed* music.

Soon I reached the county highway—the dusty, unlined road that self-organized into roughly six lanes of traffic. There were intermittent shops along its sides, concrete slabs with roofs on stilts, selling outdoor furniture and bamboo brooms. I scanned for the internet sign I'd heard was on the other side. Spotted it. Waited for an opening. Scampered across.

Oh, to scamper! I hadn't run for what felt like ages. I may not have made it past junior high in basketball, but I had excelled in other sports, all of which required something that could compensate for my lack of brute strength: speed. I was fast. The game that stuck through college and even beyond was Ultimate Frisbee. It fit my aptitudes for quickness and timing, both of which I felt in a tiny, joyful dose when crossing the road.

I missed training at what was my other temple: the four-hundred-meter track surrounding the green grass field. In truth, I had delayed my departure to Thailand by a month after quitting my job because I still played at a nationally competitive level, and I had a season to finish. Six months—the minimum on this monastic experiment—also happened to be the length of the off-season. I'd hedged. If I didn't ordain, I'd be back in time to play.

Of course, I'd be out of shape. Which was another qualm of mine with monastic life at Nanachat. How could they neglect the unequivocal good of exercise? Sure, individual yoga was allowed, which I liked, but nothing aerobic or explosive or team based. Games were prohibited. So out of spite for them and delight for myself, I maintained a jog after crossing the highway, bounding all the way to the landing of the internet café.

Kids' shoes littered the white tiles. Sliding glass doors stood open, framing a long room with two rows of computer monitors on either side. Along the left wall sat a squad of seven children, bare feet dangling from the chairs, all playing *Call of Duty*. They hardly noticed as I passed behind to the back, where I gave a few coins to a young woman behind a desk. She didn't seem all that surprised to see me, either. It hit me that she was probably used to foreigners in white robes coming over from Nanachat to check their email. She handed me a password printed on a slip of paper. I found a computer opposite the kids and typed it in.

Just like that, I was back. The internet.

And I was prepared: I flipped my diary to the page with a list of checkboxes. So far, most of my meditation sessions on my own had ended the way they often did back home: cut short because I'd remembered an item to add to my to-do list.

First, Gmail. When I logged in, I smiled at the sight of my personal account's home screen. I had customized it back when I was a consultant, so the background was a wood-grain motif. I had wanted a natural-looking theme because it was the opposite of my corporate reality. I could tell slight differences between airline rewards programs, but I longed to be more of a carpenter type like my father, who could discern hickory from walnut and pine. Now that I actually *lived* in the forest, I examined the background behind my unread emails and thought, *Mahogany?*

I clicked over into settings to find out, but the theme was just called "Wood."

One hundred and fifty-seven unread messages. Before reading any of them, I opened new tabs and checked the NBA and NFL standings, which suddenly felt important. In another tab, I opened YouTube but didn't search for anything. Then paged back to football. The Atlanta Falcons were off to another rough start, but it didn't matter. What mattered was knowing.

A green grasshopper the size of my hand zapped onto the keyboard. I yelped. The woman at the desk and the kids turned and looked up in alarm.

I shrunk and grinned and bowed to the woman and then to the kids, who giggled but spun back around to resume their games. They were all wearing headsets, and I noticed I had one, too, hanging on the corner of my monitor. I put the thin plastic band over my head, plugged it in, and typed the Game's "Too Much" into YouTube.

The sound of music in my ears was like the taste of warm butter. Entertainment wasn't allowed in the monastery. But I wasn't in the monastery. Five minutes later, I was listening to A Tribe Called Quest, "Keeping It Moving." Lake Street Dive, "Bad Self Portraits." The Weeknd, "Wicked Games." Every chant at the monastery, even my favorite one, offered a grand total of three notes—low, middle, and high—and they were always a cappella, no percussion or range or flow. I needed this.

I emailed my family. Told them how much I loved them and how much my knees hurt from sitting cross-legged all the time. I wrote to a few of my Ultimate Frisbee teammates from college with some chest-thumping declarations about how I was "about to start going hard with fasting and sleep deprivation." Which was true, but I also wanted them to *know.* Then I dashed off random notes of kindness and appreciation to people I'd found crossing my mind over the last couple of weeks. These composed over half of my diary's checklist.

On the bottom of the screen, a box popped up in the chat.

It was MJ.

I held down the exclamation mark key. So did she.

Is this for real? we wrote. Both of us happen to be logged on at the same time?

Yeah!

What time of day was it in Brooklyn?

Night, she wrote. Her apartment was hosting a party, but she had felt something in the air and gone to check her computer.

I asked what day it was.

Saturday, she said.

Had she gotten my box of letters?

Yes!

Had she opened any?

Only the one for this month, she said, even though she wanted to open all of them at once.

We said we missed each other. She asked about the clouds, what shapes I was seeing, and what messages I'd gleaned from the wilderness, luxurious questions I hadn't given myself the space to consider.

Our MO had never been IRL. We'd spent a total of three days together in person: one lunch where a friend had introduced us and one weekend when I'd visited her a month before leaving. We'd never so much as kissed. Most of our relationship had occurred over video and text, so this was familiar. On the other hand, our interactions from day one had the feeling of building toward something more. Now that I was gone, that something was in jeopardy.

This reality seemed to creep back into our awareness. Our gush slowed to a trickle. We typed goodbye and offered parting words of affection, careful to avoid the word *love*.

Her green-dot status disappeared. I began breathing again.

The remaining unread emails had lost their allure, and I began deleting them en masse. Spam. Promotions. Updated terms of service. I almost missed a message from the US State Department.

"Congratulations," it said, "you passed the Foreign Service Officer Test."

I'd forgotten all about it. On one of my last video calls with MJ, I had noticed a study guide on her bookshelf and asked what it was. She'd explained that if you worked for the State Department, you could live abroad, which was a dream of hers. The first step in the application was this standardized test. Without telling MJ, I'd found a testing center in Minneapolis and taken it on a lark the following week, mostly so that I could tell her afterward and hope to impress her with how I was spontaneous and interested in international relations, her college major.

But I hadn't expected to pass. Now, the US Foreign Service was requesting responses to essay questions so that they could consider me for the next round. In a blank page of my diary, I recorded the prompts, logged out, and left the café.

Before crossing the main road back to Nanachat, I stopped at a convenience store. At the rate I was journaling, I'd need another diary. All I could find was a purple plaid notebook with graph paper. Good enough. At checkout, some delicious contraband beneath the register caught my eye. Kinder Bueno. Hazelnut chocolate. I tossed some onto the counter.

Over the next few afternoons, I sat for hour-long stretches at the buffet tables in the kitchen and handwrote my essays for employment at the US State Department. The job entailed international assignments not of your choosing, a roll of the dice that appealed to my sense of the extreme. I knew the drill for job applications: relay boring professional anecdotes to illustrate transferable skills, inflate every achievement to the outermost edge of honesty—what everyone seemed to do. That was the game.

But I wanted to do it differently this time, to prove to myself that I had made some spiritual progress over fourteen days of monastic life. I took a more genuine approach and wrote about how, the year before, I had convinced my Ultimate Frisbee team to alter the uniforms, doing away with baggy shorts, which were the norm, in favor of spandex tights. If convincing thirty men to wear skintight, junk-hugging compression didn't prove I had the aptitude to be a diplomat, I thought, I didn't know what did. The next week, I returned to the café and submitted the essays online.

My application, rather quickly, was rejected.

But I didn't know. I had no way of knowing that when I sent off the essays, that would be my last time online for months. The rejection sat in my inbox, unread.

Meanwhile, hardly a day passed in the months that followed in which I didn't stop to fantasize about my future as a diplomat. I enjoyed the thought that maybe I would gather so much wisdom from meditating for six months that, like, I wouldn't even *need* to ordain or stay any longer as a monk. My résumé would say *former* monk, *current* diplomat.

Diplomat. God. The title sounded so sexy. Later, I paced the forest trails in my white robes and rubber sandals and wondered what I might wear to work. Probably blazers with open collars—refined but suggestive of a rugged edge. I'd stand with a martini at galas and regale the other distinguished guests with tales of my most recent assignment in Istanbul. It sounded so perfect compared with my current reality of centipedes, betel nuts, and crowds.

Other times, though, the fantasy got away from me. I couldn't choose where the State Department sent me, and I imagined being put on a covert assignment in Thailand. The mission: to live undercover indefinitely, posing as a monk at an Ajahn Chah monastery. Which would send me right back to where I was at Wat Pah Nanachat, feeling the exact same way, sour and lost and exhausted with myself. I pictured receiving the terrible news of this imaginary assignment, dropping to my knees in the middle of the street, raising incredulous arms to the sky. Rain would mat the button-down to my clammy skin. Thunder would clap in sarcastic applause. The camera would pan overhead, and I'd cry, "Is there no escape from this hell?"

GECKO

Ajahn Chah offered a template for life as a monastic practitioner: "Eat little, sleep little, speak little." By any stretch, we'd already achieved the trifecta by virtue of the schedule and lifestyle. One meal a day. Wake up at 2:30 a.m. A culture of noble silence. But it wasn't enough for me to meet expectations. I wanted to exceed them.

I took it upon myself to invent and enroll in an accelerated enlightenment program. AP Buddhism. I focused on food. I ate little, but I wanted to eat less. I dreamed of fasting for days on end. To stop eating entirely was to become self-sufficient by cutting myself off from a weak reliance upon the external world.

There were two problems. First, there was no place to honor the faster, no throne on a jungle pyramid exclusively reserved for the truly dedicated. If I fasted, then all I would do was sit upstairs in the empty dorm, twiddling my thumbs and listening to the clink of other people's spoons below. The second problem with fasting was that it meant not eating. I was constantly ravenous. If sacrificing calories didn't offer the nourishment of glory, then in the end, it wasn't worth it.

The next-best option, I decided, was to subsist as the Buddha himself had at the height of his ascetic training. A single grain of rice per day. I would pass through the buffet tables with my head held high, and the sides of my unstained bowl would glimmer with emptiness. In the crowded room of residents, eating a tiny portion would be a public signal of loftier virtue.

The only problem with this strategy was that it didn't work. When it came time for me to serve myself in the line, to see and smell and select my feast after twenty-four hours of famine, I couldn't help but take full advantage and pile my bowl above the brim.

And so, instead of eating less, I ate quickly. I set out to finish the meal first, before all the other residents, like the kid in gym who tries to win the warm-up lap. When I succeeded, I rose from my seat and inhaled to assume an air of mindfulness, not because I was aware of having lost it but because I wanted to bask in victory. I sauntered across the front of the dining area, clenching my face into what I hoped was a look of casual serenity, a look that might say, "Oh, did I win? Honestly, you know, I don't think of it as a contest."

That said, the competition was stiff. Josh was also quick. Sometimes, I caught him peeking at my bowl to check my progress against his. I despised this, and it never crossed my mind why I'd been checking to see where he was looking in the first place. If he ever finished before me, I rolled my eyes and told myself he was taking things too seriously. Classic nineteen-year-old. Eating wasn't a race, for God's sake. If neither of us finished first, then it was always another young male who did, a demographic pattern from which I drew no conclusions.

One battle I consistently lost was dessert. At the end of the buffet tables, beyond the fresh fruit, were bowls of packaged treats— chocolates, wafers, cream-filled crisps. I knew better. They'd make me feel sluggish. I was aware that the colorful packaging was designed to trigger desire, but after twenty-four hours, I was helpless and balanced as many as I could on top of my heaping bowl.

When I finished them all, I cursed myself for failing to abstain. Every day: the same desire before eating them followed by the same disgust after, a cycle of obsession and disenchantment reminiscent of watching porn. I cursed myself. If I couldn't eat less, the least I could do was eat healthy food. I cursed the treats, too. The way I saw it, candy should be outlawed at monasteries. It was the epitome of sensual indulgence with no lasting benefit. Avoiding this kind of fleeting pleasure was basic stuff, Buddhism 101. I was failing.

One day, a visitor brought a delicacy that put my jaw on the floor. A dozen glazed Krispy Kreme doughnuts. I spotted the box during meal prep. I needed to touch it. I scurried over. With one hand, I fanned away flies. With the other, I surreptitiously caressed the contours of the thin cardboard box. It was a luxury good, a sleek rectangle, white with red cursive print and green accents and clean corners—packaging a department store might reserve for a cashmere sweater.

I was so caught up in anticipation that I forgot to feel upset that Krispy Kreme doughnuts might tarnish my fantasy of a refuge detached from the outside world. I also forgot to feel curious about how they had appeared. These doughnuts and I went way back. My family had a tradition of going to Krispy Kreme every Christmas Eve. My sister and I would rest our foreheads on the glass window inside to watch the factory's conveyor belts ferry perfect rows of cake bread under a waterfall of glaze. I needed one of these doughnuts. The question was how I might get two.

Then I did the math and felt sick. There were twelve doughnuts but twenty-five monks, plus a handful of residents more senior than me. That meant more than half of the people ahead needed to abstain for me to get one.

And yet, here I was, the only person sitting right beside all of them. I could never get away with it, though. Instead, I crept my hand underneath the box and simply left it there to feel the warmth and the weight on my palm. When I was forced to depart for chanting, I withdrew as if releasing a lover.

But perhaps all was not lost. I wondered if the monks would heed the advice from a dhamma book I had recently picked up. "What we cannot relinquish," it said, "we must patiently restrain."

A new calculus struck. If no doughnuts were left by the time I reached the box, that meant all these monks who talked a big game about abandoning pleasure didn't practice what they preached. I might not get a doughnut, but I'd lay claim to the moral high ground. On the other hand, if there *were* doughnuts left when I reached the box, that meant most of the monks *had* restrained themselves. Which, I realized, meant I should, too. I had thought myself into a trap.

"Maybe," I wrote later in my diary, "the value of monastic life stems from the indulgences I'm *isolated* from (booze, internet, sex) rather than from those I'm *tempted* by (doughnuts, naps, gossip)."

I badly wanted this to be true. Isolation was cleaner than temptation. It removed choice. It forced good habits. Extreme commitments accelerated personal development. I felt a desperate need to rule my-self with an iron fist because I didn't have the energy or trust to emerge on the right side of nuance.

What I failed to spot was how the temptations I thought lacked value—doughnuts, naps, gossip—fell precisely into the three cate-gories for which Ajahn Chah had offered guidance—eating, sleep-ing, speaking. Hungry as I was for an epiphany, I missed it because I wanted a different flavor.

I never came to a final decision about whether I would take a doughnut if given the chance. By the time I reached the box, they were all gone. For a moment, I slumped at the sight, then straightened in the hopes of denying my own disappointment. I felt my mouth pull toward a scowl. Hypocritical monks. Hedonists. I decided then and there that I would never have taken a doughnut.

Then I noticed a sparkle inside the open Krispy Kreme box: un-claimed sugar crystals, a dozen circular footprints where doughnuts had once rested. Before I could talk myself out of it, I'd reached in with my spoon and scraped it along the surface to salvage what I could.

That night, I set up a bug net in the dorm for privacy—a small tent with opaque mesh walls. I'd scoffed when others had used them. We were already indoors, so what was the use? But tonight, I had a reason.

Carefully, so that none of the residents could hear, I slid one of the Kinder Bueno bars from its wrapper and ate it. The bars had been call-ing to me from my backpack ever since I'd made the impulse buy at the convenience store. And now I answered. I closed my jaws and my eyes and thought, *Heaven.*

I hoped my chewing wasn't audible. I clamped my lips and used my tongue between bites to wrap bits of the loud, crunchy wafer in a muf-fling layer of hazelnut cream and chocolate. I wanted to smack my lips and moan in ecstasy, but there were these damn people around. I re-sented them all. I ate the other Kinder Bueno bar and resented myself, too. I had officially eaten past noon and thus knowingly broken a rule for the first time. Now that the bars were gone, it hadn't been worth it. I was still hungry but guilty to boot.

At the same time, I kicked myself for not getting *more* Kinder Buenos at the store. If I was going to break the rule, then I might as well have broken it bigger. Now all I had was evidence of my crime and no place to dispose of it. There were no trash cans upstairs, and my robes didn't have pockets. Sighing, I tucked the plastic under the corner of my sleeping pad. Each time I tossed and turned that night, I wondered if the other residents could hear the wrapper crinkling.

A few days prior, the Czech guest monk had pulled me aside at the office. He had news. Soon, there would be space for me to move out of the dorm and into my own kuti. I nodded in disbelief. Second, he had a job for me. He dug his hand into an orange satchel and handed me a set of keys. Each morning after chanting and meditation, someone had to walk down to the entrance gate, unlock it, and prop both sides open so that the visitors could enter and the monks could leave for alms round. That someone was now me.

I stood taller. Surely, this responsibility carried metaphorical significance. A mere two weeks earlier, I reflected, I had entered through the gate in the dark, arms outstretched, blind in so many ways. Now, I was entrusted to bear its key.

The guest monk must have seen my eyes getting starry, because he said, "Hey. All you have to do is go open it."

From then on, around 4:00 a.m., when we rose from the forest sala and made our way back to the main area, I continued alone, past the kitchen and down the final unlit stretch to the gate. The distance from the main area to the gate was about a hundred yards, and it was as pitch-dark as it had been on the night of my arrival. For once, I experienced a sense of pure solitude on these walks. Which was exactly what I thought I wanted.

But every time I heard a rustle or a snap in the brush, I flinched. I clutched the keys in my hand, which was sweaty and smelled of metal. I pointed the tips between my knuckles like claws. I never saw anything, until one morning, a few steps short of the gate, I swore I glimpsed a figure on the other side.

Moonlight spilled through the vertical bars of the closed gate, and I shrank back into the shadows. The figure seemed to have heard me coming and hidden. If I unlocked the gate, I thought, I'd get ambushed. After a few minutes without a sign of him, I tiptoed closer and peered left and right through the gaps. Seeing nothing, I slipped the key into the slot. The lock clicked open, loudly, and in one swoop, I pulled half the gate open—fast, so that the hinges didn't groan. I turned back to fling open the other half and froze.

A man stood in the opening. He was old and hunched and Thai. He pointed something at me like a gun or a curse.

I made a choking sound, raised my arms, and backed away.

The man limped toward me, muttering some maniacal incantation. "Khan dee. Khan dee." He rattled his hand as if he wanted to drop something, and I found myself cupping my hands beneath his.

His fingers unfurled, and three pieces of hard candy fell into my palms.

The old man squeezed my hands shut over his. Then he patted my shoulder and hobbled up the path to help with the sweeping, leaving me panting in the dark, bewildered by my ability to misread a situation and unsure of whether I was allowed to eat the candy.

As promised, I moved to my own kuti. One reason I had eaten the Kinder Bueno before moving there was that I felt breaking the rule in my new place would start me off on the wrong foot. Better to squeeze in a violation on the tail end of a dwelling that, in my opinion, was itself a violation—of the solitude and silence that I felt I deserved. The dorm was a hog pen, so eating like one was hardly a crime. *Now*, though, now that I had my own kuti, I thought, I could *really* get down to serious practice.

The kuti was sublime. Just beyond the sala, the wooden hut stood on thin stilts with its back to the path. Around front were a few stairs leading to a tiny porch where I could slip off my sandals and enter. The ceiling inside was tall enough to stand but not jump, and a bug net hung from a hook. My sleeping pad used up half the floor space. The two windows had wooden shutters, and uneven floorboards welcomed each passing breeze from below.

In the hours between the work period and afternoon tea, I took to sitting in a plastic chair on the porch, straightening my back, and taking long breaths to begin meditating. The schedule had loosened since Kathina had passed, and the unstructured afternoon hours were meant for practice. My porch overlooked a kind of yard backed by a dense wall of brush. At the foot of the stairs ran a rectangular strip of dirt with an outline of small stones—a private path for walking meditation.

From my chair, I relished the view. Once I felt relaxed enough to unfocus my eyes, I shut them. My jaw unclenched. My shoulders dropped, and my ears trained to the sounds of the forest. I had made it, meditating in a hut in the wilderness.

Then my concentration would go to shit. I'd hear the snap of a twig, or the crunch of a leaf, or what sounded like the slap of an orange flip-flop against the heel of a passing monk. Within a few days, I realized I wasn't as isolated as I had hoped. My kuti was so close to the main path. I'd upgraded to my own house, but it was next to a highway.

When I heard a monk walking by, I shifted and imagined their judgmental eyes, feeling the sting of their displeasure at the sight of me in a chair instead of on the ground in lotus pose. *Back support hinders true concentration.* I was certain they were thinking it.

I certainly was. I was ashamed to need a chair. I could run a sub-five-minute mile and squat three hundred pounds, but when I tried to sit cross-legged, my knees pointed up in a V shape and trembled like the wings of a captured butterfly. I hunched and huffed and gripped my knees to avoid toppling over backward. Sitting meditation: fight of my life, fire of my groin.

The hours of chanting and meditating and eating as a group each day were strictly floor-based activities and were so grueling that I couldn't spend another minute on the ground by myself. And so on my porch, I squeezed my eyes and yelled inside my head that I could sit in a chair if I goddamn wanted to. This was *my* porch.

Sometimes, I grew so upset that I could no longer take a monk's gaze quietly. I'd hear a noise and open my eyes, which riled me up even more because peeking felt like a failure of discipline. I'd lean around the side of the porch, prepared to shoot someone a serious stink eye.

Almost every time, though, the path was empty. No one had been there at all.

One afternoon, I retired to my kuti for another attempt at porch meditation. Plopped into the plastic chair. Rubbed my face.

Time to do it, I thought, pressing my temples, forehead, and jaw. But I couldn't. I didn't want to listen to my own thoughts anymore. I stood up. Started pacing. But there wasn't space to pace on the porch. I moved to sit down again but realized that it would look crazy to any passersby if I had marched up my stairs, sat down, rubbed my face, stood up, and sat back down again.

I felt insane. I had looked forward to getting away from everyone for weeks. Now that I was alone, I wanted nothing to do with myself. I wanted to groan but realized that would look crazy, too. I squeezed my fists, bounced on my toes. My stomach sloshed in complaint. I felt like a snake with a rat lodged in my torso, and somehow, I also felt like the rat.

Maybe I needed to digest, I thought. A nap would help me be more alert for meditation, which I'd definitely do, for sure, at some point, just not now.

With my own space, I could nap as often as I wanted, and I did, sometimes three times a day. In the absence of a phone or exercise or friends or snacks or music or games or anything I might use to distract myself from myself, this strategy had become the only reliable means of escape: shut the whole machine off. Go to sleep.

Each time I awoke, I mourned the loss of that sweet, thoughtless black. I also felt ashamed, for part of the Ajahn Chah instruction was to "sleep little."

Today, though, I didn't care. I crept inside the kuti and passed out.

An hour later, I awoke and checked my wristwatch: 2:30 p.m., twelve hours since I'd woken up and gone through the motions—chanting, sitting, opening the gate, sweeping, helping with the meal, napping, chanting a second time, eating, sweeping, napping again—and now here I was, same as the day before, still here, still shackled to my mind, lugging myself everywhere I went. Teatime was something to look forward to, but it was also a false destination. Everything washed together. After tea in three hours, I'd come right back here to this empty hut with nothing, absolutely nothing, to *do.*

This is why I'm here, I thought without sympathy. *This, right now. I asked for this, to isolate the variable of the mind.* I rose and made my way back to the plastic chair on the porch to put my head between my knees.

Run, I thought out of the blue. *Just break the rule. Go for a run. A stealth jog outside the monastery. I have the keys to the gate!*

I pictured the sneakers I hadn't touched since arriving, crumpled in the bottom of my backpack in a corner of the dormitory. I could al-most feel my legs striding out on the open road, fields unfurling under a broad sky.

But I wouldn't do it, even though I'd allowed myself to munch a candy bar after noon, and even though the rule against exercise seemed dumb no matter which way I looked at it. Running was healthy and rhythmic, a form of meditation, even. It wasn't bodybuilding. I wasn't doing it for *ego* reasons. I mean, sure, growing up, I'd fantasize about sexy older women following me in their minivans down a back-street, cutting me off, pulling me into the back, and ravishing me. But that wasn't what I wanted now. All I wanted was the wholesome purity of motion, a break from this hellish stagnation.

I glanced up at the walking meditation path beyond my porch. If I couldn't run, I thought, maybe I could walk.

I was skeptical of walking. As exercise, it seemed inferior to run-ning. As meditation, it seemed inferior to sitting. I'd heard monks say you couldn't go as *deep* in walking practice. I realized that might be exactly what I needed.

The walking meditation path was shaped like an airstrip: one step wide, twenty-five long. I was self-conscious in view of the main trail, and I stomped up and back with arms holstered at my sides. But even-tually I wore myself into a rhythm and focused on how I felt more than how I looked. Slowing down, I observed the transfer of weight from the back of the heel to the wave of pressure along the arch to the push off the big toe into a floating sensation as the foot swung forward.

This was nice. And different from what little instruction I had re-ceived so far, which had been to concentrate on the breath at the very tip of the nose: coming in, going out. Monks were also fond of saying not to change the breath. "Just let it be," they'd say.

I found both strategies unhelpful. For one, squeezing my attention into the tip of my nose made my eyes cross. Worse, the method of fo-cusing on my nose confined my attention to my head, the same region of my body that generated the unending stream of thoughts, which, I wrote in my diary, was like evolution producing an animal with its mouth right next to its anus. It was bad design. And while *just letting it be* sounded carefree and untroubled, it was too passive. It gave me nothing to do.

Walking, I found, was different. The soles of my feet were the far-thest thing from my head. And I could be intentional, moving in super-slow motion, taking five minutes to walk a single length of the strip. I could step silently, bend my knees, micro-balance. I hadn't felt like this in weeks, exploring in my body rather than cooped up in my head.

Before, I'd felt like a helium balloon. A bloated head full of gas above a neglected body of string. Now I imagined myself as a hunter. A big cat. I reflected on this image, determining whether it merited a diary entry. Without realizing it, I stopped walking, stood upright on the path, and lost myself in thought, alternating between descriptions of balloons and jaguars.

Then I came to. But I didn't take a long breath. I didn't reset and re-turn to the meditation. Instead, I rushed off the path and up the porch steps. Not only did I need to record these images in the diary, but I also needed to attend to another bold idea that had struck me. I flung open the diary on my porch and began scribbling. This could be my ticket to survival in solitude: I'd write a book.

Keeping an assiduous diary would keep my mind keen. Plus, it would offer an invaluable historical record of my adventure. I wrote that word, *invaluable*, in my diary to describe my own diary.

I'd publish the diary verbatim, probably. To keep it raw. Unlike other mindfulness books, mine would tell the *real* story. Uncensored. Uncut. I'd probably give a TED Talk. Maybe start a for-profit school for certifying life coaches. I began brainstorming titles.

Within minutes, I landed on it: *Diligentle.*

It was perfect. A combination of *diligent* and *gentle*, the two ingre-dients in my special recipe for a better life. The masses would instantly recognize the yin and yang of these two previously unpaired compo-nents and see which was lacking—and which overdone—in their own lives. A single word, simple. But a new word, original. Like how tech companies used wordplay in their names. Readers would be struck with a jolt of enlightenment from simply glancing at the cover.

I was on a roll. I turned to the next page and, as I imagined was customary in the book-writing process, drafted a few blurbs from ce-lebrities for the back cover: Michelle Obama might exclaim that this was the best book she'd read in a decade and that she was so proud of this young author; the Dalai Lama might appreciate the author's deft ability to remove the rose-colored lenses through which the West so often viewed Eastern thought. In all caps *and* italics, the dust flap would promise that readers could apply this modernized trove of ancient insight to all arenas: family, romance, small business, corporations, church groups. This book would change your life!

Next, I considered the author photo. I'd want to be smiling because I wouldn't want to look like I took myself too seriously, but I wouldn't grin too wide because that would come off as overzealous. The smile would need to be wise, closed-lipped, with a knowing squint in the eyes that said, "Yes, my students, yes, I have seen the great light beyond, and it has made me beautiful, and I want you, too, to see that rapturous realm of liberation. But mostly, I want you to see me, me looking out at you from my black-and-white photo, me, a regular, humble hero who splits wood and makes hearty soups in a cabin and seems to enjoy a low profile, kind of like a father character in a movie who's grizzled and laconic and has secrets from his time in the CIA."

From my porch, I practiced this smile, seducing the young trees in my yard. I felt alive and invigorated, like a sage who, in just over three weeks of not meditating, had pierced the depths of the human psyche and survived to tell the tale.

As evidence of the Buddha's boundless compassion, people cite his life of teaching following his enlightenment. Six years after he left his wife and child, he attained full awakening while sitting at the base of a bodhi tree under a full moon. He was thirty-five years old. He'd made it. If contentment is the greatest wealth, as he apparently said, then after his liberation, he was rich. He could've abided in secluded, rapturous retirement for the rest of his days.

Instead, for the next forty-five years, he roamed what is now the India-Nepal border, gaining followers and delivering sermons on the nature of reality and the mind. His eighty-year existence alone should be considered a feat; life expectancy at the time was less than half that. The Buddha's teachings far outlived him. For the next five hundred years, his life and lessons were passed down orally in the form of chants, until they were recorded as the foundational texts of the Buddhist religion, the Pali Canon. Theravada Buddhism, which includes the Thai Forest Tradition, relies only on those oldest texts.

With subtle derision, Theravada monks refer to any later scriptures as "commentarial."

I felt conflicted about this exclusivity. On the one hand, I found it incredibly badass. It meant these monks lived as closely as possible to the code of the OG Buddha himself. Any differences between the practices of these twenty-first-century monks and the historical Buddha were merely due to inaccuracies in a more than 2,500-year-long game of telephone and translation. On the other hand, it was pretentious and rigid. It ignored the possibility of adapting as the world grew wiser about, for example, gender equality. However, what concerned me most at the time about Theravada Buddhists' narrow canon was how it threw into question the value of my forthcoming diary.

The only way out of this predicament was to wonder if my own work was special. Which was basically what I was raised to think about myself after two decades of private schooling and liberal arts education—that I was different, exceptional, could do anything I wanted, and that, whatever it was, it would *change the world*. My magnum opus wouldn't be merely *commentarial*. And so, rather than edging toward humility, I sought to infuse the everyday events of my life with even greater metaphysical meaning.

When, one morning, I surprised a cicada, and it flew headfirst into a support beam and dropped dead, I flew headfirst to my diary, where, in the tradition of pop spiritual leaders, I had fully adopted the use of the inclusive *we*.

"When we feel scared," I wrote, "we tend to run blindly, not toward anything in particular, but away from that which scares us—that which *we* choose to fear. Only with the calm release of fear can we transcend our less-evolved instincts of . . ."

I went on. In all caps at the end, I signed off with a note to my eventual publisher: "Title this chapter 'INSECT INSIGHTS.'"

For all my meaning-making, I often failed to find the lessons I could've used the most. In the middle of one night, I awoke to the sound of splitting wood. I turned on a headlamp and discovered a beetle the size of my fist, ramming itself headfirst into the corner of my kuti. I didn't want to kick it for fear of killing it, but I didn't want to grab it for fear of it killing me. I tried with a broom, but the beefy bug was too strong to be budged. Watching it repeatedly ram its head into a wall, I conjured no parallel whatsoever to my own activities. All I thought was *That's a big-ass beetle.*

I also wasn't sure what to make of my next visitor. One afternoon, I returned from the work period and spotted a massive gecko clinging to my open window shutter. It was as long as my forearm, and when it pounded across the sill and inside my walls, I shouted and peed myself a little.

To scare it away, I tried stomping. Which did nothing. It hung there on my wall with its vacant eyes locked on me. I retrieved a bamboo broom, swatted at it until it fled, and vowed never to leave my shutters open again.

After the intruders, I decided it was time for a deep clean. I tied the bug net in a hanging bun over the wood-slat floor. Cleared cobwebs. Swished the twigs of the broom through the room and the porch, down the steps, and then, for no reason, underneath the kuti in the dirt. It made no sense to clean dirt from the dirt ground, but on I went, sweeping around the kuti, then beyond it, widening my circles until I'd cleared a twenty-foot radius of every stray twig.

Later that day, a skinny monk approached me. He was Dutch, and his resting expression, I felt, was one of haughty judgment. I froze, certain he was going to critique something I'd done wrong, but he began praising the appearance of my kuti.

"It's very good," he said. He had walked by earlier that day. It was so clean, he said, that he thought I had moved out entirely.

I'd never heard him speak, and his voice—high-pitched and raspy—didn't sound like what I expected from his face. But suddenly, everything about his demeanor felt warm.

"Oh," I said. "Well, OK, um, thank you."

"So clean," he said for the second time and smiled. He raised a finger and tapped his temple. "You know, it says something about your mind."

I beamed. How could I have thought this monk was pompous? Clearly, he was intelligent and perceptive and kind, and I loved him.

"FAMILIARITY BREEDS LIKING," I wrote in the diary, happy to log a new axiom. I drew a box around the phrase, as if to suggest it might one day be printed on a sign.

That afternoon, I went to tea with my head held high. I'd cleared my home of pests and debris and received a compliment from a legit monk; I felt I'd earned some conversation.

I sat near a novice Australian monk and regaled him with the drama of banishing the gecko.

"Oh, you had a gecko?" he said. "Don't chase those away, mate! Everyone wants a gecko in their kuti. They eat all the insects. They're like guardians."

Each morning, as the bruise of sky changed from black to blue, monks could be seen wrapping themselves in their outer robes and securing their brushed metal alms bowls in a woven sling over one shoulder. Barefoot, they set out to the nearby villages to collect offerings of food.

This was alms round, the age-old tradition of monks begging for their daily bread, sworn not to eat anything that hadn't been offered specifically to them on that very day. Food connected monks to the outside world in an exchange where each side offered the other a kind of sustenance: physical for one, spiritual for the other.

For my purposes, however, alms round meant something decidedly less profound: sweeping. Every morning, for an hour after chanting and meditation, under rickety lamps that clung to the trees and buzzed, the residents searched every walkable surface around the property for every single leaf that had fallen since the morning before. Monks would join the effort for the first ten minutes or so but leave when it was time for alms.

A benefit of my recent promotion to gate opener was that walking down and back up the entrance driveway ate into sweeping time. I had taken to moseying back up the path toward the broom shed as slowly as possible, placing each foot ever so intentionally in front of the other, prepared to defend myself against accusations of indolence with a line about developing my walking meditation practice.

Alas, even at my snail's pace, I couldn't extend the hundred-yard walk into a full hour. Eventually, I had no choice but to arrive at the shed by the kitchen, where only the worst brooms remained—short shafts, split handles, missing twig bristles.

Some treated sweeping like it was a holy mission. Solemn expressions. Silence. Severe attention to every individual leaf. When their bristles couldn't dislodge a wet one, they'd kneel and remove it with thumb and forefinger.

They might as well use tweezers, I thought. I stooped to no leaf, but I also refused to give up if I couldn't move one with the broom. I'd swing at obstinate leaves like a hockey player, wearing the bristles down to the nub, failing to see any symbolism.

"Why don't we just let the leaves 'be as they are'?" I wrote in my diary. "You know, just 'bring awareness' to the leaves and 'accept their nature' to fall?"

At this hour, everything anyone did got under my skin. If someone was sweeping where I had already swept, I cursed them for implying I'd done a poor job. I hated that no one ever spoke, but then if someone whispered something, I'd frown at them for breaking the silence.

Senior monks always called sweeping *working meditation.* They added that it was an opportunity to watch emotions like anger arise. I knew this. But connecting theory to practice meant taking some responsibility, and it was a lot easier for me to contemplate the universality of a truth than it was to apply it personally.

Besides, I noticed that the monks who touted the benefits of sweeping were also almost always conveniently elsewhere when it actually came time to sweep. One day I got a chance to join them. The guest monk had approached with more news. I would be invited to accompany the monks on alms round at sunrise.

Alms round occurred every morning, seven days a week, rain or shine. Because multiple villages surrounded Nanachat, the monks split into smaller pods of around four. This morning, I'd follow the Dutch monk who had complimented the hygiene of my kuti; a casual, portly monk from China; and a shy Black pakao from England.

When it came time to go, the Dutch monk waved me into a huddle with the other two.

"OK"—he turned to me like a coach drawing up a play—"when we get out of the gate, we'll fall into single file and walk—not in a rush, but not slowly, either—along the road to the village. You don't have to worry about directions; just follow me."

I nodded and licked my lips. *Sure, sure, be quick but don't hurry, got it.* The Dutch monk concluded with a single nod, and I fought the urge to drop my hand in the middle and shout, "What time is it? Game time, hoo!"

Then he remembered something and lifted a reusable grocery bag. "Because you're not a monk," he said, "and you don't have your own alms bowl, villagers won't offer food for you, but sometimes our bowls overflow, so we'll need help carrying extra in this bag."

I took it. Sounded easy enough. *I'll do anything—coach, water boy, whatever. Let's do this. Just get me out of sweeping.*

At the gate, the Dutch monk turned right. The horizon opened into the cool morning, and I briefly stopped in my tracks at the sight of the sunrise. Having spent each morning so far ensconced in dense forest, I'd never witnessed the huge, hazy orb rising over the distant fields. At the wooden Nanachat sign on the corner, where one would turn left toward the internet café, the Dutch monk veered right.

Then, he took off. The pace would have been fine. Welcome, even. I wouldn't have minded if he had started all-out running. But the thing was, we did alms round barefoot. My feet were soft. The road was merciless. Spikes and loose rocks. No sandy patches to land a forgiving step. Head down, limping along, I stole a glance up for just long enough to see the Dutch monk leaving me in the dust.

Out of the corner of my eye, I noticed the Chinese monk accelerate by me, padding comfortably up the road to catch up with the Dutchman. Now I was sweating. No one ever passed me in anything. All my life, speed was my one reliable advantage, but now these two monks who never exercised were killing me.

I thought to check on the English pakao behind me. Maybe, as an inexperienced postulant, he didn't have tough feet like the others. But just as I wondered about him, I caught a glimpse of his billowing white robe gliding past. Incredulous, I looked to his face. He chewed on his lip as if truly embarrassed to witness my performance.

In last place now, I saw the gap widen between me and the pack: ten yards, twenty, fifty. My feet were getting pulverized. Where were the villagers who were supposed to offer us food? I wondered if the legend of monks in other traditions stepping over hot coals had a simple explanation: calluses like boot soles.

The monks were solidly out of earshot, and I narrated each tiny step. "Fuck fuck fuck fuck fuck fuck fuck."

After a mile or two, I noticed a red-and-white archway over the road: the entrance, apparently, to a village. The Dutch, Chinese, and English men stood outside, patiently waiting for me. Hobbling up, I shook my head and smiled apologetically.

Inside the village, our pace slowed to the solemn, contemplative gait I expected of Buddhist monks. Villagers lined the edge of the street, waiting on plastic mats. They removed their shoes and knelt and bowed as we approached, breaking the pose only to reach up and place handfuls into each bowl—pinches of sticky rice, wrapped candies, baggies of hot broth tied off with red rubber bands.

My feet throbbed. When our line stopped momentarily for the Dutch monk at the front to adjust his shoulder strap, I checked the undersides of my feet. They looked like ground beef. And yet, as I saw every Thai villager bow to the monks and then also bow to me, I found myself overwhelmed by gratitude. The houses in the village were small, many unfinished, with stalks of rebar sticking up out of corners. It felt clear to me that they didn't have a lot to spare but gave what they could, that they rose before sunrise every day to prepare and offer us sustenance out of respect—if not for us, then at least for the tradition we represented.

I felt unworthy of such generosity. As we made our way through the village, a rare quiet overtook my internal monologue. Wiping at my eyes, I bowed my head at the back of the line and exhaled a small prayer of thanks.

At the office after the meal, the Malaysian abbot, whose name was Ajahn Siri, gave a brief dhamma talk. He cast a spell. He could say nearly anything with his lilt and suave smile and come off sounding reasonable. He swept us along a reflection about how avoiding certain pleasures would lead to peace.

I marveled at what little I'd gathered of Ajahn Siri's life story. The only son of one of the richest men in Malaysia, he'd been raised in London and visited Nanachat as an eighteen-year-old with a plan to stay only two weeks. But something had clicked, and he'd given up a life of astronomical wealth for that of a monk. "Just like the Buddha" was the commonly whispered refrain around the monastery because the Buddha, too, had abandoned his life as a prince in search of something more. Ajahn Siri spoke seven languages fluently, and now, almost twenty years after arriving, he was stepping into the role of abbot.

Maybe it was my own training in the ever-sensible, dulcet tones of consultants that made me pause at something the Malaysian said. He was describing the view of the sunrise on alms round, that red star I'd admired earlier burning over the horizon.

It was easy, he said, to lose oneself in pleasure at the sight of it. Something as subtle and seemingly harmless as a sunrise, he said, "Even that, it can be quite easy to, kind of, *huh-huh*." He imitated gasps of delight.

He was right. It *was* easy to appreciate the beauty. But he was implying that it was wrong to do so. Of course, he hadn't used the word *wrong*. It was common to avoid the words *good* and *bad* in Buddhist circles, for these suggested dogma and duality, concepts the tradition officially eschewed. But his point was clear: if you were gasping with awe at the sunrise, you'd lost your way.

Around me, I watched the young monks and pakaos absorb this teaching. I felt I could see their faces harden. Heads nodded. Gaunt cheeks sucked in and made indentations in the bald heads, putting me in mind of craters on the surface of the moon. Which made me wonder, then, for a tradition that so emphasized the moon—celebrating each cycle by shaving heads and meditating all night, passing down legends of the Buddha being born, enlightened, and dying all on full-moon nights—for all that, you'd think it appropriate to throw some love to the sun. Sunlight, besides being the primary source of energy for life on Earth, was also what allowed us to call moons "full" in the first place. As the Malaysian flashed his reasonable grin and continued his words of warning, I felt myself recoil. Was this really the goal? To steel myself into such stoic sobriety that I might be immunized against the simple joy of sunrise? I, as much as anyone, subscribed to the idea that heavy-browed humorlessness was the path to spiritual transcendence. But when I heard Ajahn Siri promote it, I wasn't so sure.

Word spread at tea that afternoon: a senior celebrity monk was going to visit and give a Q&A. After Ajahn Siri's talk, I began formulating a question.

Our guest, Ajahn Jayasaro, was one of the two British monks who'd rolled up to Kathina in the black Benz. He lived by himself in a nearby hermitage and decided to grace us with his presence for reasons unknown to me.

His celebrity status was deserved. A monk of over forty years (double that of any monk residing at Nanachat), he was one of the youngest to have studied directly under the great Ajahn Chah before Ajahn Chah fell into diabetic paralysis for the last decade of his life. Rumor had it that in response to the early days of Ajahn Chah's illness, Ajahn Jayasaro had vowed to do *nessajik* until his teacher recovered.

Nessajik is an ascetic practice that involves never lying down. Everyone at Wat Pah Nanachat, including me, practiced nessajik once every couple of weeks for Wan Phra, a biweekly event held every half cycle of the moon where all the monastics shaved their heads and faces and eyebrows, chanted late into the night, and then stayed up all night meditating—or at least slept sitting up.

I'd done nessajik a couple of times since arriving almost a month earlier. Each time, I'd start out strong, determined to meditate all night and tap into a place of cosmic bliss. Eventually, though, after a few hours, every thought and feeling funneled into a single conviction that sleep was the only thing that truly mattered. I had leaned against walls to rest and learned firsthand how unsatisfying it was to sleep upright. As I knew from three years of flying twice a week for work, one's head flopped, mouth gasped open, and neck ached within an hour. In theory, I wanted to stay awake for seventy-two hours straight, exploring the frontier of the human mind. But in practice, by the time I'd been awake for twenty-two hours, everything was pointless, and I held but one faith, a gravitational worship of the god of prostration.

And so I was struck with particular awe when I learned that Ajahn Jayasaro, our speaker that evening, had practiced nessajik in honor of his ailing teacher every day for four years.

The man didn't lie down for *four years*.

I felt I could see the toll of those years on Ajahn Jayasaro's face. As he sat upon the dais on the office porch, his jaw was tight, his eyes deep and small and hard, with purple bags under them like battle scars. He seemed at home in his robes, and after forty years of shaving, his skin lacked the razor nicks and untanned strips along the brow that made for such conspicuous absences of hair on younger monks—and on me.

Urgent whispers swirled in the crowd below him. Monks scooted closer to the front, without regard for personal space. It felt like a sold-out concert with general admission seating.

Ajahn Jayasaro sat cross-legged and surveyed us while we settled. I'd heard another rumor that Ajahn Jayasaro, a Brit, apparently spoke better Thai than Thai people—this coming from a Thai visitor beside me who said he'd made the trip to Nanachat just for this talk. Lucky for me, though, the Q&A would be conducted in English.

The questions began. The first concerned the value of extreme practices—no surprise, given Ajahn Jayasaro's background.

He chuckled, looking back at his own history, which he didn't explain because he knew we all knew it.

"Balance is really what's necessary," he said, then went into a long story about how Ajahn Chah, when he was alive and well, had realized that he was pushing his monks too hard. "Too many monks were disrobing at that time," he said. "Ajahn Chah didn't want only the cream to survive, so he realized eventually that he needed to be running a sangha [a community of monks], not a commando unit."

There were chuckles and nods in the audience.

But I didn't move. His implication was not lost on me: having survived the intense period made Ajahn Jayasaro the cream. I, too, wanted to be the cream. Balance hadn't earned Ajahn Jayasaro his street cred, and something told me he didn't regret his youthful extremism at all. I yearned for a similarly brutal rite of passage. I wanted to journey to dangerous edges, see things I couldn't unsee, and only then, return to accept balance.

He didn't say it, but I knew Ajahn Jayasaro had also followed the historical Buddha's own example. During the six years between leaving his princely life and becoming enlightened, the Buddha had gone hard with asceticism. When he had subsisted on a single grain of rice per day, so the story went, his spine had been visible from the front, through his stomach. His skin shrink-wrapped his ribs. Finally, the Buddha had fainted and fallen face-first into feces, and only at that moment did he realize that self-annihilation was not the right path. Only then did he consider a middle way.

Maybe everyone had to learn this for themselves. I certainly wasn't taking Ajahn Jayasaro's word for it, the same way he apparently hadn't taken the Buddha's. I wanted to fall into a pile of shit and have an epiphany.

Autumn, the woman from Berkeley, raised her hand next.

"What's the difference between insight and thinking?" she said.

I perked up.

"Thinking," Ajahn Jayasaro began, "often parades as insight."

There were a few knowing laughs in the audience. One of which was mine. After alms round that morning—the road terrorizing my feet, the moment of gratitude in the village—I'd gone back and written a line in my diary about "calluses migrating from heart to sole." I'd repeated the double entendre in my head for the rest of the afternoon and felt very, very clever about it. By the evening, its charm had worn off. But the line was still stuck on repeat in my head. Hearing Ajahn Jayasaro speak, I felt a sneaking suspicion that my own diary, which initially offered the promise of crystallizing my every insight, might act as a mere extension of thinking, if not something worse.

"Insight comes from a quiet, stable place," Ajahn Jayasaro said. He added that the problem with the West's emphasis on "insight," or *vipassana* meditation, was that it neglected the other half of the equation—*samatha*, meaning "calm" or "concentration." That latter half created the conditions for insight in the first place, so it was important to pursue the pleasure of concentration, which, he said, was actually one type of pleasure the Buddha himself endorsed. "The voice of insight," he said at last, "can sound like you're speaking from the bottom of a very deep well."

I thought, *This guy's good.*

A junior monk raised his hand—the Sri Lankan with a big forehead who arbitrarily shushed people during afternoon tea.

"How do I attain wisdom?" he asked.

Inside, I sneered. Stupid question. I felt I could answer it myself. And I did, in fact, in my head, and by the time I was done admonishing the Sri Lankan and explaining to him that wisdom wasn't something one could simply *attain*, Ajahn Jayasaro had finished answering. I hadn't heard a single word.

I raised my hand.

Ajahn Jayasaro looked into my eyes and nodded.

I cleared my throat. I wanted everyone to hear this. "What role does a sense of humor play in the practice?"

A few monks turned back and frowned as if I'd said something deviant. I met their eyes straight on. I'd been waiting for this platform, especially after Ajahn Siri's subtle anti-sunrise talk. I hadn't expected to be the one promoting a sense of humor, but then again, I hadn't expected to find myself in such a crowded, grumpy community, either. My sense was that the absence of playfulness at Nanachat was cultural, not systemic—the head monk in New Zealand had joked about taking a tree trunk with him everywhere he went, and I'd read that the legendary Ajahn Chah had been known for pranks and general cheekiness.

But I also wasn't sure. I hoped my question would plant itself in the minds of the community, but I had no idea how Ajahn Jayasaro would answer.

He didn't hesitate: "You know, among the most senior monks, a sense of humor is considered *the* single most important virtue."

I leaned back in triumph. Relished a long drag of air through my nose and sought the eyes of any monk who dared to frown back at me now. *The* virtue among senior monks, he had said, which, because I had asked the question, basically meant *I* was a senior monk.

He added caveats: humor could sometimes mask cruelty, especially in a group of young men, and one should tread carefully in a multicultural context such as Nanachat. I knew he was right about the risks of humor, but my question wasn't about that. Ajahn Jayasaro had delivered the public service announcement the community needed that I never could've given myself. Which was: lighten up.

The irony, which I missed, was that I lacked the same sense of humor I accused the monastery of lacking. While I stood by the critique, I levied it with an added desperation because I fanned a dwindling flame of hope that there existed some perfect mold for me to inhabit, some shell I could find and crawl into and call my home, instead of having to forge an identity on my own. I'd wanted that certainty from Nanachat. I hadn't gotten it, and so I'd asked a sneaky question to expose what I perceived as a flaw in their mold.

The Dutch monk raised a tentative hand and asked if Ajahn Jayasaro knew any Buddhist jokes.

There were a few more frowns. This was apparently not a typical Q&A.

Ajahn Jayasaro tilted his head, said, well, no, not that he could think of at the moment, but he did know a joke about a photon going through airport security without any bags and telling the agent it was "traveling light."

I felt my hand itching to rise. I knew a joke: Two monks live in a cave. The first tires of sharing the space. He says, "Go om." The other replies, "Namaste."

But I held my hand down, not because I realized it wasn't actually a Buddhist joke (in fact, it was a Hindu one) or because I understood it might come across as insensitive, especially from me. I held my tongue because I didn't have any courage left to speak up. Besides, it dawned on me that the joke also described Nanachat too well—a crowded place with people who wished the others would leave. Like the first monk in the joke, I was tired of sharing space. Unlike the second, I was not planning on staying.

I'd come to Thailand for total solitude, and Nanachat didn't have it. While I'd begun to sense that I might be contributing to my own unhappiness, I couldn't discern *how* while I was in the presence of others. Too tightly wound were my reflexes to please—and then criticize. This much I did know: I needed vast, empty time and space to loosen my tangled impulses. There, I thought, alone at last, I could concentrate and mourn and listen. Maybe I'd even live in a cave.

A couple of days later, I heard rumors of another visitor: Ajahn Sukhito, the solemn Israeli abbot of the hermitage called Poo Jom Gom. I recalled our conversation where I'd asked if I might visit.

"We'll see in a month," he had said.

It had been a month.

POO JOM GOM

Things were looking up. The Australian novice monk who had educated me about the goodness of geckos told me one afternoon that he'd heard both of us were headed to Poo Jom Gom. While just about anyone could visit Nanachat, smaller hermitages like Poo Jom Gom had gatekeepers. One needed permission, and the rumor was that I'd gotten it.

Back on my private walking meditation path, I pranced. Rolled my shoulders. Chucked up deuces in every direction. Dancing meditation. Then I abruptly stopped. It was only a rumor. I didn't want to jinx my escape.

Ajahn Sukhito arrived in the morning in a white passenger van driven by a Thai villager. With so many empty seats in the back, I thought, surely I'd get one. And yet, still no one in any position of authority had officially confirmed my transfer. Finally, that afternoon, the genteel Ajahn Siri approached me near the sala.

"You'll come back," he said flatly. "Yes?"

I was taken aback by his curtness. He was normally so smooth and articulate, but he'd offered neither greeting nor acknowledgment that I was even allowed to transfer in the first place. I felt slighted, and had I been able to press Pause on the interaction and reflect, I might've understood why. I found Ajahn Siri inspiring, and even if I disagreed with his sunrise talk, I was hurt he hadn't taken an interest in me over the last month.

But I couldn't press Pause. I shrugged and shot back at him, "I don't know. *Anicca*, right?"

Anicca is the Pali term for uncertainty, transience, the inherent instability of all things. For me to invoke it here was to bastardize its application. I was being a punk. Speaking my mind for once, though, felt like a small step in the right direction—or perhaps too large a step, an overcorrection. I wasn't sure which, but it was exhilarating.

Ajahn Siri, classy as ever, simply raised his chin and held my gaze, as if to say, "I see what you did there."

When it was time to depart, I was first to climb into the van. The monastic hierarchy applied even to seating in vehicles. As the most junior member of the party, I'd sit in the back row. Which was fine by me. Getting in first meant no chance of getting left behind. Two others from Nanachat had been granted leave, and they climbed in next: the skinny Italian pakao named Giorgio and the Australian novice monk, whose name was Pamutto.

A small crowd of onlookers hung around outside the van, some saying goodbye, others craning their necks in search of an extra seat. One new visitor—a bearded man from Estonia—practically begged to join us. Ajahn Sukhito flicked his hand at the Estonian and shut the door.

Silently, I rejoiced. The Estonian had talked so fast the day before about his vast knowledge of Buddhist theory, dropping Pali terms left and right, quizzing other guests on their understanding of dependent origination. I bet he had special oils for his little groomed guru beard, which he had conspicuously chosen not to shave.

The van rolled down the path to the exit. Gazing out the window, I smiled and grew reflective. The head monk in New Zealand had been right: Nanachat was a good place to start. I might even miss it a little. Then again, no, I wouldn't. I imagined Ajahn Sukhito changing his mind, the van stopping, me having to return, and I knew then that what warmth I felt toward Nanachat stemmed mostly from the fact of my departure. I scrubbed myself clean of nostalgia. Best to avoid planting a seed of positive regard in the fertile conscience of the universe, lest it take root.

The van drove east.

After half an hour, we pulled over onto the shoulder. In my hurry to board the van, I hadn't noticed that a bunch of extra passengers had been loaded behind my seat in cages: rats. They'd been trapped at Nanachat. Monks wouldn't kill them, of course, so they caught them and waited until someone with a car could take them away and set them free.

As the Thai driver unloaded the cages, Pamutto asked how long they'd been held captive.

A few days.

"So, did we feed them?" said Pamutto.

Yes.

"What did we feed them?"

Cheese.

"What!" Pamutto was incredulous. Cheese was unheard of here. I hadn't seen it since arriving. "I'd live in a cage if you fed me cheese!"

I laughed. But I sensed Pamutto wasn't joking. There was something loose about him, which made me skeptical but intrigued. He was a monk, after all, and I hadn't gotten to know any of them very well yet.

At another stop to switch vans, Ajahn Sukhito had Giorgio accompany him to find a phone to call the second driver for the final leg of our trip. This left Pamutto and me to wait in the middle of a dilapidated public courtyard.

We made small talk. After a few minutes, it hit me: I was hanging out, one on one, in the boondocks of Thailand with a real monk. Just two guys shooting it in a parking lot. Even if he was only a novice monk of a year and a half, I felt I had made it to the in crowd.

We chuckled about some of the minutiae in the Vinaya, the 227 rules that compose the monastic code of conduct. After the eight precepts I had to follow, there were an additional 219 statutes fully ordained monks had to observe. Some were strangely specific. For example, they couldn't drink water while standing up. They also couldn't cross their arms while standing up. When they walked, they couldn't swing their arms too much.

"The middle way of arms," I said.

Pamutto laughed aloud, then said, "You know, I'm not sure that was as funny as I just made it, but you don't hear many Vinaya jokes, so . . ."

The smell of fish sauce emanated from the tables of tiny restaurants beside the courtyard. Enchanting but forbidden. I was traveling with monks. Monastic law applied. No eating after noon. Pamutto said he had to use the bathroom and wandered toward the restaurants to find one.

I studied the landscape. Grass sprung through the cracks in the pavement. On the far side of the lot, I noticed a dip in the topography, the trees falling away in a clean horizontal line and then rising again in the distance, indicating a canyon, perhaps, or a river.

By the time Pamutto returned, the new van had arrived. We boarded and swept farther east across more green flatness. At a small village—not more than a few rows of houses—we turned left down a narrow, crumbling street. The driver snaked the van from side to side, avoiding chickens and potholes.

At the far edge of the village lay a driveway of fresh blue gravel. The van crunched along. A stream glittered between the trees. Then the path ended. The van could go no farther. A single kuti perched on a hill to the left, tucked into a grove of bamboo. To the right, a small pedestrian bridge led over the stream, into the wilderness, and to my new home, Poo Jom Gom.

The forest of Wat Pah Nanachat was like a freckle on the sunburned back of northeast Thailand. Poo Jom Gom was different. Beyond the tiny village—population two hundred—lay miles of undeveloped wilderness, including a national park.

A cluster of three buildings composed the hermitage. Over the small bridge spanning the stream and up a stone path was a kitchen— empty, I noted, and without an upstairs dormitory. Farther up the path was a toolshed of the same build—elevated tile floor, no exterior walls, basically a metal roof on stilts. These were less buildings than open-air shade structures, like park pavilions.

Beyond the shed was the third and final structure, the sala—a stunning thatched-roof cathedral, intimate yet grand. Sheaves of palm fronds hung in layers over the roof, with ragged edges like the tipped wings of an owl. Two floors: tile on the first, then a staircase up the side with a railing made of a curving branch sanded to perfection; wide wooden boards made the second-story floor, each planed smooth on top but left with live edges and small gaps in between. Off to one side in a glass case stood a full human skeleton. Front and center, a

Buddha statue sat on a raised step in front of the building's lone wall, which was made of a flimsy lattice weave that encouraged diamonds of light to peek through like stars in a night sky.

The Buddha statue gazed beyond the hermitage and out into Pha Taem National Park. A few kutis sat in seclusion at the end of dirt trails that disappeared into the trees. I wondered if there were caves hidden deep in the park but decided to wait to ask. I didn't want to come off as overly exuberant with Ajahn Sukhito and ruin my chances. After all, I knew from my own experience leading mountain trips with teenagers that the students—boys, almost always—who were the most eager for intensity were often the least self-aware and so some of the most at risk. I was good at monitoring these boys in part because I had been one of them and, to a certain extent, still was.

Outside the van, we unpacked and carried supplies across the bridge and into the kitchen. There was a tile island with a stove. Beside it, a black, slender statue of the Buddha stood ten feet tall, one hand raised in apparent greeting. No one spoke. A breeze whispered through the bamboo and the open kitchen pavilion. The stream trickled nearby.

This is the place, I thought.

Ajahn Sukhito strode into the kitchen and looked around. His shoulders arched almost to his ears, and he turned them to regard each of us, Pamutto, Giorgio, and me. Despite his hunch, he stood well over six feet. Everyone stopped what they were doing and looked at him. Still, he said nothing. We waited.

The van was unpacked. The journey complete. I'd made it, and yet, no one had ever explicitly told me how long I could stay. As if he heard my thoughts, Ajahn Sukhito faced me and asked what I was looking for in my visit.

I stammered something about how much I liked the monastery already and wanted to focus on the practice, meaning meditation. I stopped there. Under his motionless glare, more than a few words felt like rambling.

He nodded once and said that we could see how everything felt in a couple of days. He did not say I was welcome to stay longer.

"The schedule here can be more . . ."—he paused—"demanding." He watched for my reaction.

I offered a somber nod, one I hoped would communicate both a respectful understanding of the gravity of his concern but also a confidence in my ability to handle it. As far as I could tell, the schedule seemed like a dream. No chanting in the morning, and I'd get to go on alms round with the monks every morning at 6:00 a.m. After that, we'd sweep a bit, meditate as a group in the sala until the meal, work for a couple of hours, and then, around noon or so, have the rest of the day to ourselves for practice. It didn't sound demanding to me at all.

For afternoon tea, Ajahn Sukhito said, I could find a plastic bin in the kitchen pantry and serve myself when I pleased.

"One or two cups," Ajahn Sukhito said, his eyes boring into mine, "not three or four."

Three other monks lived at Poo Jom Gom, too, and they greeted our arrival. An older white man appeared in the kitchen. He was quick to inform me that he had only ordained recently, in his fifties.

"Just barely an Ajahn," he said with a shrug and a chuckle. The accent and modesty seemed Midwest American. Sure enough, he was from Michigan.

The next monk was from China. Roughly in his sixties, he also seemed to have ordained later in life, for he bowed to Ajahn Sukhito as if he were junior. He nodded once to me and did not speak.

The third monk was a novice from India, rotund and genial, in his thirties. His name was Badacharo, Bada for short. Later that day, we got to talking while watering trees during the work period.

I asked him what he'd done before ordaining.

"Citibank," said Bada. "Customer service."

I titled my head in surprise.

Bada grinned and said, "But local. So we never would have spoken."

I grinned back.

"But nevertheless," he said, exaggerating his Indian English accent, "thank you for your continued membership with us, sir; you are a valued customer, and I hope you have a truly wonderful rest of your day."

We both laughed so loud that when we heard a rustle in the leaves, we ducked and went silent. Ajahn Sukhito's stern energy permeated the hermitage. One could never tell when he might appear and cast a disapproving eye. His intense demeanor may have been tailored to temper the joy of the residents, all of whom, I noted, seemed happy.

But too late. I could not be tempered. Once supplies were packed and I'd dropped my backpack inside the kuti I'd spotted near the pedestrian bridge, I found myself alone, with hours of free time ahead of me. The fantasy had become a reality. I was truly off the grid, nestled in endless forest with my own simple dwelling and a strict teacher.

I hiked into the national park. Drank in the tall, dry forest. Waist-high grasses waved with the wind like a sea of arms in concert. A precarious suspension bridge spanned a slot canyon above a creek. Trails curved through leaves and grass and sand and stone. After a while, the canopy lifted, and my heart leaped at the sight of a wide-open vista—a rocky plateau; long, flat views; and a few massive boulders balanced in Daliesque shapes, worn from years of air and water. Cairns sat like cookies baking in the sun. The smell of moisture rose from the earth. That night, I fell asleep with a smile.

The next morning, I waited on the stoop outside my kuti to meet the monks for alms round. All of us would go except Giorgio, whom Ajahn Sukhito had instructed to stay back and sweep. From my stoop, I could see Giorgio across the stream and through the thin trees. He was a lone figure in a simple robe. The swish of his broom on the stone path made the only sound in the quiet of early morning. I could envision this image translated into a watercolor painting. I could finally understand sweeping's meditative beauty, especially when I wasn't doing it.

The monks appeared on the bridge. Each held his brushed metal bowl in an orange sling in the crook of his right arm. I hopped down from the porch, grinning, half expecting a pregame huddle or a morning greeting, but Ajahn Sukhito stared me down without so much as a nod. I straightened to attention, then fell in line behind the monks.

I'd been outfitted with a new set of white clothing. A baggy shirt, massive loose pants with a sash to tie them around my waist, and an outer robe that was an actual twin bedsheet. I limped along the gravel behind the four monks, carrying another reusable mesh bag. Ajahn Sukhito had advised me the day before to watch for when his or any of the other monks' bowls got too full. If they did, I'd scurry up to the front and take some of their load.

I peeked up at the village as we exited the monastery. Along a straightaway, villagers already knelt on mats on the pavement outside their homes. Many had placed covered goblets at their side, containers to keep sticky rice warm.

It struck me then that not one of the residents of our tiny rural hermitage was Thai. For a moment, I feared the thought of Thai people grousing behind closed doors about a bunch of foreigners appropriating their customs, but then, for the second time, I saw the villagers' deferential reaction to our approach. Heads bent to the pavement, hands to hearts, bare knees on hard ground. Almost every house had someone waiting for us out front, and I remembered with disbelief the widespread respect I had heard Thai people held for forest monks—and the pride from having birthed a tradition that had gained such an international following. It was a common refrain that the king of Thailand, a beloved figure who was admired almost as a demigod, would himself bow down before forest monks.

The villagers bowed to me as I passed, and all over again I felt confused, unworthy, and then awed by the power of the tradition I was representing. I'd fantasized about this kind of adulation, but now that it was real, I felt not the wings of being worshipped but the weight of being trusted.

Roosters waltzed about the village streets and stopped to scream good morning. Puppies, actual adorable puppies, tumbled over each other in a ditch. I was in heaven.

On alms round later that week, I saw a boy walking toward us. Shirtless and barefoot, he held a whip-stick in one hand and, in the other, a long leash connecting a line of four water buffalo. He led them down the street, and I marveled at the boy's ease in walking on the rocks. I still staggered over every step, but I was getting the hang of it. Thankfully, this village's road had some forgiving patches of sand.

A bell hanging from one of the buffalo's necks clanged slowly in time. As they clopped and swayed past us, we hugged the opposite shoulder to give them space. Massive animals. I could hardly believe their size, and I turned to watch them go, neglecting the front of the line, where a villager was offering a bouquet of flowers to Ajahn Sukhito. The line had stopped. I almost ran smack into Pamutto.

I glanced ahead to see Ajahn Sukhito already peering back, waiting for me to remember my one and only job. I peeled off the back and made a beeline for him, reminded of fartlek runs in cross-country, the back of the line sprinting to the front. In my hurry, I took my eyes off the road and stepped with a squish into a fresh buffalo patty.

Warmth rose to my ankle. I removed my foot with a soft squelch. The monks beside me tried not to acknowledge this mishap. We were supposed to keep our heads down at all times on alms round.

But I hoped they saw. I wanted them to see how unfazed I was. I looked up at Ajahn Sukhito, shrugged, and forced a quiet chuckle that I hoped would communicate something like "Ah, it's just digested grass. I'm so wise and tough, I can actively appreciate humor in the face of adversity. Also, please let me stay here forever."

As Ajahn Sukhito handed me the flowers and his extra sticky rice, I met his eyes. For a moment, I felt, they gleamed with approval.

Joy! At the back of the line, I wiped my foot in a patch of grass but didn't care if I had to wait to get clean. I planted the bouquet in the sticky rice at the bottom of the mesh bag, and the flower stalks poked out the front like baguettes in a picnic basket. I leaned toward them as we carried on and inhaled deeply, smelling the petals, feeling like I could skip the rest of the way.

Every day, I was completely alone from noon until sunrise the following morning, when I would join alms round, meditate, eat, work, and then be all alone again. Gone were the chants. Gone were the crowds. Gone were all my grievances. I had made it. Nature. Solitude. Quiet. I'd gotten exactly what I thought I wanted, and within a week, I hated it.

I had run out of distractions. I'd stopped hiking in the park because Ajahn Sukhito had said it was frivolous to explore every day and because I'd sweat in my robes. Laundry was a task I preferred to ignore until I absolutely couldn't. One had to clean robes by hand in the stream, which dwindled at this time of year to a brown trickle. The dry season was upon us. Mid-November. Pools in the pockmarked riverbed had been cut off from the diminishing flow and stood stagnant, evaporating along with whatever swimming creatures were unlucky enough to be trapped inside.

There was an unexpected trouble with finally securing solitude: I had no one to blame for my unhappiness but myself. I had escaped from Nanachat, the busy heart of the tradition, and landed in its distant fingers, but they were wrapping themselves around my neck and beginning to squeeze.

By the second week at Poo Jom Gom, every problem boiled down to one: food. Every day, on my own for hours, I raced with desire. Give me enchiladas. Bathe me in queso. Inject me with tikka masala. Restaurants of the past called to me like long-lost loves: Neapolitan classics from Punch Pizza in Minneapolis, hot slices on the patio from Fellini's Pizza in Atlanta. I fantasized about my own unique concoctions: grilled peanut butter sandwiches dipped in a puréed soup of chilled banana milk. I drew diagrams of future delicacies in my diary:

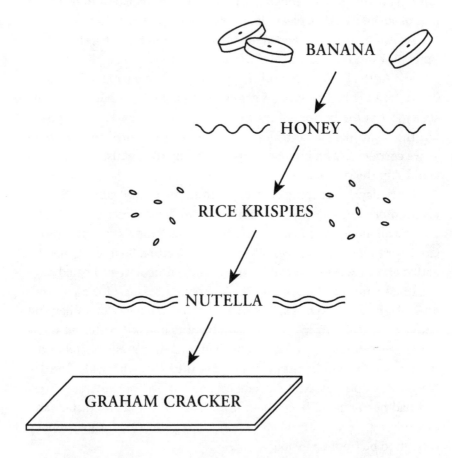

On alms round, while I felt the weight of trust from the villagers, I also felt the weight of the food I carried. In the back of the line, I thought about how it had been over twenty hours since I last ate and about how physically close I was to the food, separated by millimeters-thin layers of mesh and clothing. Sometimes I hugged the bag to my sternum and imagined osmosis ferrying calories through robe, bone, and muscle and into my stomach. Even when I let the bag dangle and brush against my leg, the skin on my thigh broke into a sweat from the warmth of sticky rice and curries. I despaired, for I knew four hours yet remained until the meal.

Back at the monastery after alms round, I reluctantly dumped the contents of my bag into a blue plastic bin that waited for us on the kitchen table, then rushed off to help Giorgio sweep, as far from the kitchen as possible, no longer able to bear the proximity to what I couldn't have.

Around this time each morning, I heard the whine of a small motor coming up the gravel path. It was Yupin, a woman from the village who prepared the meal each day. The monks may have gathered sticky rice and treats and bags of broth, but that wasn't all we ate. In fact, it was hardly any of what we ate. At Nanachat, a whole team of local women volunteered in the kitchen beneath the dormitory to feed upward of eighty people. Here at Poo Jom Gom, there was only one woman, Yupin, and she cooked for eight. Alms round was a lovely ceremony, but it wouldn't have fed us. As at Nanachat, women made the place run.

Bright eyes. Maybe forty years old. Straight black hair, always in a ponytail. She drove a motorized trike with two wheels in the back that framed a wooden bed to carry her supplies—rice cooker, pots, pans, fresh vegetables, and multiple platters she had prepared ahead of time. The frame of the trike barely fit over the pedestrian bridge, and I wondered if one had been customized for the other. She pulled over the bridge, parked right outside the kitchen, and set to work.

Yupin's arrival triggered the next section of the morning schedule: group meditation. Up at the sala, the five monks and Giorgio sat on the step of the stage, facing the same direction as the Buddha statue behind them. I wasn't a pakao, so I sat on the main floor, facing them—an arrangement that felt like an interrogation by a panel on high.

Each of us sat on one circular cushion, except Ajahn Sukhito, who, as the abbot and most senior, reclined at the far left on an orange pillow that was a veritable throne. It sported armrests that cradled his elbows and knees as well as, sweet lord, a backrest.

Ajahn Sukhito started by lighting a stick of incense beneath the

Buddha statue. Then we silently fell into meditation. Eyes were closed, but I felt watched. As I tried to meditate with the group, I heard throats clearing, floorboards creaking, and occasionally, dishes softly clattering from the kitchen. After about an hour, Yupin clanged a bell, signaling to us up at the sala that the meal was ready.

On the first morning, I treated the sound of the bell like a starting gun. I popped up from my cushion and made my way to the stairs. But then I realized no one else had stirred.

Bada, the collegial Indian, opened one eye to meet mine. He tilted his head toward Ajahn Sukhito, then closed his eye again. And so I learned the unspoken rule that no one could get up for the meal until Ajahn Sukhito did.

What followed was an excruciatingly slow process. We were so close to eating, but the ringing of the bell seemed to indicate the start of not a sprint, but a marathon.

Every day went like this: full hour of meditation, bell, then . . . nothing. On my cushion, I watched Ajahn Sukhito's eyelids flutter, as if he were slowly returning to consciousness from some faraway place. But then he wouldn't return. His eyes remained closed. The flutter, apparently, was involuntary, a movement that must have accompanied a state of concentration so deep that he preferred to sit for minutes after the bell, which I knew damn well he had heard. No one could be in *that* deep.

Sometimes I wondered if the flutter was a conscious pump fake, a teaching tactic designed to make me *think* he was about to get up, thus giving me an opportunity to deal with impatience. At the same time, another part of me knew these final minutes before the meal were where I might make the most progress in meditation. Like the final rep in a workout, all the mental training throughout the day led up to this test of how well I could keep my cool at the point of greatest fatigue.

Ten minutes after the bell had rung, a couple of monks might shift on their cushions, as if hoping that creaking the floorboards might gently remind our leader it was time to get moving. Pamutto stretched his neck. Giorgio sat stiff as a board, acting all stoic and undisturbed, but then broke his pose at every tiny sound to see if it came from Ajahn

Sukhito's side of the sala. By twenty minutes, any noise set eyes opening and heads to turning to see if it had originated from the abbot.

I often began to feel offended on behalf of Yupin. Hadn't she told us the meal was ready? Weren't we disrespecting her effort?

Ajahn Sukhito sometimes sat fluttering his eyelids for thirty-five minutes, all of which I spent guessing his motives and watching his breath more than mine.

After a couple of weeks, I noticed that my mouth watered every time the bell rang. I had become a Pavlovian dog. With nothing else to do, I began to examine the watering. It started with a welling sensation high in my neck and ached as the waters rose. I salivated and swallowed so much that I wondered if it was possible to hydrate myself. I grew certain that the monks could hear my constant swallowing, which made me self-conscious, so I'd try to stop, which somehow seemed to make my mouth water even more.

Eventually, Ajahn Sukhito cleared his throat and started to rise. All of us then knelt, facing the Buddha statue, and briefly chanted our gratitude to the Buddha, dhamma, and sangha—the "three gems" of Buddhism, referring to the Buddha himself, his teachings, and his disciples, respectively—bowing once for each. Then we bowed three more times—not necessarily to anyone specific, just the standard three-bow transition for standing up or sitting down. With each rep, my impatience grew, and my bowing form deteriorated.

I sped down the stone path toward the kitchen like a kid at the pool who knows the lifeguard is watching. I passed the food—two tables lined up end to end, a pot or two of rice, a few platters of saucy dishes, a single plate of fruit or sweets—and assumed my position beyond the tables on a plastic mat in front of yet another Buddha statue, to which I bowed three more times before sitting. There, I waited for the monks to serve themselves.

Somehow, Ajahn Sukhito disappeared every morning between the sala and kitchen for another five minutes. To pee? To taunt us? I never knew. Even the other monks seemed like they were trying not to look impatient, standing in line with their hands clasped around their bowls, trying not to stare at the spread before them.

Ajahn Sukhito strode in through the trees rather than on the main stone path, adding to the mystery of his whereabouts. Then, his outer robe often wouldn't be secure. He'd stand on the tile, unapologetic, fluffing his robe, wrapping his shoulders, and tucking his coil under his arm. *Then* he would serve himself, and the others followed.

But not me. As a resident, I sat on the ground, as did Yupin, who was on the other side of the kitchen. From the floor, we watched the monks fill their bowls and carry them back to the sala. It was from this angle that, one day, I noticed Giorgio, the Italian pakao, slipping cookies and miniature bananas into his pocket on his way up the path.

He could do it without even looking. Giorgio! He was the person who moved in the most intentional and spiritual way, his thin head always held high, a look of resolute serenity painted on his face. I thought back to Giorgio's actions during my very first meal at Nanachat—he had been the last pakao to serve himself, the one who had hesitated at the dessert section, snatched one treat, and then snuck another one as he turned to flee.

This time, Giorgio slipped treats into a pocket by his thigh, where his hand just so happened to graze in his natural gait. He had room on top of his bowl, so these were treats for later. Incensed, I imagined Giorgio off by himself, acting the part of the forest monk while he peeled his little banana and crumbled his cookie over the square of cloth he was always folding so delicately—not a handkerchief, I thought, but a napkin! I hated the way he swept (too hard, I decided, no longer fit for a watercolor painting). Clearly, I thought, he moved with the forced grace of someone compensating for transgressions.

I was unaware that I was as hungry for self-righteousness as I was for food. I spent so much time over so many vacant afternoons thinking about him that I briefly understood something else: his behavior showed struggle. He, too, was having a hard time.

Compassion briefly flickered in me, but the ember wouldn't catch. As soon as I felt for Giorgio, I wished he'd get caught—or that *my* white pants had that same side pocket.

Yupin and I followed the monks back up to the sala to sit in front of the monastic panel. Ajahn Sukhito made small talk with Yupin. Between spurts of conversation, he gazed out at the treetops beyond the railing of the sala, leaving us hanging in silence while he considered another topic. Eventually, he nodded once, cleared his throat, and straightened, cueing the others to begin the pre-meal chant.

It began with a slow, solo intro, all in Pali. The rest of the monks and Giorgio joined in a quiet chorus. After a couple of minutes, they concluded with a drawn-out phrase, "Balaaam," which I actually found beautiful, perhaps in part because it marked the end.

Yupin and I responded with a mumbled, twenty-second chant of our own, bowing during it at specific times, then bowing three more times to stand up again and go.

And then I was off, gripping the railing to prevent myself from skipping stairs, walk-running down the stone path to the food table, grabbing the top bowl from the stack, and serving myself. I carried my bowl three steps from the table to the plastic mat where I sat as Giorgio tucked away his treats. I faced the Buddha statue, put the food aside, and bowed three more times to sit down, my fastest yet—and also my twenty-fifth, twenty-sixth, and twenty-seventh bows of the morning.

At Nanachat, a resident told me something Ajahn Chah said: "Once you understand food, you're done." *Done* as in *enlightened*. There was a lot of that at Nanachat, guests trading good-sounding monk quotes of dubious accuracy. Another guest had responded to the Ajahn Chah quote with something *he'd* heard from a different monk that seemed to confirm the first. The monk said his practice advanced to the point that he could maintain total moment-to-moment mindfulness at all times of the day, with only one exception: the meal.

All that may have been true. But at this point each day, I wasn't concerned with the mind. I was concerned with the stomach. Like an animal, I descended upon the bowl. In the first minute, I ate as if exacting revenge. In the second, as if I'd won a championship, restraining the urge to pump my fists, rub sauce over my bare chest, and scream that anything was possible.

I built up so much anticipation for the food that it was hard to focus once it arrived. Every day, half my bowl disappeared before I felt like I had tasted a thing. Similar to a vacation, my enjoyment was greatest before eating and afterward. I tried to savor it by counting the number of bites because I'd heard this was a good mindfulness practice and wondered if it would help me draw out the experience. But that was all I did—*wonder*. In the abyss of the afternoons when I was hungry again, I imagined counting bites, but in the moment, on the mat the next day, by the time I was free to feed, I forgot.

After the initial spasm of gorging, I grew tender with the food, remembering it wouldn't last forever. The clink of the spoon became a soft cymbal to accompany the rhythm of mastication. In these moments, I was so absorbed in eating as to be thoughtless, a state that I confused with pure mindfulness. The difference was, while I ate, I was unaware of the *absence* of cognition—and so unappreciative of it.

I forgot to breathe. I forgot to count. I forgot the commitment to counting I'd written in my diary, just like I'd forgotten about having written the same commitment the day before, and the day before that. I wanted to remember. I wanted to reflect on the hundreds of people and thousands of hours involved in planting and growing and harvesting, packaging and shipping, and purchasing all the ingredients for this single bowl of food, not to mention Yupin preparing it.

But I couldn't do it. Yupin would eat a small bowl of her own on the floor on the other side of the kitchen, and when she finished, the sight of her rising to begin doing all the dishes inspired in me not gratitude but fear, for the meal was almost over. I cherished the textures—the fibers of eggplant, the gumminess of rice, the sweet lubrication of sauce.

One day, I felt something sharp and located it with my tongue. It was hard, like an uncooked grain of rice but bigger. With my thumb and forefinger, I pulled out an open staple—not the thin kind used for office paper but the thick ones used in construction, whose tips taper into dagger points. Yupin would have been horrified. What would I even say? It didn't matter. Besides, the most important thing was that I still had food in my bowl. I placed the staple next to my bowl and continued eating.

Each day when I finished, I helped Yupin with the dishes. I ferried all the pots and platters from the table to the island while Yupin filled three sinks with water, one soapy, one warm, one cold. She scraped and washed; I rinsed and placed each dish on a drying rack overhead.

She spoke almost no English. Whenever I did something poorly, like leave a soapy spot on a dish, she'd furrow her brow and say, "Mmm!" Her tone was stern but playful. I'd make an apologetic sound, and once I corrected my error, she'd grin and say, "OK."

Which is to say, she spoke more English than I spoke Thai, although we taught each other small phrases over time. *Sak pha* was what we were doing—"washing." *Kop khun ka*—"thank you." *Moat*—"ant." Except it wasn't exactly Thai that I was learning. When Yupin tested my vocabulary, pointing to some object in the kitchen and raising her eyebrows, she'd say, "Speak Lao."

Laos was nearby. I later learned that the northeast region of Thailand has its own language called Lao, also known as Isaan, which happens to be the name of the region, too; that area shares more in common culturally and linguistically with Laos than with the rest of Thailand.

I didn't care what language I learned so long as it helped me communicate with Yupin. Sometimes she held up an object with a quizzical look, wanting me to teach her the English word for it. When she asked one morning about the rubber rake we used to wipe the tile floor clean, I paused. I couldn't think of a better synonym, so I made a show of sighing to inform her I was about to deliver difficult news.

"Squeegee," I said.

She feigned looking crestfallen. "Skee-jwee—no. No, no, no." She waved her hands, burst out laughing, and practiced saying it almost every day thereafter.

For my part, I didn't possess the same self-awareness of my limitations. One word in Isaan could have five meanings based on its tone. So if I thought I was nailing my pronunciation of the word *eat*, I might well have been saying the adjective meaning "short" or even the verb form meaning "to wag a dog's tail."

Every once in a while, Yupin brought a flock of six or so kids from the village. They rode in the bed of her moto, fidgeted in the sala when watching the monks chant, and giggled while Yupin and I tried to communicate.

Each day as Yupin packed up, Ajahn Sukhito would make his way down to the kitchen to speak with her in a slow, methodical Isaan that he had learned over his twenty years as a monk. I often felt awkward as a third wheel, lingering close by at the island, but soon realized I performed an important function. The presence of a second male enabled Ajahn Sukhito to converse with Yupin. Monks weren't allowed to be in the presence of a woman alone. Giorgio could've done it, but

I was pleased to be the workaround to the rule, in part because I was skeptical of it.

I also enjoyed watching them interact. They seemed to genuinely like each other. Although Ajahn Sukhito generally remained as deadpan as anyone I'd ever seen, here he broke into the occasional smile. Yupin bowed while she spoke, bobbing forward and back as all Thais did with monks, asking him questions and responding to his with her hands clasped as if in prayer.

Each had occupied their respective roles for upward of four years. Four years of quiet daily chats after the meal. Observing their cordial dynamic and understanding nothing they said, I let my mind drift.

Yupin might chuckle, and I'd feel a vague sense of safety in the company of their relationship. I found their controlled banter relaxing, as if they were parents. I never noticed how my enjoyment of their bond conflicted with my ideal of solitude. Sometimes I imagined a fracture between them, perhaps because my own parents had divorced a couple of years earlier. But the flare of tension I felt from this thought was soothed by the knowledge that Ajahn Sukhito and Yupin were, in one sense, interchangeable. When one or both moved on, another abbot and cook would step in. The monastic system was more durable than any person or pair. I could appreciate the solidity of their roles, the abbot and the cook, the two sides of monastic symbiosis, exchanging spiritual for physical sustenance. Each held demanding roles that required sacrifice. Still, I couldn't help but squirm, knowing only one side got the glory. The history of Poo Jom Gom would enshrine its lineage of abbots. Yupin wouldn't get so much as a footnote.

Yupin would then climb onto the trike, rev the engine, and wave goodbye. As the sound of the moto faded down the gravel road toward the village, I'd look around the clean, empty kitchen, hardly able to believe that it was all over, the meal I had spent all day looking forward to. I was invariably still hungry but had more than twenty-three hours until my next bite.

Yupin also assisted with mail delivery, although the hermitage rarely received any. At one letter every few weeks, I was the most active user. There wasn't a mailbox, so I'd hand Yupin an envelope when I had one to send, stamped and addressed to friends or family. I'd given the address of Poo Jom Gom to my parents and to MJ, the woman in New

York, and all three had sent letters back. It struck me as a feat of global cooperation that anything could reach the hermitage at all. Poo Jom Gom's address was a stack, six lines tall, of phonetically spelled-out Thai words that Ajahn Sukhito himself had needed to puzzle out for me in English with a pen and pad.

I never saw a mailperson, either, so whenever I got something, Yupin simply handed it to me directly when she arrived in the morning. One letter from MJ arrived forty-six days after its postmark in Manhattan, and until then I'd never appreciated the miracle of operations that reliably sent slips of paper around the world without them so much as getting wet.

My father's first couple of letters contained a page of updates in his clean cursive on the changing seasons in Atlanta, the inaugural year of the college football playoffs, and his progress in building out the basement of his new house. I hung on to every word, no matter how mundane, reading them twice, three times, four—a temporary fill in the void of my days.

I must've written something to him about how hungry I was, because one day, a package arrived. Mail came seldom enough, but a package was unheard of. I opened it alone inside my kuti at the end of the gravel driveway by the stream. At a small desk with a plastic chair that I used for writing and, less often, meditating, I opened the package and gaped.

Inside was a Tupperware container filled with unthinkable bounty: twelve KIND granola bars and an assortment of TAZO tea bags. They shone golden light upon my visage.

I shut the container and forced myself to turn away. It was after noon. I began pacing the tile floor. There was a bed in the corner—a stick-frame twin with a matted purple-and-green comforter. I wasn't allowed to sleep in it. Ajahn Sukhito had said that it was reserved for "distinguished guests," which didn't bother me. I already knew I wasn't allowed to sleep on a bed—eighth precept. Besides, I didn't *want* to sleep in a bed. I wanted to be a rustic and disciplined Man Who Needs Nothing. I was miffed about the existence of a bed at all. The presence of such a luxury detracted from the ascetic image I was trying to cultivate.

Worse, the guest kuti had its own toilet—a real American-style, sit-down toilet. The cinder-block outhouse everyone else used across the stream had the standard tiny stalls with porcelain holes in the ground. My toilet lived in its own room the size of my entire kuti at Nanachat. The bathroom separated my room on one side of the building from a second bedroom on the other, in case another guest were to visit. It was unoccupied, but I never looked inside. Doing so would've forced me to acknowledge that by monastic standards, I wasn't living in a simple hut but a two-bed, one-bath palace.

What I loved was that my desk was peeling and wobbly; that I didn't have toilet paper; that there was no electricity. *These* were the details that made me who I wanted to be—Severe Religious Wanderer—and these were the only ones I included in my diary.

I wrote in the diary every night, convinced I was digging deeper into wisdom, carefully constructing a self and circumstances that I hoped would serve as an impressive spiritual résumé for posterity. At the same time, a small, nagging suspicion was growing with each page I filled. The act of writing was mutating, I feared, from an attempt at illumination into a means of procrastination. I wasn't meditating.

I worried about none of that once the KIND bars arrived, though. My dad had outdone himself with this treasure chest. Twelve magnificent bars. I didn't have water for the TAZO tea, which was fine. The bags were pretty but useless. Tea has no calories.

He had also included a multipage Wikipedia printout on local snakes. "Just being a dad," I could almost hear him say. I skimmed it once, if only to distract myself from the KIND bars for another few minutes.

It stated that most snakes in Thailand are green and live in trees. *Low risk*, I thought, although I did notice one on the list, the Malayan pit viper, that apparently hides in brush.

Bada, the novice Indian monk formerly of Citibank, had recently explained to me the hierarchy of venomous creatures. Black ants were bad, causing pain and swelling, but they were at the bottom. Scorpions were higher on the list. I'd already seen a few delicate brown ones tucked into the corners of buckets of soil. I'd also spotted a beefy, armored black scorpion on the tile of the shed, although it had turned out to be dead. Above scorpions were giant centipedes. Here, Bada had paused and told a story of a monk at Nanachat getting stung and then begging for his foot to be amputated.

"Otherworldly pain," Bada said of the centipedes, and I recalled the one the size of a corn dog that I let scramble by my foot at Nanachat. I'd had no idea.

Cobras were at the top of the list. Apparently, so was the Malayan pit viper. Their venom could kill.

But the KIND bars. More than dangerous animals, these posed a real dilemma. On the one hand, I had learned my lesson after the night of the Kinder Bueno. I hadn't broken the rule about not eating outside the meal since. But I wasn't ready to offer the bars to the other monks, either.

I continued pacing the room. I chewed my lip and scratched my head. Dusk had fallen. I lit a candle and admired the soft orange light glimmering off the plastic wrapping.

Technically, I thought, the precept was "no eating after noon," not "no eating outside the meal." I also knew monks were forbidden to store offered food overnight, but that was a finer-point rule, which, for me, was probably optional. Eating outside the meal was certainly against the spirit of the rule, if not the actual rule, but I didn't seek clarification. I needed to be able to claim ignorance, if only to myself.

Then my thoughts took on what I hoped was an imminently reasonable and rational tone. It was probably fine, even advisable, if I ate one bar when I woke up alone at 3:00 a.m., yes? That was before noon. It was a gray area. After all, my dad had *offered* me these KIND bars, in a way. And hey, eating a little snack might help me wake up and meditate. They could aid my practice. Really, they could! Smoothies had been allowed in New Zealand, so why not granola in Thailand? Sweet baby Jesus, a tiny taste would make the maw of morning so much more bearable.

I stopped pacing at the desk and stared down at the goods. The KIND bar packaging was partially transparent, taunting me with a view inside. Coconut flakes glistened. Artisanal sea-salt crystals lay seductively across beds of dark chocolate.

To eat or to offer? I decided not to decide. I'd figure it out in the morning.

Normally, I struggled to rise on my own at 3:00 a.m., with nowhere to be for another three hours. But the next morning, I popped right up with no trouble at all.

For the hours before I accompanied the monks on alms round at 6:00 a.m., it was quiet. I tried to meditate during this time, but the external silence had a way of amplifying my internal monologue. Sometimes it grew so uncomfortable that I gave up after only a few minutes of attempted meditation and slept for three more hours until I heard the crunch of gravel coming from outside, at which point I gasped awake, threw the sheet around my torso, and scurried out the door to catch up with the monks.

But the quiet this morning was different. Total. My heel jittered above the floor. Insects fell silent outside, and I pictured them leaning out on their branches toward my hut, as if they knew what I might do and were listening for the crinkle of wrappers. I lit a candle at the desk, slid the Tupperware in front of me, and studied it.

No, I thought, *meditate first.* Most mornings, if I managed to stay awake, I spent much of the time deep down in some rabbit hole of fantasy: concocting triumphant sports plays in which I prevailed against all odds, considering the best condiments for tacos, or rehashing times I'd been wronged and then rehearsing all manner of sharp replies. Then I came to, minutes later, leaning sideways off the chair, teeth clenched, knuckles white.

After a few minutes of such meditation, I turned, crouched over the package, and ate a KIND bar. It happened so fast. The whole experience was over before I really knew it had begun. Next thing I knew, all I had was a wrapper, eleven KIND bars, and nothing else to show for it.

What the hell? I thought. *They had better not all disappear so fast like that.* Hunching in candlelight, I licked the wrapper clean, folded it gingerly into a square, and regarded the other eleven bars.

OK, I thought, *let's be strategic here. I'll eat* two *bars, then offer the other ten. So that means I can eat one more now.* I shrugged and nodded, which must have looked a little crazy to the audience of bugs I still imagined peering in my window, watching me shrug and nod at a box of granola bars as if I were engaging in sensible dialogue.

I tried to eat the second one more slowly. Between bites, I paused to read the ingredients. What *was* soy lecithin? Could I taste the chicory root fiber? The address of the KIND company's HQ was printed on the back. New York. Maybe I could get a job with them when I got back? Surely, they'd love hearing about the time I inhaled their product in a far-flung corner of the world. Maybe they'd make me, like, a brand ambassador. Maybe I could write them a letter from here. Maybe they'd send more bars in the mail.

Coconut almond. Lord have mercy. I hated swallowing because I hated saying goodbye. When each mouthful disappeared into the tasteless black hole of digestion, I felt cheated.

The following morning, without hesitation, I rose again at 3:00 a.m. sharp and ate two more bars. *All right,* I thought afterward, *new plan: I'll eat four, then offer eight to the monks.*

But later that day, I forgot to bring the remaining bars to the kitchen to offer. It just never crossed my mind. I don't know. It was weird.

The next morning, I judged that a clean, even split made the most sense. That was it: I'd eat half and offer half. Six for me, six to offer.

Four days later, I offered the TAZO tea.

Between the meal and work, there was a transition period of around fifteen minutes. The time was unstructured, but it was understood that everyone would go brush their teeth. Which felt downright sadistic. Rushing off to erase the sacred memory of taste felt less like self-care than self-flagellation. We scrubbed away the evidence of eating as if guilty for the gluttony of existence.

Normally, I liked brushing. I even extolled the virtues of flossing to feel luxurious on camping trips. But here, I was so hungry and obsessed with food that I decided not to brush my teeth. The resource was scarce, so I saved what little I had. Like a squirrel with full cheeks, I scurried through the work period and into the afternoon with my tongue free to explore and remember the good times of the meal. Sometimes, if I was lucky, I dislodged a tiny, tasty morsel.

Then I got greedy. At the meal one day, I tucked a packet of vanilla shortbread cookies into the waistband of my robe. While doing dishes with Yupin, I was nervous it would slip out. But it stayed in place, and when Yupin left and everyone else scattered before reporting back for work, I retreated to my kuti with my bounty hidden.

I crept inside my kuti to the bathroom. It never crossed my mind that this version of seclusion—a dark room behind two closed doors I would've locked if I could—differed so diametrically from the open, expansive ideal of seclusion in a vast wilderness I told myself I needed. Then again, my fantasies of spiritual achievement had never included hiding in a bathroom to house a pack of cookies.

Perched on the edge of the toilet, I beheld the treat. The wrapper was sky blue, and the Thai text was a fun marshmallow font. With two hands, I found a perforated edge, twisted, and slowly opened down the seam.

Inside, two rectangular cookies lay across each other like lovers. I slid the first cookie out, held it so that all ten fingertips could touch its chalky texture, and proceeded with small, furious nibbles. The shortbread's initial crumble and crunch balanced a delayed sweetness and softening. Without a shred of shame, I used my tongue to spread a coat of chewed-up food over the outsides of my teeth as if I were spackling a wall. This way, taste and texture would linger long after, even if I knew everything would eventually disintegrate. *Anicca.*

Like the KIND bars a week earlier, this post-meal consumption fell in another gray area. Or so I decided to believe. We brushed our teeth around 11:00 a.m., so this was, again, technically before noon. I wasn't *trying* to break the rules. I was trying *not* to break them. I just needed more than ten minutes of eating time every twenty-four hours.

Had I examined that notion, I might've wondered how it could be that I'd seen so many monks who were stout. Far from emaciated, there were plenty of people on the same schedule and diet as I was who seemed to enjoy a surplus of calories. Granted, they were mostly older, with slower metabolisms, but it still pointed to the possibility that I had enough food. What I really wanted was time.

So I took the damn cookies and ate them slowly on the toilet for another ten minutes, then didn't brush my teeth afterward. And not just once. A few times.

OK, ten times. Maybe I did it for two weeks. I was struggling.

Afterward, I would cross the bridge, hike up the stone path to the shed, and report to Ajahn Sukhito for my work assignment.

There, he would stare at me, saying nothing, observing me with the piercing eyes of a psychic.

Like a stoned high schooler returning home after curfew, I'd think, *He knows.*

Our mouths might have one conversation:

Me: "Is there anything I can do?"

Him: "Yes . . . [thirty-second pause] One . . . bit and piece . . . could be . . . to water the fruit trees. Take a bucket from the stream and water them."

Meanwhile, especially during the pause, our eyes held another conversation:

Me: "Um."

Him: "I know *exactly* what you did."

There were tales of monks who had developed psychic powers. In these moments with Ajahn Sukhito, I believed. Mind reading was one of a handful of supernormal powers that the Buddha himself supposedly gained on the night of his awakening, and some present-day monks apparently had, too. I'd heard senior monks discuss the possibility of acquiring psychic powers upon enlightenment, although it sounded random who did and who didn't, as if the manufacturer normally pushed out the stock-model enlightenment but sometimes got spontaneous with add-ons—"Mind reading for you! Knowledge of past lives for you!"

One of the four worst offenses for a Buddhist monk is to falsely claim possession of psychic powers. The other three are murder, sex, and theft. These four compose the *Parajika* offenses, the gravest category, requiring the offender to disrobe immediately and for life if committed. The Pali word *Parajika*, which to my ears carried a severity reminiscent of a Voldemort spell, roughly translates to "defeat."

What made me shiver with intrigue was that the offense is to *falsely* claim psychic powers, meaning the rule leaves room for the possibility of real ones. If a monk who claimed to have them actually did, then that was totally cool. He could stay.

I didn't really believe in psychic powers, but I did believe in the near-magical power of deeply trained attention. In my own tiny way, I had grazed these benefits a few years earlier. After one month at Vimutti in New Zealand, a week of which was spent in silent retreat, I had returned to college and aced every class of my last semester. I was less stressed and more productive than I'd ever thought possible. The effect had worn off after a few months because I thought I was hot shit permanently and neglected the cause: meditation. But I never forgot what it was like to be able to concentrate with such direction and endurance. It felt like a superpower.

It didn't take deep mental training to notice my anxiety during Ajahn Sukhito's extended silence. Shame sat heavy in my neck. I felt my eyes widen and my head pull back, as if trying to display the picture of innocence. In an attempt to compensate, I found myself stifling the impulse *not* to look like I had something to hide. I must have looked like I was choking, and in a way, I was.

Meanwhile, Ajahn Sukhito remained completely still, allowing me to squirm in guilt. His silences felt cruel at first, but over time, I began to see there was something more going on. The effect of our daily interaction cracked open a new door of perception. I started to glimpse part of what he probably saw plainly, which was that my body was constantly offering subtle signals that corresponded to how I felt, and this was happening whether or not I knew it or liked it.

Physical adjustments mirrored mental movements, I realized. I began applying the idea elsewhere. In meditation, I began noticing that sometimes I shifted my physical position in response to uncomfortable thoughts. The more I observed what went on below the neck, the more I saw parallels with what happened above it. As an athlete, I thought I was already good at listening to my body: I could lean forward and know if my hamstring was strained or just sore; I could tell which pains were alarming and which were brutal but bearable.

But I'd never noticed much in the way of the body's emotional signals until I felt shame bend my neck and anxiety literally tighten my chest. Little by little, I found I could settle my awareness in part of my body, say, my abdomen, then listen there as if with a stethoscope and discover what I was feeling without relying on thinking. The words of the mind worked in tandem with the sensations of the body. But with an important difference: the body didn't lie.

I'd been in the monastery for a matter of months, so I could only imagine the quality of attention that might develop over twenty years in robes. For all I knew, Ajahn Sukhito read me like a children's book: my avoidance of his eyes, the detritus I'd pasted onto my unbrushed teeth, the way I nodded and rushed out of his sight as soon as he finally gave me a task. I didn't know if he was trying to teach me a lesson, but I learned one anyway. Having a secret was exhausting.

And perhaps he saw far more: that I was barely surviving; that I was losing weight from choosing not to eat enough at the meal, yet also sneakily stress-eating whatever I could get my hands on at off-hours before noon. He could've seen the moisture on my fingers and understood that I had licked them and pressed them into the corners of the cookie wrapper to gather every crumb. Maybe he saw all of me, and that was why, out of compassion, he said nothing.

One evening, he invited me to have a conversation. I couldn't believe it. I had been in Thailand for nearly two months, and this would be my first formal consultation with a monk.

We met in the kitchen. Before we could bow and sit, it began to rain—unexpected for late November and the first drop since the storm that had sidelined the moto driver and me en route to Nanachat from the Ubon bus station.

Under the tin roof, it sounded like we were inside a snare drum. Ajahn Sukhito opened his mouth to say something, then thought better of it. He'd have to yell. Instead, he pointed up to the sala, where the thatched roof wouldn't amplify the noise.

I followed him into the rain. Along the way, he maneuvered various containers to catch the rainwater, removing lids from standing jugs and setting bowls and pails out in the open. I helped him waddle a few basins into position under the corners of the sala to gather runoff. I didn't care that I was wet. I was excited to spend any time with him.

We stood on the sala stairs, looking out at the rain. Thirty seconds went by. Itching for conversation, I blurted, "Do you always collect water?"

"It is . . . my hobby," said Ajahn Sukhito.

The rain intensified. Seeing this, he nodded once and turned up the stairs to the second floor, where, each morning, we meditated as a group. In the middle of the room, we centered two cushions, mostly protected from the wet gusts blowing in from the sides.

Together, we bowed three times to the Buddha. Then he turned to face me, and I bowed three times to him. I knew to do that much. He sat on my level with the stage as his backrest. I didn't know whether we needed to chant next or if I could start talking, and if I could, what I would say.

He asked me to tell him about myself.

The question made so much sense that I was taken aback. He knew almost nothing of me, and yet it felt like he knew everything about me. I had expected to jump right into Buddhist philosophy.

I found myself dusting off the script of my professional trajectory as I might for a job interview, but then, all that seemed irrelevant. Instead, I told him about stumbling into monastic life at Vimutti as a college kid hungry for any kind of travel, about how meditation and monastic life had unified a lot of things that had become important to me—wilderness, sports psychology, concentration, trying to be kind— and that I had come to Thailand to go deeper and experiment with solitude.

When I finished, he looked away for as long as I had spoken, nodding slowly, as if replaying my full answer in his head.

Then he spoke: "A little bit of background . . . about me."

Again, this made so much sense that I hadn't expected it. I hadn't wanted to breach some code by prying into his personal life, but now that he'd gone there, I felt rude for not asking. I also didn't realize it then, but I assumed that Ajahn Sukhito was who he always had been—a static figure of authority, not someone who had once been a pakao, or a layperson, or a child.

After his required service in the Israeli army, he had traveled to an ashram in India, then tried out Zen Buddhism, and finally ordained at Wat Pah Nanachat at age twenty-five. He said he liked the word I had used—*unify*. For him, the Thai Forest Tradition had unified the wisdom and inclinations that he had gathered.

I let his comments linger in the air. At this point, I knew better than to rush in on the heels of anything he said. The rain on the thatched roof slowed to a patter. A soft evening light whispered through dissipating clouds. Under the dripping eaves, I could see the four legs of a double rainbow. We both looked at it for a few minutes without comment.

Then I said I was also twenty-five.

He turned to me, said that he thought I was older than that.

This made me feel proud, which, I realized, placed me squarely back in the realm of a twenty-five-year-old.

Ajahn Sukhito decided to address something I had said earlier. "Some monks romanticize solitude."

I had mentioned reading an essay by the head monk in New Zealand, titled "Alone on a Mountain." I'd loved it and craved the experience.

"Total solitude can be excellent for *samadhi*," he said, referring to calm, "but it can also give people wrong views, maybe dead ends or blocks they cannot get around. In solitude, people can develop strange, obsessive habits."

He paused here as if remembering an example or inviting me to imagine one. He continued, "It's actually more beneficial to training to be in *community*, to *surrender* to community." He emphasized these words as if they had saved his own life.

This, especially coming from such an introverted monk, left me perplexed. But then, thinking back through my own life, I found I had to agree. The most valuable experiences of my young adulthood were things I could never have done alone—the month-long instructor training course in the Wrangell Mountains of Alaska, a few special Ultimate Frisbee teams, my first steady romantic relationship, even the monastery in New Zealand. I hadn't been alone for any of those. At the same time, I felt I was ready to *graduate* to solitude and independence. I'd come to Thailand to learn supreme self-sufficiency because the world was unreliable. Divorce. Death. I expected Ajahn Sukhito, of all people, to get this.

But he went on. "*Friendship* within one's spiritual practice is critical. Being of benefit to a community, too, which means being connected. Solitude is still a big part of life here: there's the free time, and each meditation session offers solitude, even if fifty other people are sitting with you." After a long pause, he snorted and said, "*Alone on a mountain*," repeating the title of the essay I'd read. He shook his head.

My eye twitched. First, I'd never heard a monk diss another monk. Second, I realized that in all my cherished visions of myself as a spiritual guru, I had been either alone or in front of an audience. I'd never really considered having friends.

"Of course," Ajahn Sukhito went on, "in any intimate community, even a small one, it can be quite difficult at times."

I wondered if this was a subtle acknowledgment of the culture back at Nanachat. Maybe Ajahn Sukhito had wanted to escape himself, and that was why he was here. But I wasn't going to probe.

He asked me next about the schedule. "I have an instinct for who will find Poo Jom Gom conducive, and I felt it when I met you for the first time at Nanachat."

I said I enjoyed the schedule, which was almost true. I liked the *idea* of it. The reality was more complicated. "I keep thinking about how we have everything we need here," I said, "which makes life easy in a way. But it's still so difficult sometimes. I don't know. I guess I'm starting to see that it's only hard here when I make it hard."

Ajahn Sukhito grunted in affirmation, waited a few seconds, and said, "Yes. That is a true insight. But it can take learning over and over again: we say it, we think it, we keep learning it, and eventually, there is an actual *transformation* in the mind where we *stop* making things difficult."

At the word *transformation*, he flipped his hand as if turning a doorknob.

Night had fallen. I could only see his silhouette before me. We scooted our cushions so close to one another that our knees almost touched.

He asked whether I had any questions.

"Many," I said, then forced a chuckle. "But it's getting late. I can save them." I wasn't sure he really wanted me to ask a question. We'd already been talking for over an hour.

He paused a long moment, then said, to my relief, "Perhaps one."

Now I took the long pause. I felt an itch to fill the space with hums and head tilts, but I stopped myself. If anyone could handle silence and stillness, it was Ajahn Sukhito. I didn't have to take care of him. So I sat motionless, waiting for thoughts to form.

I heard myself start talking: "I have a question about grief. I'm trying to learn how to watch it and experience it, not push it away, but not dwell on it, either. I've also started to feel more kind because of it, which I don't really know what to make of. Sorrow can feel addictive sometimes."

I trailed off. I hadn't really asked a question, which wasn't uncommon. Rather than personal inquiries, laypeople often offered broad topics to monks in Q&As. That way, monks could discuss psychology in general terms, and the audience could translate the particulars to their own lives. But I was also hiding behind this convention, and he picked up on it.

Instead of launching into a treatise on grief, he asked softly, "Is this in regard to . . . something in particular?"

"Um, yeah," I said. "The deaths of a few people I was close with, especially one younger friend."

He nodded and grew quiet—ten seconds, twenty, thirty. I sensed that this particular pause might have been an act of generosity, a chance for me to calm down, which, as the silence stretched on, happened. My breathing had slowed by the time he spoke, and I was ready to listen.

"To contemplate," he said, "means to think, to feel, to experience, to allow without getting caught up in something or pushing it away. It's important to bring a balanced mindfulness to the experience of grief or, for that matter, to any emotion. It's a skill worth cultivating. Grief is a teaching on dhamma, on the way things are."

And now I felt my chest closing in. I knew what was coming next, and it was a lesson I didn't want, a lesson about how, because I experienced grief, I simply wasn't yet enlightened. It would go something like "Noble ones, knowing that all things arise and pass, do not fret too much about anything, even death, for they have risen above suffering."

Ajahn Sukhito went on. "We experience loss and know, on some level, that all things eventually leave. If there is grief, that means there is longing, and that means sorrow at separation, which is actually," he said, "a *mature* feeling."

I straightened.

"We have these feelings for experiences, places, possessions, animals, but they are always strongest for people," he said. "Grief can generate a lot of positive emotions, like an increase in generosity and kindness, which you said you had experienced since the death of your friend."

I held my jaw closed to keep a sob from escaping.

"Sometimes, people can get caught in grief for years, even lifetimes, which," he added tenderly, "is unfortunate."

We sat together and listened to the ripples of our conversation settle. Then he gave a small bob of his head to indicate that he was finished talking. I thanked him, we bowed to the Buddha and I bowed to him, and then we said good night.

On the way back to my kuti, I paused on the little bridge. The stream had swollen from the rain. The clouds had cleared. The stars and crescent moon were sharp, and I noticed a stone bench across the gravel. I went to it and lay on my back to keep admiring the sky. Placed one hand under my head, another over my chest.

We had talked for two hours. I could've cried with gratitude. I felt the slow, gulping rhythm of my heartbeat under my fingertips. Slow, I thought. Really slow. I checked the green-lit digital watch face to count out a minute and measure my heart rate.

It was thirty-four beats per minute. I had to double-check. Sure enough, thirty-four. I didn't know whether to be proud or scared. I'd had a heart problem a few years earlier. *Pericarditis*, they'd called it, finally giving a name to my summer of chest pain and specialist visits. The other word the doctors attached was *idiopathic*, a fancy way of saying, "We have no idea where this came from."

My fingers crawled along the soft spaces in between my ribs, searching for the slightest sign of tension. But I could sense none. Under my hand, my body felt relaxed, reinvigorated, like the stream I could hear flowing nearby. Even at my most fit, my heart rate had never dipped below sixty. Now, after not exercising for two months, it had dropped to nearly half that. Maybe monastic practice was working. Ajahn Sukhito had given me an endorsement to feel. Maybe I was somehow taking one of Ajahn Chah's sayings literally, "Use your heart to listen to the teaching, not your ears."

Checking my watch once more, I paused at the date, "TH NOV 27," and laughed. I'd completely forgotten it was a holiday. Smiling up at the star-dusted sky, I felt a second flush of gratitude for Ajahn Sukhito. Perhaps he had known that his American guest would appreciate company on Thanksgiving.

CHILL

Ajahn Sukhito had talked about learning and relearning lessons until, eventually, there was an actual transformation. That was all well and good, but I didn't know what there was to learn from hunger. The only transformation I could imagine was the groundbreaking discovery of a missing section of the Pali Canon extolling the virtues of dinner.

I was tearing my hair out. Literally. My plug-in razor ran out of battery a couple of weeks after I arrived at Poo Jom Gom. I located the monastery's single electrical outlet—by the pantry in the kitchen—but it didn't work. While I relished the reputational cachet of living without electricity, I was less enthusiastic about having to shave my head, face, and eyebrows like everyone else did, with a single loose blade and a bar of soap. When I finished for the first time, I had unleashed a blizzard of dandruff and drawn a roadmap of blood. Neglected tufts remained behind my ears, and I looked like one of the feral dogs with mange I saw during alms round, slinking around, hungry for scraps.

My new tactic to combat hunger was to wake up even earlier, around 2:00 a.m., which shifted the meal deeper into the day, increasing the number of hours spent anticipating the meal, which were far more bearable, and decreasing the time spent agonizing over its passing.

I was losing weight and losing my mind. Afternoons were interminable. I delayed opening mail until loneliness brought me to the brink. One evening, I opened a letter from my grandmother with a cartoon cut from the *New Yorker*: two figures sat on a picnic blanket and stared at a piece of cake. The caption read, "Now we wait." I was indignant. This was torture too close to home. It took me a day to realize the picnickers were anteaters.

Letters were few, and ultimately there was nothing to do but meditate, to actually do the thing I'd gone there to do. I tried sitting in the plastic chair by the peeling desk, but I grew restless and claustrophobic and fled outdoors.

At the streambed, I found a depression in the rock and sat on a sandal for a cushion. *Time to meditate,* I thought, *for real.* I set a timer on my watch for an hour, closed my eyes, and heaved the sigh of one who knows the cause is already lost.

Around eight minutes later, I fidgeted, stood up, and grumbled about not being able to stick it out for even ten minutes. Each day, the same cycle. I raged at myself for spending so much time *thinking* and *writing* about concentration rather than actually *concentrating.* I thought back to one of the signs posted on a tree at Nanachat. A quote from Ajahn Chah: "If you have something bad-smelling in your pocket, wherever you go it will smell bad. Don't blame it on the place." I sulked at the stream, seeing the movement of my mind in that of the water bugs, restless and darting nowhere across the surface. For so long, I thought solitude—resplendent, desperado solitude—would remove all obstacles and pry me open to nature's pristine lessons. But solitude had not rid me of suffering. It had rid me of excuses.

I checked my watch. A measly six minutes had passed. For the fiftieth time that day, I calculated the hours and minutes remaining until the next day's meal. Cravings swelled in my skull for foods I never ate: Twinkies, olives. Time dripped like a broken faucet. I checked my watch again. Four minutes had passed. Agony. Time was not fluid. It didn't even drip. Time was the rock, sedentary and impenetrable and hot and stupid.

One afternoon, I took off the digital watch and began roaming the riverbed, in search of a boulder to lift overhead and use to smash the thing like a primate cracking a nut. Finding nothing suitable, I trudged to my kuti and tucked the watch into a pocket of my backpack with the other items I never used: phone—dead, electric razor—dead, wool socks—useless.

Better, I thought, to be unaware of time than addicted to it. "Isolation > temptation," I wrote in my diary, for the eleventh time. Without a watch, I hoped to cleanse myself of the twenty-four-hour construct entirely. Without concentration or contentment, fantasy presented the only escape from insanity, and so I imagined living in bare-wristed harmony with nature, forgetting the day, the month, the year, even. Whenever I needed to know something, I'd simply crouch in the forest, smell a pinch of soil, then squint at the sky and nod in understanding.

The only time I never forgot was teatime. The trip to the kitchen each afternoon felt like a jailbreak. Yupin would fill a thermos with hot water and leave it beside a plastic box containing the supplies: a few types of tea, unsweetened cocoa powder, and a small glass jar with brown sugar. If I was lucky, Yupin left a juice box, either apple or cranberry.

Sometimes, Giorgio took tea in the kitchen, too, and on rare occasions, we happened to arrive at the same time. Initially, my heart leaped at the sight of another soul, but then it landed in a puddle, for my brooding head produced a rain cloud over the prospect of human interaction. Forgetting Ajahn Sukhito's advice on friendship, I felt Giorgio's presence soiled the purity of my solitude. Unable to coerce my free time into meditative bliss, I didn't think I had earned the right to relax, much less socialize. So I drank a quick cup with Giorgio, found myself enjoying it too much, and then stomped back to my kuti to continue going crazy.

Most afternoons, the kitchen was empty. Without the activity of the morning, the stillness of the surrounding forest dissolved the feeling of shelter. Hot breezes swept across the tile. Bamboo leaves shuddered and clicked. A task kept my mind at bay, so I took sips often, and I made them small.

Once every couple of weeks, on Wan Phra, Ajahn Sukhito allowed a snack—but only one. I found it waiting beside the thermos and tea box in a tiny bowl: a lonely, individually wrapped gummy, hardly bigger than a jelly bean.

One bean. I would've been furious if I wasn't overjoyed. The wrapper was white with red Thai text, mimicking the gummy's white shell and luscious red filling. As much as I despised the ritual around the daily meal, I found myself ritualizing the consumption of my biweekly bean. And although I failed to track the number of bites in the morning meal, I found out exactly how many I could get from this tiny treat. Seventeen. I studied every ingredient on the wrapper the way I'd done with the KIND bars. In what must have been a mistranslation to English, the slogan shouted in all caps: "GOOD TASTE OF THE FASHION LIFE."

One afternoon, Yupin left a surprise: a pineapple juice box. This merited special treatment. I hiked around the pantry to the bamboo and stream, sat, and dangled my legs off the edge. After sweeping my area free of twigs, I punctured the box, careful not to let a drop go to waste. I twirled the straw like a paper umbrella and brought it close to my nose to smell the fruit. Before partaking, I pored over every line of text on the box, from the branding on the front to the numbers along the barcode. After all, I thought, you read the card before opening the gift.

Monastic life was largely devoid of text. This was by design. The way my eyes crawled over the packaging, I understood how words could be sinkholes of craving. Senior monks talked about "sense restraint" as a key to maintaining focus. Ajahn Chah had given the image of trying to catch a lizard from a den that has six holes from which to escape. Five of the holes were the senses, and monastic life helped you plug them. By restraining the stimuli of the eyes, ears, nose, mouth, and body, one could keep a vigilant watch over the mind.

I knew this. But I also *really* enjoyed the taste of this pineapple juice. Between tiny, savoring sips, I didn't know whether the satisfaction I felt from making a special occasion of it was heedless extravagance or harmless pleasure. I furrowed my brow. After two and a half months of monastic life, I knew something else: overanalyzing my experience ruined it.

Just stop already, I thought. *Relax. Enjoy this.*

Below the ingredients on the box were instructions: "For best taste, chill."

I'm trying! I thought.

Even sleep no longer offered a reliable getaway. I dreamed I was outside a café in a quaint European city with cobblestone streets when, suddenly, terrorists began shooting. While others fled and the bullets flew by, I reached across the table, willing to die for a bite of someone else's French toast.

Another night, I awoke to the sound of a vibration.

Vvvt-vvvt. Two buzzes.

I sat up. An animal outside? No. It had come from within the kuti. Another beetle inside? I replayed what I could remember of the noise, which was strangely familiar.

Then I understood. Lifting myself from the floor, I crossed the room to my backpack and unzipped the pocket that held my electric razor. It was off. Under the wool socks, beside the discarded digital watch, was my cell phone.

It was impossible. I hadn't touched my phone in eighty days. It had no service. It should've been dead. It should've been off. It should've at least been set to silent. Inconceivably, I had gotten a text.

FREE PIZZA WITH ORDER OF GIFT CARD! A promotion from my favorite restaurant in Minneapolis, Punch Pizza. Please reply STOP if you no longer wish to receive these messages.

I doubted my reply would go through, but I needed to send a plea into the universe.

STOP, I wrote. PLEASE.

I tried to write myself into a breakthrough. In all caps, over and over, I wrote in my diary that I *had* enough food. But brute force didn't work.

One evening, a memory startled me into considering an alternative. I recalled a story from a childhood friend. At a summer camp, a counselor had lined up the campers shoulder to shoulder, told them to raise a hand as if taking an oath, and then gone down the line, pushing his palm into each of theirs. Naturally, each camper pushed back, matching the force. Except one. She absorbed the pressure and let the counselor's hand push hers back. The counselor asked if she had any marital arts training. Sure enough, she had a black belt.

Maybe, I thought, *I need to stop pushing so hard.* This, I was certain, was the unlocking I needed. On a fresh page, I wrote the moral of the story and underlined it: "Nonresistance is both wisdom and power."

For a moment, I leaned back and felt both wise and powerful. Not only would this realization solve my problems, I thought, but it would be a major turning point in my bestselling diary.

In fact, it was neither. Unbeknownst to me, I had written the exact same story of the black belt's nonresistance one month earlier. Same arc, same pseudo-insight. Worse, it wasn't even the second time I had written this anecdote in the diary. It was the third. Trying the same thing in the hopes of a different result: instead of writing my way out of insanity, I was charting a path into it.

When I sensed the uselessness of writing, I wrote commitments about stopping. "NO WRITING FOR THREE DAYS!!!" The irony was not lost on me. As if I might be able to hide something from myself, I tried stashing the diary in unusual locations, deep in the bottom of my backpack, underneath extra candle boxes in the desk, far underneath the bed reserved for distinguished guests.

Monks describe five hindrances to meditation. I understood them visually and had written them this way:

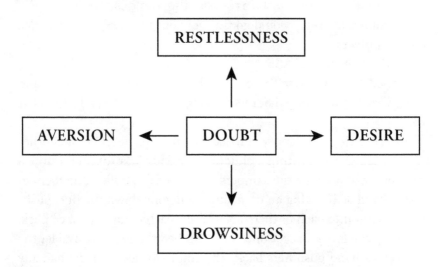

They are generally referred to as "the hindrances," which makes sense because they affect more than meditation. They are also hindrances to happiness. Desire approaches; aversion recoils. Energy is depressed in drowsiness and elevated in restlessness. Doubt sits in the center, questioning everything. Sometimes I could label my own struggles: *food—desire; writing—restlessness*. But I didn't know how to use that information. The best I could come up with was to clench and think, *Stop that!* Or I tried nonresistance but then heard myself saying phrases like "just acknowledge what is" or "allow my truth," which sounded like a parody of some new-age yoga class. Awareness, by itself, was a dead end.

There were, in fact, strategies I could have used for dealing with hindrances. Drowsiness, for example, could be counteracted with thoughts of mortality to give rise to a sense of urgency. Lust could be met with contemplation of bile and decay. But I knew none of that at the time. In the face of suffering, I ran. I ran from meditation, just as I had run from Nanachat, just as I had run from my whole life back home in the US. I could scoff at the cicada who flew headfirst into a beam, I could write a metaphor about how *other* people would be wise to run *to* instead of run *from*, but I couldn't take the lesson I taught. It was so easy to call out in others what I missed in myself.

I didn't want to write, so I fled to the stream one afternoon and sat with my legs dangling in the water. Glancing up at the position of the sun, I guessed it was 1:00 p.m., barely. Days at Poo Jom Gom felt like months. My knees trembled, and I watched the small concentric circles cast out, bounce off each other, and spread smooth like a tablecloth. That made my mouth water. Another pang of hunger surged, and I despaired at the injustice of yet another sixteen hours without—

Wait, I thought. *Am I actually hungry right now or just thinking about food?*

Closing my eyes, I tried dropping awareness from my head into my stomach. There, I felt around, checking my gut for the physical sensations of hunger.

To my surprise, there were none—no ache, no growl. It was quiet. My body wasn't hungry. Huh.

For the rest of my afternoon outdoors, food cravings remained, but I had glimpsed a place where they didn't exist. What had been an infinite, enveloping desire now had a border at the neck.

That night, I tried to keep the body involved and give walking meditation another go. Pacing the dirt strip outside my kuti at Nanachat had temporarily quieted my mind, so I lit a candle, set a line from the desk across the room, and practiced going back and forth at a brisk clip. Warm-up laps.

With the candle at my back, my shadow loomed on the far wall. When I walked closer, it shrank to my size. Which meant the figure grew behind my back when I walked away. This gave me a shiver, and I spun around halfway across the room to find him staring at me, eight feet tall, heavy fists, thick neck. Watching me with a blank stare. I waited for him to make a move that I hadn't. His weight shifted. Had mine? I ran toward the wall, shrinking him to scale. It helped to see his thin, panting frame, and I touched his shoulder and searched his face for solace or similarity. But it was flat and cold, and I suddenly realized I was nose to nose with this creature. He had lured me in.

It was ridiculous. It was my shadow. But I was freaked out and alone and losing my marbles. Still, I decided not to blow out the candle for fear that the figure would still be in the room, and then I'd lose track of him. I backed away in small steps off the line I'd set for walking meditation, dispersing the shadow's human form, and I sank into a corner on the floor.

I'd read once that solitary confinement was the worst form of torture, and I thought, *Yes*. This was the hardest thing I'd ever done. This was definitely extreme, I thought. Like, if I were to get captured on assignment for the State Department, this would be good prep for that. I pictured being thrown into a dank cell with peeling paint and a single buzzing light bulb. My captors would shut the door and feel confident I'd crack. But when they left, I would just straight *handle* it, divulge zero state secrets, and meditate the whole time in peace.

I caught myself. *No, no*, I thought, *real solitary would be brutal.*

I stood up and thought, *Yeah, gloriously brutal.*

Pacing again, I stroked my chin. Where might the Foreign Service send me to work? Slovenia? What cities were even in Slovenia? Reykjavík? What would my kitchen look like? How much of a stipend would I get? Would a local sheep farmer give me wool socks and a sweater and call me by some cool nickname that he'd shout to me from his wheelbarrow whenever I passed him in his field?

Before I knew it, I was seated at the desk, drawer open, candle box lifted, diary out. I clicked the pen and began compiling a list that felt critical and strategic:

- • FSO location? Rent covered?
- • Research Slovenia—cities, temperature, precipitation, typical cuisine?
- • Sheep/wool?

Without access to email, I still had no idea my application to the Foreign Service had been rejected.

At the end of three months, I had to renew my visa. This meant leaving the monastery. While I welcomed the thought of novelty, I was nervous. I'd leave in the morning and miss the meal, meaning no food for forty-eight hours.

Before alms round that day, Yupin arrived early. Ajahn Sukhito met us in the kitchen to translate: Yupin would take me, along with her husband and kids, to a bus stop outside of town. From there, I'd take a public shuttle to and from the visa office. Yupin had shopping to do with her family and would pick me up at the same stop later that day. No plan for food was discussed, and I didn't ask. *Eat little; speak little.*

When we reached the bus stop, Yupin handed me a plastic container with rice, chicken, and steamed mini bananas.

Breathless, I said, "Kop khun ka," *thank you.*

She grinned like she knew I'd been thinking about it all along.

We confirmed the plan as best we could, pointing to the ground at the bus stop and saying, "Here," to indicate step one, the drop-off. Then we waved our hands as if into the future to show step two, our respective errands. Finally, we pointed back to the ground, again saying, "Here," to confirm step three, the pickup.

"OK?" she said.

"OK," I said.

From the driver's seat, her husband chuckled and kept his hand on the wheel. Her two kids in the back seat literally pointed at me and laughed, which felt appropriate. I looked like an albino stick bug being released from captivity into the wild. They drove off, and I wrapped myself tighter in my bedsheet.

Immediately, I ate the dish, including every grain of rice that hid in the divots around the container's edge. The bus, when it came, was an old van with pink curtains inside the windows. It dropped me at the visa office, where, inside, I stood in the doorway, squinting at the glare of the overhead light reflecting off the white linoleum floor.

Luckily, the employees at the visa office knew exactly what to do when a bald foreigner in robes showed up looking confused. They ushered me to the front of the line, expedited my approval, and stamped my passport. I walked out in less than twenty minutes, awed once again by the bureaucracy-deep respect afforded to the Thai Forest Tradition.

Ahead of schedule, I shuttled back to the pickup point. At the corner stood a tin roof on crooked posts. Between them hung an off-white thread hammock with chickens milling about in the dry brush. Across the street I noticed a market, bustling under tarp roofs.

Yupin's plate had been so delicious but so small. I had some time before they picked me up, plus some leftover cash from the visa run. It was well before noon. Fifteen minutes later, I returned to the hammock with plastic bags on each arm. I binge-drank a six-pack of chocolate-soy-milk boxes and chowed down on a heap of cookies and dried fruit. Then I tossed every carton and wrapper into the garbage across the street, afraid Yupin would be disappointed to find me looking like a busted piñata.

Rocking in the hammock, I committed to recording in my diary the full menu of what I'd consumed. The memory of this feast would continue to sustain me. I ran through the list—*six-pack of soy milk, twelve dried bananas, vanilla cookies*—when, without warning, a new thought landed like a splash on a flame.

It said, *Who cares?*

I stopped rocking. In that moment, I was blessed with something lovely and long overdue: boredom. Not a clever construction of words or reason, but a release born of exhaustion. I never wrote the list in my diary because this new voice interrupted my fascination with food, and I finally believed it.

Back at Poo Jom Gom, I began to meditate for hours at a time. The idea occurred to bring the plastic chair from my desk out to the small porch of my kuti. The porch, I discovered, offered a divine kind of balance. I could be rooted to the structure but available to the breeze, no longer floundering back and forth between the exposure of the out-doors and the claustrophobia of the kuti. It had taken three months, but food cravings had evaporated, and I felt almost peaceful.

One day, after I'd settled into meditation, I heard someone clear their throat.

Pamutto, the forty-year-old Australian novice monk, stood at my steps.

"Er, hello there, Grant," he said. "I, erm, well, I know I'm supposed to be over at my kuti, and we're not really supposed to socialize, and I don't mean to bother your meditation . . ."

"No, that's fine," I said. I wanted the interruption to be annoying, but I couldn't hide a hint of relief. "What's up?"

"Well, I was wondering if I might use the other room of the kuti, seeing as it's unoccupied, to write a letter to my parents, seeing as that room has a desk and chair and my kuti is nothing but a floor, and I've been having these back issues." He winced and arched his torso as if to prove it. "It's a rather important letter," he said.

"Sure," I said. "I don't know if permission is mine to give, but yeah, go ahead."

He bowed and smiled so kindly that I thought he might cry.

Over the next three afternoons, he came back to write in the vacant room. I'd hear him cough and adjust his chair, and I wanted his presence to be a disturbance, but curiosity about his letter was cracking my commitment to the solo curmudgeon act.

On the fourth day, I heard him get up, slide the chair against the desk, and close the door to leave. But I didn't hear the crunch of footsteps receding down the gravel.

"Grant?" he said.

I glared at the trees and tried making a sour face. But then I bounded around the corner and said, "Yes?"

Pamutto stood with a sheaf of pages in his hand. "I just finished up with the letter and wanted to say thanks."

"You're welcome," I said.

He made a subtle wave goodbye but made no move to depart.

"Letter's done, huh?" I said. I, too, felt inclined to chat.

"Yeah, well, as done as I can think to make it." He looked down.

"Actually, I'd be curious what you think. See, it's a letter to my parents to tell them I'm gonna ordain."

Pamutto was a novice monk, not yet fully ordained. A novice followed ten precepts compared with my eight. The main difference between his position and mine, other than his robes being orange, was that he could not handle money. Ordaining as a novice generally carried a one-year commitment in the Thai Forest Tradition. The next step Pamutto was referring to was the big one: 227 rules and a lifetime commitment.

"Oh," I said.

"Yeah," he said, "and actually, you've got this interesting perspective because you know the monastery life, but you haven't been in it for so long to kind of erase the outside perspective. Maybe you'd be interested in giving it a look?"

He'd hit me with a one-two combo of flattery and intrigue. I couldn't say no. He left the letter with me and said we could discuss it the next day.

I read Pamutto's letter as if it were my own. Almost as much as I had imagined what it would be like to ordain, I had also envisioned how it would feel to tell my family I wouldn't be coming back. I pictured them visiting me in Thailand, walking tentatively up the Nanachat driveway, then hugging their emaciated, hairless son. Then I remembered I wouldn't be allowed to hug my mom because physical contact with the opposite sex was forbidden. The actual rule, as I understood it, was specific to contact *with lustful intent*. However, the practice in Thailand was far more strict. It had come to encompass any physical contact with women whatsoever. When female villagers made offerings, they had to use a special cloth to avoid even the slightest incidental grazing.

The extreme was appealing in theory. But applied to hugging my own mother, or sister, or grandmothers, I grew furious. Later, I'd learn that some monks hugged their mothers in private. This exception made the norm even more absurd in my eyes, partly because I still craved an existence of total puritan certainty with no space for nuance. But underneath that grievance was another feeling I didn't quite recognize—or didn't want to: a distrust of a community that would bar such a harmless expression of filial love. And beneath that was a small hard fear that this monastic existence wasn't the one for me at all, which would leave me adrift. I was intensely curious to see Pamutto's rationale.

His folded pages were thick. If his goal was to say, "Dear Mum and Dad, I've decided to ordain as a monk," then he took twenty pages to get there but never arrived at all. He recapped his story, which they surely knew already, about how he'd gotten stranded in Thailand while sailing because of a boat malfunction. To burn time while the boat was in the shop, he'd visited a cheesy mega-monastery in Bangkok. They gave him bright-orange robes and ordained him on the spot, along with a couple hundred other tourists who wanted to be Monk-for-a-Day and post pictures about it on social media. For most people, that was the end of it. But Pamutto had nowhere else to go, so even though he had no knowledge of Buddhism, he remained at the monastery longer. One day, they invited an Ajahn from the Thai Forest Tradition to visit and give a talk. The Ajahn happened to be Ajahn Jayasaro, the famous British monk I'd seen arrive for Kathina in the black Benz and who had answered my question about a sense of humor being a virtue. Unsurprisingly, Pamutto was blown away, so much that he asked if he could go with the Ajahn to his monastery, thinking he might stay somewhere more inspiring for another week or two while he waited for his boat to get fixed. Ajahn Jayasaro took him to Wat Pah Nanachat. And now, eighteen months later, someone else had taken the boat, and Pamutto was still in robes.

That was where the letter ended. No next step. It seemed like he wasn't telling his parents he was ordaining as much as he was trying to convince himself to go through with it.

Which is what I told him on my porch the next afternoon. "It's really interesting," I said, "but it almost reads more like a letter to yourself."

"Hmm," he said. "You're right to pick up on that. That's kind of why I'm here at Poo Jom Gom, actually. I'm a bit overdue, you see. Novices are supposed to ordain after a year. I've been going on eighteen months, and Ajahn Siri is pushing me to make a call. It's just really full-on, you know? Full ordination. Life commitment."

"I do," I said. And I did. Signing up for life, like other aspects of the monastic tradition, sounded great in theory, kind of the way medical school had appealed as I approached college graduation. Both offered a prestigious, prolonged answer to the question of what to do, which at the time struck me as more burden than privilege. Much was expected. Being a senior monk, being an attending surgeon, both seemed settled and striking. Then again, my uncle was a surgeon, and I'd shadowed him and peppered him with existential questions until he had said that, actually, most of his peers who finally emerged from medical training were bitter, entitled, or both. The monastic training presented a similar risk. The first five years were especially restrictive. You were glued to an older monk supervisor called a preceptor. Your travel was severely restricted. You had to close your bank accounts. Full-on, as Pamutto said.

I added, "I think about whether I should ordain quite often. Honestly, I waste a lot of time thinking about it."

Another benefit of a porch: conversation. Pamutto brought out the other plastic chair from the kuti, and over the next few days, we chatted. It felt illicit. *Afternoons are for practice,* I thought with a tight jaw. But then again, Ajahn Sukhito had encouraged friendship.

We had what the other wanted. For me: an insider's perspective on monastic life, someone who was deeper in but also open about their doubts. Pamutto had lived a full forty years of life before ordaining. He'd done what I often considered, which was to ordain later if a more conventional route failed. He told me he had lived in London, owned two cars, made lots of money, gotten divorced, partied hard, and sometimes woken up on his bathroom floor. In other words, he was relatable.

For him, I offered a listening ear. He was on the cusp of a major decision, and he needed to talk to someone who wasn't a monk or a villager. He'd acclimated to the multitude of superficial challenges of monastic life, but now he faced the big hesitation: family.

"What am I going to do if I *don't* ordain," Pamutto said one afternoon, "go home and say, 'Hey, Mum and Dad, it's me, your forty-year-old son, back to live in your house'? What *job* would I possibly get after having lived this way? Like, something in *marketing*?"

We guffawed. "That's exactly what I think about," I said.

"And what am I going to say to my friends?" he said. "Like, 'Hello,

I'm completely different now.' I would be utterly lost in a bar. And *women*, oh boy, I don't even want to begin thinking about that."

I did. "Do you think it's possible to live celibate on the outside?"

"I think about it, yeah. Like, have a little studio apartment near my parents and go to work, do something I enjoy, something that's *good*, you know, not like *marketing*, and just live simply."

I didn't really know anything about marketing, but I was happy to jump on board and assume it was all spin and fluff, the opposite of what I needed to believe *I* would do outside the monastery walls, which was something *honest* and *essential*. Emphatically, I agreed with Pamutto, oblivious to the countless marketing teams that understood the appeal of a slogan like "Live simply" and how susceptible I was to it.

"That's what I think about, too," I said, "a minimal life. But with celibacy, I just have no idea how realistic that is." I did not mention that if and when I left the monastery, I might travel with a woman. MJ, the woman in New York, had written me a letter saying she could meet me in Bangkok.

"Yeah," Pamutto said, "and there's nothing like that warm body next to you in bed."

"I keep writing all these ideas in my diary," I said, "like, how to have my cake and eat it, too. Spiritual lives I *could* lead on the outside, re-creating this place, basically—nature, meditation, solitude, sparse technology—but then adding the things I want to keep, like dinner and family and pranks and dance parties and occasional psychedelics."

Pamutto laughed. "Oh, I've got *loads* of journals I've filled up over the last year. Sometimes I even think about publishing them, but then I go back and can barely get through a few pages before I have to stop. They're awful."

Somehow, staring epiphany in the face, I turned away. "Yeah," I muttered, then thought, *Pamutto's diaries probably are kinda bad; that's why mine'll be so valuable.*

Alone one afternoon, I returned to the streambed, feeling shaky. I stopped at a divot in the rock bank, slipped off one rubber shoe for a cushion, sat, and began to cry. Something about Pamutto's unlikely path to Poo Jom Gom invited reflection on the unlikelihood of my own. I'd been fighting for three months—first for solitude, then the ability to tolerate it. I'd finally adjusted enough to feel a sudden flood of appreciation for the place and the people. I felt a tenderness toward Pamutto, a fellow traveler led by luck and pain. He was, I realized, a friend.

Which put me in mind of those I'd lost. My instinct when crying is to curl inward and clench as if wringing tears from a towel. But the privacy of wilderness was expansive, and I realized I had nothing to hide. No one could see or hear, so I pried my crossed arms open and turned my palms up and made noise. Eyes on the streaks of clouds overhead, I cried for the beauty and the tragedy and the relief of fully allowing a feeling.

Eventually, I said aloud, "What is happening to me right now?" And in a small and gradual moment of progress, I didn't try to answer.

A month after our first conversation, Ajahn Sukhito invited me to have another, again in the sala. As the evening sun softened, without a single word between us, we met at the bottom of the stairs, made our way up, set cushions opposite one another, and bowed to the Buddha statute at the front of the room.

After bowing to him, I let another quiet minute pass before asking about writing. Despite the quote I had heard at Nanachat about being "done" once you "get" food, I was still struggling. The discomforts of craving food had vanished, but the discomforts of craving insight via writing had intensified.

"Writing can be useful," Ajahn Sukhito said, "if it's contemplative, dhamma related. It can clarify and organize, and you can use it to re-visit your . . . selves. It can even be a substitute for talking, because even 'together' time here isn't all that social."

That had been true in my experience. Writing had at times given me a second voice outside of my own head, a tiny surrogate community.

"But," he went on, "beware not to develop 'writer's mind.' It can distract from meditation when we think, 'Oh! I need to write that down.'"

He suggested I give it up for a period of time to see what it brought up for me.

I didn't tell him I had already tried that and failed because I thought my head would explode from so much wisdom piling up unrecorded. I said, "OK, I'll try that."

I had a follow-up question, but I waited, as was customary in conversation with Ajahn Sukhito, for silence to reestablish itself between us. I took a few long breaths and stole glances at his face to see if he looked ready to move on.

Then I said, "I keep thinking about intentionally giving up other things I enjoy, too . . . to, like, *supercharge* the practice or get on the fast track beyond indulgence in pleasure, but when does that kind of thing slip over into indulgence in pain?"

I was pretty sure Ajahn Sukhito would brush this one away. As such an intense person himself, he was most likely going to say, in a Buddhist way, "No pain, no gain." And part of me hoped for that answer. Extremes offered simplicity. A warrior needed only to fight.

Instead, he smiled and spoke softly, as if explaining something to a child. "Ajahn Chah, later in his life, de-emphasized special practices like fasting and focused instead on *consistency* of practice."

I had a small sinking feeling. Common sense was never glorious.

"*The myth of the forest monk*," he said theatrically with a hand gesture for added flair, "the person who *goes off* and does *intense* things and becomes some *special* teacher. Western competitiveness and self-criticism often influence the desire to push oneself. But really, we live in such a restrained environment *already* that it's OK to engage with . . . and even enjoy . . . certain things, like the meal."

I was crestfallen. A part of me still believed that the path to enlightenment was a battle that involved progressively greater feats of annihilation—and that joy was a necessary casualty. I was also confused because I recalled Ajahn Siri's warning about enjoying the sight of the rising sun. Most of all, though, I knew Ajahn Sukhito was right.

"Sometimes," I said, "when I think up some intense way to push myself, I notice that the very next thought is of telling my friends about it."

Ajahn Sukhito gave a rare chuckle, almost a laugh. "Yes," he said. "This is long-term training, so the spurts of intensity, fasts, et cetera, are not really all that important. It can be good to experiment. But not push. That's the middle way."

He looked away. His eyes roamed as if running over his own thoughts.

I waited. I'd gotten to know Ajahn Sukhito well enough that I could tell when he wasn't finished talking. Sure enough, he had heard something more in my question, something I hadn't.

"A competitive nature," he said, "can influence people for *years* without them realizing, young men especially." The way his eyes softened made me wonder if he was speaking from personal experience. I imagined him as a young monk, racing others through the meal as I had. He continued, "It can hinder a real sense of connection . . . and teammateship with others at the monastery. It's a big difference between Western and Thai cultures."

Hearing Ajahn Sukhito re-emphasize the importance of friendship in monastic training, I felt a kinship with him, born of respect but also a growing affection. For someone so uninterested in ensuring his audience was at ease, he was not cold. In fact, the more I'd begun to find ease myself in his long pauses, the more I'd sensed that he exuded a subtle, unflinching kindness. This, too, was a departure from Western culture, at least from my own upbringing, where one learned to perforate conversation with frantic affirmations. As a new consultant, I had received explicit coaching to double down on my already overdeveloped impulse to please. *More* nods, I was told, *more* smiles, *more* validating utterances to show *more active* listening. And it had been effective, in a desperate, superficial, productive way that fit the context. But here, at Poo Jom Gom, in a world with no clocks or clients, we could behave differently. Goodwill could have a straight face. I could watch Ajahn Sukhito as he watched me, without expression. It was intimate. I felt known. And as I grew comfortable in his presence, I felt I could know him.

Next, I asked about the unexpected swells of emotion, which had become a regular occurrence.

"Some afternoons," I said, "I've been going to sit by the stream and, I don't know, just overflowing with gratitude to the point of, like, uncontrollable sobbing. I'm not really sure what to make of it. Seems healthy, but it's really strong."

Ajahn Sukhito took this in. "Long ago," he said, "I heard a

layperson ask Ajahn Sumedho how to know if their spiritual practice was advancing."

I remembered Ajahn Sumedho—Ajahn Chah's first Western disciple, the legendary monk whose bowl I had dropped rice into back at Kathina.

"His answer," Ajahn Sukhito said, "was more frequent and increasing depth of gratitude."

He let this sink in before continuing. "So that's a good sign. However, there are things to watch out for: feeling *unworthy* or constrained or suffering over not being able to *repay* those to whom you feel gratitude. Those are neurotic responses. Let gratitude flow naturally. Don't force its cultivation. There is a word—*katannu-katavedi*—in Pali that basically means 'to know what has been done.' It combines gratitude with generosity. The two go hand in hand."

This didn't make a lot of sense at first, that those two would be connected somehow. But then again, I had noticed a recent shift in the fantasies I entertained. Many remained personal—*me as an island, me as a revered meditation teacher, me doing great things*—but some new ones were based in generosity. I found myself planning an elaborate celebration for a friend's PhD, a party of appreciation for a kind roommate, a surprise visit to my high school Ultimate Frisbee coach's house to read him a heartfelt letter.

To deepen a sense of pleasure in generosity felt like progress. But I'd also heard monks say the mind would do anything to avoid sitting still in concentration. It seemed everything had a potential shadow dependent on intent. Distractions could become more refined. In place of food, I now craved munificence.

"And with regard to . . . *big moments*," Ajahn Sukhito said.

I felt a catch in my throat. Big moments were still what I was after, epiphanies that bypassed the slog of incremental growth.

"They can be good. But they may not be markers of progress. They can be born of delusion."

He looked away to the smudge of orange at the edge of the sky. The tips of the trees had gone dark like extinguished candles.

"Patience and kindness," he said. "Those are markers."

SAUNA

Ajahn Sukhito told us one morning that we all would be attending a ceremony at Wat Pah Nanachat.

I sensed danger. Novice monks, pakaos, residents like me—all of us were subject to immediate relocation. I feared him pulling me aside and telling me to pack my bag. To my immense relief, he said nothing, and I climbed into the white van the next day feeling certain of my return. I'd also left my backpack in the guest kuti, which, I felt, was like calling dibs. I'd been extra clever, too, and stashed the diary in the backpack, preventing myself from writing for the two or three days we would be gone.

Despite my conversation with Ajahn Sukhito, I hadn't been able to stop writing. In fact, it had gotten worse. I obsessively recorded every passing thought, contorted my own ideas into truths I deemed universal, and adopted the insufferable voice of the self-help evangelist. It was addictive. My diary had turned into the worst thing, the cultivation of a brand. Nearly everything I wrote eventually flowed back into the same rut: my word, my thesis, my title to shock the world: *Diligentle. Writer's mind*, just like Ajahn Sukhito had warned. I was happy to force a break.

Bada, the genial Indian, hunched under the van roof and plopped into the back row beside me. We searched our waists for seat belts. There were none. We looked at each other. Bada shrugged and crossed himself.

A Buddhist monk making the sign of the cross set me laughing. I didn't see Bada much, but whenever I did, he was playful. I'd seen him a week earlier carrying an umbrella that was missing the fabric canopy and consisted of only the thin spindles and metal joints. I'd given him a quizzical look, and he hadn't missed a beat. He pointed up to the sala and said, "It's for the skeleton." He was a novice like Pamutto, but he didn't seem conflicted about monastic life at all, so I never asked.

Returning to Nanachat felt like coming home after a semester of college. I was equipped with an inflated sense of maturity. I'd left the nest and grown new feathers, and I intended to strut. I was an insider now. I sat in the back seat of vans, giggling with monk friends. When we arrived, I hopped out, stretched my back, and tried to survey the surrounding landscape with a nostalgic look. I sauntered around the kitchen and the dorm and the office, hoping the new batch of residents understood I was a regular.

To my chagrin, another layperson was soaking up all the attention. A stranger: a white American in his fifties or sixties, I guessed, wearing cargo hiking pants that zipped off at the knee—an immediate red flag, as far as I was concerned. He had thin curly brown hair and an obnoxiously loud voice. Most curious, he had an actual following. Everywhere he went, Thai villagers trailed him, bowing as if he were a monk.

Turned out, he had been a monk. And not just any monk. Years earlier, he'd been the abbot of Wat Pah Nanachat. The head honcho of the whole damn place. After more than a decade in robes—thirteen years, I heard someone say—he had disrobed. He'd proceeded to live a whole new life since then, and now he had returned to attend the ceremony and show his old digs to his wife, who accompanied him.

Perhaps he also intended to show his wife to us. She had long, straight white hair, held her chin high, and avoided eye contact. At first, I felt she flaunted her presence. At one point, she found a flat boulder in the middle of the roundabout, the most visible public place in the entire monastery, and lay across it and took a nap. I was outraged. She was haughty and insensitive. What never crossed my mind was how strange it must have been to be in her position, to join your husband, a former monk, at his old monastery, where you might be ogled by a gaggle of celibate monks, blamed as the reason for the loss of a member of the brotherhood, and feared as the embodiment of the desires that could derail a monk's fragile commitment.

It wasn't fair. And yet it was the question on my own mind. In fact, for all I knew, I could've been the only one grappling with the question of whether I might leave and find love, the only one who viewed her as a threat, because it was *my* commitment that was fragile.

Then again, it might not have only been me. The chilly reception from the other monks stood in stark contrast to that of the adoring Thai villagers. There was a palpable suspicion from the men in robes. Which cast the wife's public nap in another light. While I felt offended, I also felt it was badass and courageous of her, and I relished the discomfort visible in the other monks, who kept their distance from the couple. The former abbot had been more senior to most of the monks at one time, but now he was nothing in the eyes of the hierarchy. Back at zero. He made no deferential moves toward them, and I saw that he received no official greeting. Instead, monks' eyes darted in his direction. I overheard anxious chatter at teatime. It was as though a handsome ex had shown up to a party unexpected.

I was so absorbed by this couple and the shock waves they were causing that it took a day to register the rest of the place. Some things hadn't changed. Josh was still there, duckfooted and eager as ever. The prim Malaysian abbot, too, Ajahn Siri, still efficiently delivered work assignments to a whole new batch of lay visitors, who themselves had crammed into the dorm above the kitchen and whose awkward frowns suggested they were just as frustrated as I had been.

The deep forest sala was different. Stone pillars had been erected around the perimeter in honor of the occasion I learned we were here to celebrate: the fortieth anniversary of Wat Pah Nanachat. There were visiting monks I hadn't seen before. The darker robes of one caught my eye. They were maroon. While some variation in color was normal, given the Thai Forest Tradition's process of hand-dyeing robes, these departed from the normal spectrum. I watched this monk from afar with curiosity. Much was familiar—shaved head and eyebrows, slip-on sandals, robe to the ankles—but something wasn't. And then it hit me. It wasn't a monk. It was a nun. I hadn't seen a female in robes. I hadn't thought it possible in the Thai Forest Tradition. I resolved to watch for an opening to hear her speak.

The bustle around the ceremony rivaled that of Kathina. Visitors, preparations, crowds, even a mobile kiosk in the driveway serving Thai iced tea. Despite the commotion, I felt a sense of reunion with those I recognized. I was glad to see Josh. I caught the eye of another monk with a familiar face and smiled.

He smiled back. He was a young American monk—tall, thick-rimmed glasses, comfortable presence. Not someone I had interacted with much in my first month at Nanachat, so I was surprised he recognized me. More shocking, he walked straight over and placed a hand on my back in greeting.

For a moment, I froze. Touch was rare. In fact, I'd had no physical contact since arriving at the monastery almost four months earlier. I found myself pleasantly melting under the pressure of his hand. Flooded with gratitude for this small gesture, I opened my mouth, found I could say nothing, and so returned his warm smile. I wasn't even sure of his name.

"Yanissaro," he said, reintroducing himself. I told him mine.

His left hand pressed on my shoulder and neck like a dog resting its head on my lap. "You've really been taking the teaching of non-self to heart," he said, looking at my frame, which had gotten thinner since going to Poo Jom Gom. "Literally, man. You have less 'self.'"

I had lost weight, but we both knew the teaching of non-self wasn't about that. His eyes twinkled. I couldn't believe it. A monk at Nanachat was dishing out some lighthearted shit-talk. The interaction couldn't have been further from most of my experience with Nanachat's seemingly disgruntled, antisocial residents.

I wanted to play along but found I was out of practice. I chuckled, looked around in search of something funny to say back to him, then blurted, "How've you been?"

If Yanissaro noticed my awkward transition, he kindly chose not to show it. He shrugged and said he'd been well.

"What's been going on here at HQ?" I heard myself say, hoping to feel like an old-timer.

"Oh, you know," he said. "Meditatin'. Eatin' every now and then. The usual."

I nodded and glanced around again in search of something cool to say. I settled on "Yep."

"Seriously, though," he said, "are they feeding you enough out there?"

"Yeah. I guess I've just been trying to eat less during the meal."

"Well, too much less and you might disappear. Have you been fasting?"

I shook my head. "I've been thinking about it, though. Have you done it? You recommend it?"

His eyes lingered on me an extra moment, as if trying to glean my motivation for asking. "It's a thing. You start to feel really light by the fifth day."

"Light?"

"Yeah, it happens to most people. You kinda break through the aches and pains and the habits of thinking about food after the first few days, and eventually you feel this sense of lightness."

I remembered those aches and pains and habits—although I'd felt them for a few months before feeling any sense of lightness, not a few days. I also recalled Ajahn Sukhito's caution on special practices. Still, I was curious.

"So," I said, "is it nice or, like, helpful for meditation, er . . . ?"

"Honestly, it's just a thing that happens," he said. "Kinda cool, but not critical."

I figured I'd take his word for it. "How's Josh doing?" I said. This also made me feel like an insider, leaning in and asking about others with raised brow and lowered tone.

Yanissaro caught my eye with a knowing glance. "Josh is . . . Josh." He smiled. "But you know, he's got a good heart. Or something. He's generous. He used the last of his money on a visa run recently with a few other monks to buy them all ice cream."

I was stunned, and then touched, and then a little jealous. "Wow" was all I could say, thinking about how on my visa run, I had blown all my money on a feast for myself.

"What about this former abbot guy in the zip-off pants?" I said. "What's his deal?"

At this, Yanissaro took a long, diplomatic breath. I'd hit a nerve. "Yeah." He exhaled, shaking his head. "No one seems quite sure what to make of him."

That spoke volumes. I narrowed my eyes and nodded in

understanding. "And what about the person in the red robes?" I said. "The nun?"

Yanissaro lightened. "She's visiting from Amaravati, the branch monastery in England. A bunch of their other monks are here, too. But she's senior. Worth following around. You should listen to her if you get a chance."

At the next meal, I watched the nun. She was in her sixties, I guessed. She waited patiently at the back of the line while the senior Ajahns served themselves, then the middle monks, then the novices and the pakaos. Even though she had to have been senior to some or even most of them, she ate last. I couldn't help but be skeptical about the order, especially for a tradition so attached to hierarchy.

Later that afternoon, I returned from a walk in the forest to the sound of laughter coming from the kitchen.

There was the former abbot in his zip-off pants. He lounged in a chair in the open area, entertaining questions from local fans and lay-people, all of whom sat on the ground beneath him. My first thought was that there were no chairs in the kitchen, so how the hell did this guy have one? Worse, I noticed a growing crowd gathering around him, hungry, I imagined, for any scrap of instruction during a busy period in a monastery where guidance was in short supply.

I hid behind a bookshelf but stayed within earshot. Grabbing a dhamma book, I acted like I was reading. No way was I going to kneel and give this dude the pleasure of enlarging his audience. He seemed to be enjoying it enough already.

"You know, the first thing I noticed about Ajahn Sumedho," he said, referring to the most famous, respected Western monk as well as the original abbot of Nanachat, "was his ankles. They were huge!"

The crowd offered respectful, surprised chuckles. The man in zip-offs laughed the loudest.

"Yeah! His feet were all swollen," he went on. "He kinda had *cankles*, and I thought to myself, I thought, 'Boy, if I ordain, I hope I don't get feet like that!' Ha ha!"

All afternoon, it went like this. People fawning over Mr. Zip-Offs, who basked in their adulation with the comfort of one who feels he deserves it. A few villagers brought him and his wife a meal. A meal! Despite the meal only a few hours earlier and despite openly violating the precept of not eating after noon, the man and his wife sat in *chairs* eating *at a table* off *plates* using *forks* and *knives*, none of which anyone ever did. All the while, Zip-Offs talked with his mouth full and cackled at his own jokes.

Surely, the man who had once run this monastery knew its rules. His disregard for them struck me as a sad attempt to suggest that he'd *graduated* from the constraints of monastic training, when really all signs pointed to him having flunked out. What didn't cross my mind was that I might've been extra offended by Zip-Offs because he spoiled a fantasy I had quietly stoked—that I might get to leave the monastery but *also* get to keep the prestige of having been a senior monk. I wanted both, again, and he was evidence that I couldn't have it.

Zip-Offs drew all my ire. So much that I didn't have the emotional capacity to dislike the ceremony honoring the fortieth anniversary of Nanachat that night. Normally, a multiple-hour ritual of chanting and circumambulating the deep forest sala would've at least bored me, but this time, I kind of liked it.

The next day, I returned from another walk to find the nun sitting with a crowd in the same spot Zip-Offs had occupied the day before. I noticed she didn't have a table, food, or as large of a crowd. Notably absent, too, were any Thai people. But present were all the female overnight residents as well as a few of the men.

I heard one of the laypeople ask, "Will you be giving a formal talk during your visit here?"

She was hosting an informal Q&A. I crept closer.

"Oh," said the nun in a charming British accent, "they haven't told me that I will, I'm afraid. Thailand isn't quite as . . . enlightened, shall we say, as England." She grinned, and the others laughed.

I stood by the bookshelf and wondered what she meant. Only later would I learn that in Thailand, ordained Buddhist nuns were not considered valid. The first ordination of nuns in the Thai Forest Tradition had occurred only six years earlier, in 2009, at a branch monastery in Australia. The move by the male Australian Ajahn was met with fury by the establishment. A group of monastic leaders convened in Thailand, headed by none other than Ajahn Sumedho, the most senior Western monk and founder of Nanachat. They condemned the Australian abbot, banished him from the Thai lineage, and formally cut ties with his monastery.

But the story had taken a strange twist next. Shortly after the controversy in which Ajahn Sumedho had punished the monk who ordained nuns, he began to ordain nuns himself. At another monastery he founded in England called Amaravati, which was where the nun visiting Nanachat for the anniversary celebration lived, he set forth on ordaining women under a set of conditions they referred to as the Five-Point Agreement, which unequivocally established all female monastics as junior to males—so totally subordinate that the most junior male monk would rank above the most senior female. That was why the nun went through the food line last.

The lengths to which the monks went to exclude or put down women made me think of the *Calvin and Hobbes* comic strip. When those two barred girls like Susie from their tree fort, it was cute in a limited, boyish kind of way. But it was something else entirely when a group of old men congregated in their own forts among trees and unanimously decided "No girls allowed," or when pressed, "OK, fine, you're allowed, but you're below us, all the time, forever, no matter what." The measures struck me as draconian, and when I learned about them, I found myself wishing the monks' mothers could smack some sense into them, if only their mothers were alive and physical contact allowed.

At the time, though, I knew none of the history of the ordination of women, so I only felt two things: a vague unease with the established order and an interest in this nun who persevered in spite of it.

Another layperson asked, "How is it at Amaravati these days?"

As she answered, I crept into the group circle and sat on the floor.

"Rather dreary now, actually. Rainy, dark, that kind of thing. But in terms of the bhikshuni order, it's growing," she said, referring to the order of nuns. "It has a gradual momentum, you know. You can't go around being angry all the time . . ." She laughed brightly and then abruptly stopped. "But you also can't stop working for progress."

Her balance of levity and severity was captivating. After a couple more questions, I felt my hand rise.

"I've been reading about the cultivation of positive states of mind," I said. "How can I make them stronger and last longer?"

"Oh"—she chuckled and waved a hand—"don't worry about that."

My face grew hot.

Then she looked me dead in the eyes and said, "Just appreciate them when they arise."

I knew she was right. I was embarrassed and bowed deeply, then kept my head lowered to hide from everyone else's eyes. Maybe she had been able to tell what I'd been angling for—some complex, intellectual road map—and so had given me what I didn't know I actually needed: to be humbled and reminded, once again, of wisdom that, once spoken, seemed like common sense.

That evening, I caught wind of a rumor: the monks were going to fire up a sauna. I didn't know Nanachat even had a sauna. Day visitors wouldn't be allowed. Most residents didn't seem to have gotten an invite, either. Pamutto had given me the tip. At dusk, we walked down a series of trails to a clearing. Flat stones made the ground, and a cauldron sat off to one side; I assumed this was where they boiled bark from the jackfruit tree to dye the monks' robes. Thick orange candles flickered in glass boxes around the perimeter.

Inside, there was an air of loose relaxation akin to a locker room. A few shirtless monks reclined on a bench, bodies steaming. Others toweled off outside the sauna, a low cubic structure with small, fogged windows. Most monks, it seemed, had already come and gone. Pamutto and I removed our robes, folded them, and put them on an empty bench. Without orange undergarments, I felt timid in my lime-green Patagonia-branded briefs, but there was no other choice. I tiptoed barefoot across the stones to the sauna and followed Pamutto in the door.

The heat was so intense inside I could barely breathe. Steam hung low, and white tiles covered every surface. I was so immediately drenched in sweat, I thought I might slip as I made my way to sit on a ledge. Across from us were two monks, both broad-shouldered and shirtless, orange underskirts drenched. I recognized one as Yanissaro, the young American with whom I felt friendly. The other monk was a senior Ajahn from the Netherlands; I recognized him because he wore transition sunglasses. As we entered, I heard the slap and squelch of wet skin and cloth on the tile. He lay on his stomach on the highest ledge.

"Is right here good?" I heard the Dutch monk ask.

"Sure, that's great," Yanissaro said, standing, turning, and pressing his hands onto the monk's lower back.

Junior monks, I knew, washed the feet of their elders as a sign of respect and care. But I had never imagined a massage like this. Full body, deep tissue, lubricated by sweat and steam. Yanissaro was not a small man, and his palms produced grunts from the Dutchman underneath.

The ceiling dripped. I wiped my eyes and peeked at Pamutto beside me. Like me, he was staring and trying to look like he wasn't. The whole scene struck me as such an obvious allowance of pleasure that I began to wonder if I was witnessing something illicit.

But I caught myself and began drafting various defenses: this was *generosity* for elders, *healthy* for muscles and friendship, and it came from an *intention* of veneration. This wasn't sexual.

Then again, it *was*. Sensual, at least. Two half-naked, slippery men, bathed in lambent light, one rhythmically kneading the flesh of the other with the deliberate, intimate focus only a monk could bring to bear. The action was so hot that the Dutch monk himself had to pause for a moment. He sat up and said, "Yanissaro, where did you learn to massage like this?"

Yanissaro shrugged and said something about a class he'd taken back before ordination.

The Dutchman took a deep breath and resumed his position, and then they got back to business. As they continued, I found myself reflecting. Monks weren't allowed to touch or even risk touching women, but a deep-tissue sauna massage was allowed? What about gay monks? How did a massage jibe with Ajahn Siri's dhamma talk a few months back where he warned against the simple pleasure of appreciating a sunrise? If sensual pleasure was the enemy, then what was I to make of the moans echoing off the walls in this late-night rubdown?

I understood that the closer one looks into anything, the more contradictions appear. Still, I couldn't shake the dissonance between what was said up front and what was done in the back. Perhaps the whiff of hypocrisy reminded me of myself. I craved the clarity of a total ban on pleasure but also wanted a massage and would've accepted one without hesitation if Yanissaro had offered. More than that, I had lived two lives for as long as I could remember, one up front that was polite and prestigious and scared, and one behind closed doors that was messy and uncertain and ashamed. I wanted one life, not two, and I'd thought that if anyone in the world had figured out how to make enough peace with themselves to achieve this, it would be Buddhist monks.

The appeal of a total prohibition on pleasure was its simplicity. I could wrap the rule into a stoic, spiritual-warrior package: Man Who Needs Nothing. But the truth was, ever since the accident, I hadn't been sure how to hold grief and allow space for pleasure. I wanted all or nothing, so I found the nuance of the massage infuriating.

Yanissaro slid both hands down the Dutchman's spine. He patted him once on the lower back and said, "All right, that'll do it."

The Dutchman rose. I lowered my head to make it seem like I hadn't been studying their every movement for the last half hour.

Yanissaro left, and the Dutchman began rolling his towel and heading for the door when Pamutto spoke. "Er, Ajahn?"

The Dutchman turned, blinked, and said nothing.

"Erm, well"—Pamutto stood—"I'm wondering if I might ask you a few questions."

The Dutchman's posture visibly slumped.

"See," Pamutto went on, "I've been a novice for coming on eighteen months now, and I'm feeling the pressure to fully ordain. But it's really full-on, you know, and I know you disrobed at one time—"

"I was just leaving," said the Dutchman.

For a moment, I saw how life as a senior monk might not be as glamorous as I imagined. Every time you wanted to chill out, you got pelted with existential questions. Even among younger monks, or maybe especially, there was no refuge.

I was light-headed and way past my raisin point but nearly as desperate as Pamutto to hear about this Dutch monk's experience. I remained seated, hoping my presence would go unnoticed.

"All right." The Dutchman sighed and sat back down. "What do you want to know?"

Pamutto essentially asked for the monk's life story, which he then gave.

The Dutchman had ordained in his twenties, spent four years as a monk, and then disrobed. At this, I perked up. I pictured him moments after his official disrobing, standing outside the Nanachat gate in cargo shorts and a T-shirt, looking at the outside world with a rolling suitcase in his hand, thinking, *Oh, shit. What have I done?*

Which turned out to be accurate. "Almost immediately, I knew disrobing was a mistake," he said.

"Yeah, see, that's exactly what I'm afraid of," said Pamutto. "Once you've lived this life for any amount of time, how can you go back and return to anything close to normal, because what's normal to me now is so totally different than it used to be."

Sweat dripped in spurts from the tip of my nose. I realized I was nodding in agreement.

"Right," said the Dutchman. "Some do it, I suppose, like this former abbot person you may have seen . . . gallivanting around Nanachat right now."

"I know," said Pamutto gravely. Among the sangha, it had become even more clear that Zip-Offs garnered suspicion, although the official reception seemed to be one of cold, diplomatic welcome. At best, everyone seemed to think Zip-Offs was lost. At worst, he was a traitor. My aversion to the man had deepened, perhaps in part because this reassured me of my distance from him. Surely, if I despised him, then when I left, I couldn't turn into him.

"Of course, you can always come back," said the Dutchman, "but you have to start all over again. There are monks I was senior to when I first ordained who are now senior to me by five years."

"That doesn't seem like it should affect my decision," Pamutto said, "but to be honest, I absolutely have thought about that, too."

So had I. I had imagined leaving, standing in my T-shirt outside the gate, and returning to the US only to discover that I no longer fit in the outside world. I imagined coming back to Thailand then, finally certain of the decision to ordain, and who would be waiting with a smug grin but Josh, gloating about his seniority.

"And then there's family," said Pamutto. "I'm at the point where my parents are getting older, and I'd like to be able to take care of them. And just spend time. But if I ordain, I won't have hardly any mobility for, like, five years."

The Dutchman conceded the point but offered a trade-off. By ordaining, he said, you lived by example. Your actions rippled out to family and friends. The Dutchman's mother, for example, had begun to meditate because of his ordination.

Sweat stung my eye. I tilted my head sideways in skepticism. This was where I had heard other conversations about ordination end up—the question of family followed by the reassurance of a ripple effect. The message was "This is better for them," which I wanted to believe because I could barely stand the idea of disappointing anyone, especially my parents. I was a peacekeeper. But I couldn't deny how unsatisfying the ripple-effect answer sounded. What if losing a member of the family *wasn't* better for them? The harder answer was the more honest one: people ordained because they wanted to.

I wanted more opinions. To my surprise, I found myself wondering what Zip-Offs might say. He had lived thirteen years in robes and then left.

The next morning, I thought I might get to find out. I learned Zip-Offs would give a formal Q&A the following evening. The monks seemed to grant this stage reluctantly, out of respect for the office of abbot rather than the man who had formerly held it.

But we were scheduled to return to Poo Jom Gom. We would miss the talk. Pamutto begged to stay an extra day. Ajahn Sukhito, with an expression that bordered on disgust, flatly said, "No."

Before our departure, Pamutto and I took a walk and commiserated. Loosened by disappointment, we gossiped.

"I'm not sure how to ask this," I said, "but are there . . . frictions within Nanachat? Or am I projecting all of it?"

Pamutto paused a moment, then smiled. "You're right to wonder, actually. Thank goodness Ajahn Siri is starting to take over now. People call the last ten years at Nanachat *the dark years*." A decade earlier, he explained, the loud German abbot had been appointed to the role, surprising everyone, not just because he lacked charisma but also because he had only been a monk for nine years at the time. "The abbot of *Wat Pah Nanachat*," said Pamutto, "not even an Ajahn! Can you imagine?"

"He did rub me wrong," I said. "The whole 'It's terrible and idiotic out there beyond the monastery' bit doesn't really resonate, you know?

It's a straw man; like, there are plenty of kind people and good things on the outside."

"You don't know the half of it," Pamutto said. "Imagine what it was like when he had no experience. People were disrobing left and right. Ordinations plummeted. Senior monks left."

Now that he said it, I had noticed that not a single monk with more than twenty years in robes lived at Nanachat. Monks left at their first opportunity. I had done the same thing.

The best part of coming to Nanachat was getting to leave again. That afternoon, we boarded the white van with Ajahn Sukhito and hit the road.

Pamutto fidgeted in the row ahead of me. "I really would've liked to see that talk. It'd be interesting, well, rare, you know, to hear from someone who disrobed . . ."

Ajahn Sukhito stared ahead at the road.

Pamutto grumbled, "A former abbot, especially."

Ajahn Sukhito said nothing.

Pamutto kept on. "He did strike me as a little off, though, that guy. I don't know . . ."

"Yes," Ajahn Sukhito said. The back of his jaw tightened.

"You know," Pamutto said, "I overheard him talking about how he wants to write a book about his life. Kind of a lot of 'self' in that . . ."

Pamutto was baiting Ajahn Sukhito. His statement also veiled a question. I knew Pamutto harbored similar considerations of writing his own book about his experience in a monastery. He had all those journals. But *self* had negative connotations. *Non-self* was what everyone was going for. I, too, had a diary and considerations of my own, and even though I'd sworn off writing for the last few days, I found I was leaning as far forward as my seat belt would allow.

Ajahn Sukhito only shook his head in disbelief. "To have studied *directly* under Ajahn Chah," he said. "He must have some kind of incredible *kamma*."

This was a burn. "To have inherited such karmic fortune," he seemed to say, "and then waste it."

I leaned back in pleasant surprise. This was why I preferred Ajahn Sukhito—he chose honesty over diplomacy, the opposite of my own programming.

But as we drove on in silence, I grew pensive. Ajahn Sukhito's implication was that my own presence in the Thai Forest Tradition was the opportunity of a lifetime, so if I left, I'd be wasting it, too. It didn't occur to me that almost every pious follower of an ideology spouted something akin to "This is the one true path." Even if I didn't believe such a thing existed, I desperately wanted it. More than enlightenment, I craved certainty, a calling, a mission I never doubted.

I gulped. Had I been able to see that I was feeling doubt, I might've approached it as I had hunger. I might have slowed my breathing in the back seat and dropped my awareness into my gut, where the noise of words couldn't obscure the signals of sensation.

But I didn't see it, so I fell back to trying to think my way out of a problem I had thought myself into. If Nanachat wasn't for me, and people weren't allowed to ordain at hermitages like Poo Jom Gom, then maybe I could ordain at Amaravati in England? Or what about some other Buddhist tradition that wasn't so rigid? Ordination was still on the table, I thought with a clenched jaw. It had to be.

CAVE

Ajahn Sukhito had cautioned against "big" spiritual moments because they might not be valid measures of progress. But I still wanted them, especially because if I wasn't going to ordain at Nanachat, that meant I wouldn't ordain on this trip to Thailand. Only a couple of months remained.

I needed to double down and get results. Maximize the extraction of insight. I'd fast, find a cave, and pull myself through grief into wisdom. I'd contemplate death and then write something about it that blew minds and changed everything for good. Although these old, anxious ambitions had receded over the previous month, they surged back with a renewed intensity as my mind raced on the van ride back from Nanachat.

But when we returned to Poo Jom Gom, there was a new guest whose demeanor upset my grim ideal. A senior monk. He wasn't a celebrity. He was a Canadian, and although he had the trappings of grandeur—over forty years in robes, personal study under Ajahn Chah, and being one of the founders of the Thai Forest Tradition in the West—he was different. Casual. He chuckled all the time. If you called him by his full name, Ajahn Tiradhammo, you'd expect him to wink and shrug and say, "Just call me Uncle Tira."

He was short and pudgy. He oohed and aahed at the meal spread each morning, of which he got first pickings, ahead of even Ajahn Sukhito, who was Tira's junior by twenty years. If Ajahn Sukhito was the slim, stoic, Buddha-type monk, then Tira was the other type—the fat, laughing Budai.

Tira was jovial, informal, and, I decided, insufferable. Who was this tourist, I thought, this freeloader, this bowling-ball monk who rolled around the world from one meal to the next, arriving to warm welcomes and cutting to the front of every line? He rubbed his hands together and leaned over the platters and said, "Huhuhuhu!" Didn't he understand that pleasure was the enemy? Was he really so spiritually advanced that after almost half a century in robes, he could simply enjoy himself? Ajahn Sukhito had once said it was appropriate to enjoy some parts of monastic life. Surely, he didn't mean this much.

And yet I, too, found a nascent sense of ease upon my return to Poo Jom Gom, despite the grand ambitions. When we pulled in and crossed the pedestrian bridge, I felt refreshed, even at home. I shaved off my eyebrows with minimal bleeding. During free time, I meditated. I knew where the thin brown scorpions hid along the edges of the bins of gardening soil in the shed. I remembered which branch our resident kingfisher preferred as a tree stand to hunt over the stream. I could tell when the fruit tree needed water because it drooped and looked sad.

We cared for many trees throughout the monastery, and I felt compelled to check in on them each afternoon. A big part of dry-season work consisted of satisfying thirsty plants. I'd spread straw around the base of trunks for insulation, fill buckets from the stream, and listen to the liquid trickle down into the dirt. This work actually felt like working meditation.

I grew particularly fond of a bodhi tree. It stood in its own plot in a place of honor, the literal center of the hermitage between the sala, kitchen, and work shed. I fluffed the straw around its trunk and lingered after emptying the buckets to admire its leaves. The tree was young, its life measured in decades rather than centuries. Its skinny trunk accentuated the broad splendor of its leaves: lush green, as large as my hand, each with a tip that extended into a long tail that put me in mind of a string beneath a heart-shaped kite.

It was strange that such an austere tradition would take the bodhi's ornate leaf as one of its symbols. It was custom for every monastery to plant at least one bodhi tree, and illustrations of the leaf appeared on many back covers of dhamma books. But the kind of leaf that better aligned with the severity of the Thai Forest Tradition, I thought, was the fallen leaf, whose brown-orange colors inspired the hue of monks' robes. That leaf represented detachment. It fit my stoic ideal of discipline. I never reflected on the fact that it was lifeless. Instead, I idolized stories of somber men who endured hardship with a heroic grimace, like the Buddha himself during his six years of wandering and starving and falling face-first into feces. I considered his voluntary deprivation not as an overcorrection but as the essential ingredient to growth. I didn't reflect on how he had finally sat, one full-moon night, at the base of a tree and awakened to the fact that he'd been pushing too hard. That there was a middle way.

The tree the historical Buddha had leaned against was a bodhi—with the Sanskrit word *bodhi* meaning "awakening." Some believe that very tree is alive today in northeast India. A 2,600-year-old giant crowning a temple in Bodh Gaya, it's the oldest known specimen of *Ficus religiosa*—Latin for "sacred fig." On the night of the Buddha's awakening, the tree would've been smaller—maybe around the size of the one I watered at Poo Jom Gom every day.

Its leaves were vibrant and lovely and fragile. Even if I didn't consciously reflect on the bodhi when I watered it, I was drawn to it. After I finished, I ran my hands down its trunk and caressed the leaves with my thumb. There had been a subtle shift below the level of my consciousness. Despite my drive to double down on deprivation, I had started to enjoy myself.

In addition to working meditation, I also grew fond of cleaning after the meal with Yupin. Now that I wasn't bemoaning the loss of each food scrap we scrubbed from the dishes, the routine together had become lovely.

One morning, beside her at the row of sinks, with my hands plunged into soapy water, I felt a tickling sensation between my legs. With wet hands and white robes and no towels in sight, I couldn't grab or brush, so I tried itching my crotch with a dry elbow. The tickling became a piercing stab. I suddenly realized it wasn't an itch but a scorpion or a black ant sinking its pincers into my scrotum.

I jumped back from the sink, yelping, splashing, beating at my robes with both hands. Plates clattered. Yupin gasped. The village kids she'd brought with her that day froze. The spiny offender dropped from the wide leg of my robe. It spun across the tile and came to a halt in the middle of the floor.

It was a fruit stem.

Everyone looked up at me.

"*Yai moat*," I said, meaning "big ant." My first joke.

Yupin doubled over laughing. She said it again and again, *yai moat*, possibly because it was funny, but just as likely because I hadn't said what I thought I'd said. She understood nonetheless and shook her head and repeated it up until the moment she sped off on her motor trike down the gravel with the kids and the leftovers and the clean dishes.

After cleaning and work meditation came the wide-open afternoons. Once torturous, they had become almost pleasant. I'd begun meditating for around eight hours a day.

Having finally found a rhythm of dedication, I allowed moments of rest. I hadn't explored the national park since my first week, so one day, I went for a hike.

For the first half hour, I followed a familiar trail. I'd already crunched along the fallen leaves under the forest canopy, around boulders and over the rickety suspension bridge that spanned a slot canyon. But this time, I wanted to go to where the path and the trees ended.

Eventually, I got there. Beyond the shaded edge of the forest was a vast plateau of rock. I had reached this point before and turned back, not wanting to venture too far from the hermitage and lose my way. But what had felt like the end now felt like the beginning.

Cairns dotted the uneven rock expanse. Normally, a hiker or visitor could connect dots on the landscape like this to signify a route, but here, they were too numerous and scattered to be of use. I also noticed an unusual ornament sitting on top of many of the cairns: poop. Not human but seemingly from a medium-size mammal, baked dry in the sun. Before stepping out of the shade, I wondered which was more likely: that some being had squatted directly over the cairns or that they had gone about collecting feces and balancing it by hand or by paw.

Either way, there was no clear path. I decided to proceed slowly straight ahead, turning around every few steps to remember where I'd come from. Without a trail or landmarks, it would be easy to get lost. I tracked the angle of the afternoon sun for bearing. Lines swirled in the rock as if the landscape had melted during the wet season and hardened in the dry. Small shrubs huddled in divots of sand. At one point, the ground split, and I found myself straddling a fissure in the rock that plunged twenty feet deep. On either side, I noted wider sections that could swallow a distracted hiker. I felt the hairs on my neck stand. No one would find me if I fell.

I moved forward with caution. With the sun to my left, I followed a dip in the horizon, crossing the plateau toward what I decided was the northeast rim. There, I met a new line of forest, and although it offered no trail, its border with the plateau gave me something to follow. I continued north, checking the sun, watching the rock, and peering into the forest to my right. I didn't know what I was looking for. Then I saw something.

A few steps into the woods stood a tree with an orange cloth tied around its trunk. Surely, this was a marker of some kind, I thought, and stepped into the forest. The knot was a double overhand, and the ends hung around the waist of the tree like the belt of a bathrobe. The cloth was bleached so stiff by the sun that it cracked under my touch.

I looked in every direction but still could discern no path. I felt I'd found a clue of some kind, so I couldn't just return to the plateau. But the canopy made orientation difficult, and the gradual dip in the other direction had grown steeper. I decided to bushwhack in parallel to the plateau. Soon, I found another tree with an orange belt. This one was deeper into the forest, and I hesitated, then checked the watch I'd brought for the hike—an hour had passed since I'd gone off-trail. I was testing the limits of my memory for safely finding my way back. Plus, the horizon behind the trees cleared to open sky, which suggested I was near the edge of a cliff.

But I figured I could go a bit longer. Up a small incline near the border of the plateau, I found a third belted tree. The spot was elevated and sparsely treed, and although I could see no more markers, I paused at an unusual shape on the ground. A few rocks higher up the incline formed a corner. I stepped up and found myself on the end of a walking meditation path. Unkempt but undeniable: a perfect rectangle of rocks framed a track, thirty steps long and one step wide, like a secret airstrip hidden in the bush.

I wondered if I'd crossed into the territory of another monastery. If I was intruding, a monk might pop out from behind a tree. I crouched and listened, motionless. All was quiet but for the whisper of the warm breeze. A lone meditation path didn't make sense. I felt a burgeoning thrill. There had to be more.

I stepped beyond the path, but the rock rolled into a steep drop. I inched forward, avoiding loose leaves and sand to keep traction and get a view of what lay ahead. To one side, I saw a row of stones that were stuck onto the sloping face. The size of a fist and equally spaced, they were too regular to be natural, and I realized they were globs of dried concrete. Steps.

I got on all fours and crawled toward them. Reaching one foot down, I tested the highest one with my weight. It held. I did the same with the second. When the third proved solid, and the fourth, I had backed down the slab far enough to get a look. I stopped breathing at what I saw. In the distance, a thousand feet below, a huge brown river swept through green forested hills.

That wasn't all. A couple more steps down led to a long pair of two-by-fours that bridged a twenty-foot drop onto a boulder, beyond which was a mouth in the side of the cliff.

A cave.

An overhanging slab the size and shape of a bus protruded from the plateau above, sheltering a rustic dwelling. In the back was a ledge with a huge orange candle and a warped, dusty frame with a photo of a monk. Closer to the front was a wooden platform like a coffee table, which I took to be a bed. The four legs rested in small porcelain saucers, as if the table were wearing shoes. In each saucer was black tar, creating a moat, I realized, that prevented bugs from crawling up to where someone would sleep.

Dazed with the enormity of this discovery, I took a seat on the platform. The river below had to be the Mekong. It was too big to be anything else. Which meant the stretch of forest on the other side was Laos. I tried to meditate, but I couldn't close my eyes. For an hour, I grew still and breathed slowly and feasted on the view before finding my way back to the hermitage.

The next day, when I described the cave to Ajahn Sukhito, he said simply, "Yes. The cliff cave."

That was it. No offer to let me move. As usual, I'd have to approach the issue slowly and from the side with him. A day later, I slipped a reminder into our conversation that I had experience in leading trips in the backcountry. Then, after another day, I asked if he wouldn't mind if I tried staying out in the park. He said maybe. I didn't press. The next day, he came to me. If I wanted to, he said, I could sleep out there.

This was big. This was the culmination of my monastic fantasy. That day, I gathered supplies: a sun hat from the shed, my digital watch for an alarm, and an extra robe for a bedsheet. No more inflatable sleeping pad. The cave had a trash can and a yoga mat that I would unroll for cushioning. I filled a one-liter plastic bottle with water from the stream and stashed it, along with a juice box, in the same mesh bag I carried behind the monks on alms round. That very day, I retraced my steps, and ninety minutes later, I made it to the cliff cave, my new home.

I'd arrive each afternoon after the work period, sweaty and in need of a shower. There were no monastic rituals around bathing, as far as I knew. Back at the hermitage, my own had consisted of occasionally filling a couple of buckets I used for watering the trees, carrying them away from the stream, and pouring one over my head before soaping up and then pouring the other over myself afterward to rinse off.

But there was no water source at the cave. The Mekong was visible but distant below the cliff. All I had was the one-liter bottle. In the same storage can that held the yoga mat was an old bar of green soap. I stood on a far ledge each afternoon, removed my robes, doused myself with a conservative splash from the bottle, and lathered. Then I carefully rationed the remaining liter until I was clean. I air-dried, spread-eagle, bald eagle, shivering in the breeze, reveling in my memory of the phrase *alone on a mountain*.

After bathing, I meditated until sundown, then slept on my back on the yoga mat on top of the platform, with my robe bunched in a few places to cushion under my knees and elbows. A week into the new routine, I gave myself a break. I was sore from sitting and sleeping on the platform, and I felt a cautious appreciation for moments of repose. After all, rest from my strict meditation schedule had led to the discovery of the cave. So one evening, I pulled two new items from the mesh bag: a lighter and tube of lotion I had spotted on the supply shelf back at the hermitage pantry. Tonight would be special. By candle-light, I'd give myself a foot massage.

With a crunch and a spark, I lit the lone dusty candle, whose or-ange column of wax was as big as my thigh. I pulled my knees up to my chest on the platform and gazed east. At dusk, the sky and the forest and the river melded into shades of navy. I relished an exhale. I had made it. I'd upgraded to a dwelling even more remote and rustic, an actual cave where other legendary monks had lived before me.

Surveying the vast wilderness, I couldn't help but wonder if the majesty of my outer world reflected a certain corresponding *inner* majesty as well. Perhaps my spiritual accomplishments over the last few months had manifested all this beauty before me. I hadn't fully bought into the idea of karma, but now that it seemed to be working so well in my favor, I was tempted.

I'd been logging as many as nine hours of meditation per day, and my ankles were sore from sitting cross-legged. I opened the tube of lotion, squeezed a generous dollop into each hand, and set to rubbing both bare feet.

This was paradise, I thought, and finally, I wasn't letting myself get in the way of enjoying it. If I wasn't going to be grim, I might as well be luxurious. This small shift felt like progress, and it was, but it didn't occur to me that it carried similar risks to my ego. No sooner had I started massaging my feet than I found myself wondering if a villager on the other side of the river could see my glow on the cliff-side and, perhaps, sense the presence of a Significant Spiritual Being. Maybe they'd feel the deep admiration for me that I, in that moment, felt for myself.

Never mind that the existence of such a villager would've sul-lied my ideal of pristine solitude. It didn't occur to me that although I wanted to be alone in the wilderness, what I also wanted was for people to *know* about it. Solitude was great. An audience was better. Again, I wanted both. I kneaded my feet and allowed my pride to swell. I was really getting it, I thought. *This* was self-care. This was the mid-dle way.

My feet absorbed the lotion quickly. I went for more but hesitated. The tube was small. Maybe I'd save the rest for another time.

No, I thought. Why not be kind? Why keep grinding myself down in the name of discipline? It felt good to treat myself. I squeezed more lotion into one hand, then shrugged and emptied the entire tube. This, I thought, *this* was *Diligentle*.

I could no longer see the river below. I'd left my diary back at the hermitage, but I knew I'd write about this moment later. Allowing myself more lotion was a breakthrough. A profound insight, even, on self-love. I rocked in a slow rhythm, thumbs pressing along my Achilles tendons, working the arches, slipping my fingers between each toe.

My feet were thoroughly coated, but I still wasn't getting any slide. In fact, dirt was peeling and rolling off my skin. I furrowed and brought the empty tube up to the candlelight to read its label.

It was covered in curly Thai script. I understood nothing.

Then I spotted a hair of fine print I recognized as English. Squinting, I brought the tube of lotion close to the candlelight. Then I caught the smell of spearmint on my hands as I read the word: *toothpaste*.

While I experimented with rest, I continued with exertion. Each morning, I left the cliff cave at 4:00 a.m. to make it to the monastery for alms round at 6:00 a.m. The first time, I got lost and almost panicked. The next few trips, it felt magical, turning along faint forest paths, crossing the moonscape of the plateau, and arriving at the hermitage by the first suggestion of sunlight. After a couple of weeks, the trek became a commute. Once again, having barely achieved another degree of comfort, I felt compelled to disrupt it.

I'd gotten too comfortable, I thought. If I wasn't getting better, I was getting worse. Gone and forgotten was the insight that lighthearted moments had often led me to where I wanted to go. I decided it was time to fast.

A fast would get two birds with one stone: be intense, plus skip a few commutes. I wouldn't have to hike in the dark or return in the heat. I'd stay at the cave all day. Work from home.

Ajahn Sukhito gave permission, and I chose February 7, the following day, in honor of my dad and sister's birthday. For forty-eight hours, I'd meditate on my cliff in uninterrupted bliss. I couldn't wait.

One thing about leaving the cliff cave before sunrise every morning was that I hadn't fully appreciated the cave's orientation to the east. When I noticed the clouds turning pink and the horizon brightening ahead of my perch on the platform, I stretched my arms and welcomed the light.

However, the direct glare of the sun soon transformed the cave into an oven. There was nowhere to hide. Within minutes, I fled. The plateau was hardly better, but I settled on a rock and tried to resume meditating. Small black gnats that I had never encountered in the afternoons hovered in a thick cloud around my face, nestling between my lips and exploring my nostrils. I knew they were harmless. We experienced them back at the hermitage, too, around this time of day during group meditation in the sala. But there, the monks shared vials of a menthol solution that we rubbed across our lips and brows that somehow worked as a natural insect repellant. The substance also aided in meditation, for its minty-cool smell accentuated the sensations of breathing.

But I didn't have that solution. It was just me and the woods, exactly as I thought I had wanted it. I had no choice but to lift my robe from my torso and wrap it around my head. This preserved my orifices but transformed me into a mummy, baking in a makeshift sauna and blind to the glimmering Mekong I'd been expecting to enjoy looking at all day. Sweat dripped into the crease of my stomach and pooled in my exposed belly button, where gnats congregated and bathed.

If I had hoped to push myself to the brink by spending an entire day without food or, whoops, drinking water, which I'd forgotten, then I was succeeding. But rather than breaking through difficulty as if it were a fever, I spent the entire day sinking into mean thoughts. Yanissaro had described light and bright feelings around the fifth day of a fast. I'd never find out. By the end of the day, all I'd discovered was something I had already been told, that extreme practices like fasting didn't guarantee an epiphany. Which itself could have been the epiphany, but I missed it. Despite my experience and better judgment, despite Ajahn Sukhito telling me that one of the markers of progress was patience, I was still convinced insight came from heroic feats that could later be summed up in a clever turn of phrase. I continued to envision my life as a blockbuster movie in which I was the main character, and I expected the completion of tidy narrative arcs roughly every ninety minutes.

The following day, I returned to the hermitage to find Pamutto smiling.

"Oh, man, you missed quite a day yesterday," he said. "A couple of Sri Lankan visitors came and offered all these fresh, homemade cakes and fruit pies. Mmm."

I stared at him. Many thoughts flashed through my mind over the next second. It had been forty-six hours since I'd last eaten, and he knew it, and this was what he led with? Was he joking? Was he lying? Was he trying to torture me because he was jealous that I'd done some awesome spiritual-warrior shit by fasting alone in a cave for two days?

He wasn't lying. The one day I'd stayed away, a chef had visited the hermitage. But I wasn't upset. I couldn't muster the energy for that anymore. The reality of the last two days had been so unenjoyable and humbling that I could only laugh. Pamutto's face was genuinely delighted. He was excited to tell me. And after two days on my own, I found I was happy to see him.

There was a calendar in the kitchen propped on a small table by the pantry. I'd been eyeing it all February. For one, it showed the lunar cycle, so I knew in advance which day I'd shave my head, eat my one gummy bean, and stay up late, meditating for Wan Phra. For two, it told me how long I had left at the monastery—less than two months. I performed these calculations sneakily, as if I could hide from myself the fact that I wasn't going to ordain. *Not this trip, at least,* I thought. The third reason I had paid extra attention to the calendar was because the last day of the month, February 28, 2015, was the first anniversary of the car accident. When the day arrived, I wanted to make something of it. If ever there was a time to sift through the ashes of the past and forge some new diamond of understanding, this was it.

I was disappointed to discover that the moon wasn't going to be full on that day. I couldn't decipher any special meaning from the moon cycle, nothing that suggested that the day would be what I hoped, a turning point, or closure, a new beginning. According to the calendar, it was just another night. No matter, I thought. I'd *make* it special.

When the day came, I returned to the cave, meditated until sunset, and then climbed up onto the plateau, my diary in hand. Normally, I didn't bring the diary. The forced time apart offered a welcome reprieve. But writing—and the thought of writing—still strangled much of my time. Back at the monastery, in free moments between activities, I stole away to my backpack, where the diary lived, to relieve myself of the thoughts that had built up since the prior day's entry.

At a boulder on the open expanse of the plateau, I took a deep breath, looked up at the pink dusk sky, and opened to a blank page. On the anniversary of the day that changed everything, I felt sure something else would change again. I'd built up to this moment. I'd quit the job, bought the flight, ridden the twelve-hour bus, paid my dues at Nanachat, found Poo Jom Gom, and discovered an actual cave in the wilderness. Something *had* to become clear now. And when it did, my pen would be there to record it.

"Dear James," I wrote, then glanced skyward, offering the cosmos a chance to answer. Maybe a symbolic gust of wind or a bolt of heat lightning. But nothing came, and the golden light of evening slipped away. Feeling rushed, I scribbled half a page outlining what I had done that day. I couldn't believe it, but I felt bored. With myself. Which made me angry. If I couldn't even access sadness, how was I to break through it? I forgot the advice I had so freely dispensed to others, that grief came and went unpredictably. It never occurred to me that my impulse to give advice was an anxious tic to soothe myself without admitting that I was the one who needed soothing. It was so much easier to preach than to practice.

I dropped the pen. Slapped the diary on the rock. Growled. I considered screaming. Maybe exaggerating a display of anger could incite the kind of cinematic climax that began with a cursing of heavens and gnashing of teeth and ended with collapsing onto one's knees in a state of beautiful, depleted acceptance? But even my growl sounded hollow. I tried scrunching my eyes but couldn't wring a tear. *Dry season,* I thought.

I shuffled back to the cave, plopped down on the platform, and stared absently at the Mekong. I'd met James once by another river, the Mississippi. On a sunny Saturday in Saint Paul, we'd thrown the Frisbee at his old high school football field, then brought Jamba Juice and a sack of weed to a secluded spot he knew that overlooked the river, a bench at the end of an overgrown trail. He'd packed a bowl, and we'd coughed and giggled about girls and parties and how to balance homework, for him, and work, for me, because I'd graduated a few years ahead of him. Even though he was younger, I admired this quarterback-handsome kid, with his crescent eyes and his stories of paddling the Arctic and his endless stream of earnest questions.

He had died on a Friday night. I'd lost interest in giggling and girls and parties and work. I'd fled from my old life and succeeded. I was a world away, sitting high up on a bank of a different mighty, mythic river, and it didn't matter. I was still lost, and he was still gone.

A squawk from behind made me duck and yelp, and a large-billed crow flapped overhead. I slumped, and the crow's laughter echoed off the rock. High above, the moon stalled, a waxing gibbous, the least poetic of phases, an uneven hump of stone like the one on which I sat. I shut the diary. There was nothing I could say.

Deep in the dry season, there were fires in the forest. Some days we worked to prevent them by cutting fire breaks, which were like hallways chopped through the forest to create gaps that could stop the spread of flames. Giorgio and I donned gloves and carried machetes into the woods and hacked at dense clusters of bamboo.

Other days we put fires out. They weren't raging infernos but small ground fires whose origin I never understood. Giorgio, Pamutto, Bada, and I grabbed twig brooms from the shed and set off into the woods. When we located a fire, we tossed the tails of our robes over our shoulders and bashed the flames with our brooms. We cycled in and out, retreating to cooler air to mop our sweaty skulls with our robes. Once we tamed a fire, we sat together on boulders nearby, monitoring the embers and chatting with the looseness earned by physical exertion.

One afternoon I said to the others, "What's the story with Ajahn Tiradhammo?"

"He's a wild man," Pamutto said, then recounted a tale from a previous visit to Poo Jom Gom. Tira, the pudgy senior Canadian monk, had gone on a firefighting party like ours and disappeared. A monk had gone searching for him, turned a corner, and found the seventy-year-old stark naked, pouring sweat, beating at another fire with his own robes.

Suddenly, I found my feelings about Tira shifting. Maybe I liked him after all.

The next day, when I overheard Tira telling Ajahn Sukhito in the sala that he'd like to visit some of the caves, I perked up.

Some of the caves? There were more?

"Grant has been staying at the cliff cave," said Ajahn Sukhito. He then turned to me and said, "Why don't you spend the work period today with Ajahn Tira. Maybe check on the supplies in the caves, do some cleaning."

That afternoon, Tira and I set out with brooms and a bag with a couple of juice boxes for afternoon tea.

Tira hiked fast. With tentative glee, I noted the way he *didn't* clasp his hands in a contemplative bundle or seem intent on establishing silence as our default. Instead, he chatted. Nonstop. He'd stayed at Poo Jom Gom many times, he said. He loved checking out the caves.

By the time we reached the plateau, I was feeling limber. "Hey, I have a question," I said. "All these cairns have dried . . . poop on them. What's that about?"

"Civet cats," he said matter-of-factly. "They shit on cairns. Yeah, they like shitting on high places or something. You know, some people make luxury coffee from beans that civet cats shit out." He wiggled his eyebrows and grinned.

I'd never seen one of these cats, nor had I heard anyone swear in months. Tira, unlike nearly every other senior monk, didn't seem allergic to conversation. I could ask this guy anything.

"What do I do if I get bit by a snake out here? Just get back to the monastery as fast as I can?"

"Don't run," he said. "If you run, the venom pumps faster through your blood to your heart, and you die. Breathe and move *very slowly* back to the monastery. Don't exert yourself."

That frightened me for a moment, but I was too excited to dwell on it. The questions came spilling out.

"What's your favorite cave? Or what's the quietest cave out here?" I asked.

He smiled. "That would be the tea cave. Which is where we're headed."

It sounded so civilized and cozy. *Tea cave.* I rubbed my hands together. *Huhuhuhu.*

"But first," he said, "there's another little one I wanna stop by."

We turned left around the side of a nondescript hill I passed every day. On the backside was a tiny cave, like a single scoop had been pulled from the rock face. Inside was a hobbit-type home with only a square table for sleeping and meditating, not even enough room to stand.

"I spent a couple of months in here once," he said.

I bent down and peered into the hole. I turned back to Tira, expecting to hear him recount some great difficulty he'd faced during that period and recap the insight he'd gained from it in the end.

But Tira only shrugged. He turned away to keep hiking and said, "Looks the same."

I gaped at him, then ducked back inside the cave to study it once more. I searched the walls for faint carvings that might offer a shred of a story, but they were blank. Tira reminded me of the guest monk back at Nanachat, the Czech with a square head who told me, while shoveling dirt, that he wanted to be a monk because he liked the lifestyle. There was something similar and extraordinary about Tira, some absence of the impulse to place himself at the center of an epic messianic tale. He seemed a lot happier for it. I jogged after him to keep up.

I had another question. "I read something you said in a dhamma book in the kitchen, that the search for sensual pleasure causes the most trouble for the most people most of the time." I trailed off. I didn't really have a question. I just wanted him to elaborate.

"Oh, you read that, did ya?" Tira said. "Didn't know that was even still in print, huhuhuhu!"

"The idea made a lot of sense to me. I mean, I thought about food nonstop for like three months."

"Oh, is that so? Yeah, there's food, and there's lust, but you learn about each desire as you practice. There's kind of a hierarchy to them. For instance, if you're struggling with lust, just fast," he said. "It'll go away like that." He snapped his fingers.

"Wait, what?"

"Yeah, it's like magic. Food is just one level more basic on the hierarchy of needs or whatever. If you're hungry, you won't be horny!"

And I realized he was right. For those three food-obsessed months, I had hardly felt a sexual urge. We laughed. When Ajahn Jayasaro had visited Nanachat, he said that a sense of humor was the key virtue. Tira didn't need to say it, because he lived it.

We passed the turnoff for the cliff cave and continued deeper into parts of the forest unfamiliar to me. The grade turned into a subtle descent heading north. Trees sprouted from the plateau in increasing density. A small trail appeared around the side of a boulder, and then, in the middle of nowhere, we stopped at a small wooden gate.

It was as high as my knees. We creaked it open, then walked down a trail and into a haven tucked under the slope of the terrain.

The tea cave. Like the cliff cave, it was long and shallow. A huge roof of a boulder spread like the wing of a plane over the familiar furnishings: a walking meditation path, a wooden table wearing porcelain shoes, a large orange candle, and a plastic bin full of supplies.

There was no sweeping view of the river, but the place instantly felt like home. The gate we'd crossed ran on as a decorative fence that drew a perimeter around the mouth, giving the impression of a yard, even though what was inside was the same as what was outside. Like a sleeping animal, the cave was hidden in the trees.

"This is quiet," I said.

Tira saw my big eyes and said, "Oh-ho yeah, buddy. Primo!"

"I might move out here at some point," I said.

"You should," he said. "The cliff cave has the views, but it also has the boats."

He was right. The vista at the cliff cave included the occasional fisherman. The sight of their skinny boats far down below was welcome, but the sound of the handheld trolling motors carried up from the water.

A few evenings later, I heard something else from my perch in the cliff cave: the sound of thumping bass. From somewhere under the trees in Laos, an invisible venue equipped with a commercial-quality speaker system began blasting music that reverberated off the walls of my cave with the volume and clarity of a concert. Between beats, a whining synth expanded and contracted like a digital zipper being pulled back and forth. It took me less than a second to recognize the song, Psy's international hit "Gangnam Style."

I sat up. I hadn't heard music in months and was too stunned by its sudden appearance to remember it was against the rules. Caught off guard, I forgot about how I was supposed to be training myself to grimace in silence. But Tira's levity had rubbed off on me, and I was tired of being solemn. This wasn't a disruption. It was a gift.

The song ended as abruptly as it began. Cut off, unplugged after only the first six seconds of instrumental crescendo, as if the whole thing had been an accident or a test. I never got to hear Psy's deep, movie-trailer voice, but I remembered the nun from Amaravati's guidance to appreciate what arises, and I decided to be grateful instead. I had begun bobbing my head to the beat, and now that it was gone, I pressed my palms together and bobbed once more, slowly, deeply, into a bow toward Laos, bestowing a small, distant blessing of thanks onto whoever it was who had pressed Play.

ZEN

Before I could relocate to the tea cave, I had to leave the country altogether. I'd been in Thailand for five months and needed a visa extension to stay through six. Not that I was at risk of government detection
out in the middle of nowhere, but we followed the rules, which dic-
tated that I couldn't simply bop over to the local office. This time, I had
to cross the border.

Savannakhet, Laos, was the closest town with a visa office. Plenty
of non-Thai monks had made this same trek before, and Ajahn Sukhito
outlined the plan: I'd take the bus over on Friday, get the stamp, and
be back by evening. But things didn't go according to plan. When I
handed my passport over the counter at the Savannakhet office, the
clerk kindly informed me that my visa would be ready the next business day. The next business day was Monday. All of a sudden, I had to
spend the weekend in Laos.

"No, no," I said, there had to have been a mistake. I hadn't brought
anything but my passport and wallet.

But the small man behind the glass only smiled and shrugged. I
glanced over my shoulder at the line of people waiting behind me, saw
compact cars zipping up and down a two-lane road, and realized I had
no idea where the town was and no phone to help me find it. I asked
the clerk. He pointed right, then waved me away and beckoned the
next customer forward.

I had no way of letting Ajahn Sukhito know. Staring at my feet,

I realized what I'd be wearing for the next three days—white robes, black knockoff Crocs, no change of clothes. Then I remembered I was in public without hair or eyebrows. A shorn sheep put out to pasture. I flapped my arms, sighed, and started toward town.

Vendors on mobile sidewalk stands peddled baguettes, an influence from French colonization before Laos gained independence in the 1950s. I hadn't seen bread for months. I hesitated at one stand, smelling the grain. The prospect of buying a baguette with my own money and being free to eat while I walked down a busy street felt like too many indulgent variables at once. The last visa run where I'd binged on food had felt like an intermission, but this one felt like a trial run. I was out on my own in the world now, unmoored, and I was scared of how I'd navigate. Caution was key. Besides, I told myself, I needed to find a place to sleep, and the afternoon light was fading.

Streetlights turned on over tangled nests of telephone wires. After about an hour, I stopped at a roadside hostel. I met a host and followed him down a hallway to a private bedroom with a tile floor and a plug-in fan. I sat on the edge of the bed and wondered what to do. I considered going back out to explore but opted instead to simply close my eyes.

For another hour, I meditated. Out in the street, I felt shy and exposed. I also *wanted* to feel different, to prove to myself I was changed and wouldn't relapse into mindless habits. I meditated for a second hour. Then a third. At one point, I heard a dribbling sound from inside the room and opened my eyes. A lizard the size of my forearm padded up the wall and disappeared behind a flat-screen TV. A lizard didn't bother me anymore—I knew it was a guardian for insects—but I considered the TV. I hadn't even noticed it when I walked in.

Oh, why not just check it out, I thought. The fan stood in the corner, swinging its head back and forth in disapproval. But what the hell—I'd already meditated, and every channel was bound to be Laotian soap operas anyway, probably without subtitles. I flipped it on.

Sure enough, the content was local and indecipherable, and each time I changed the channel, there was a four-second delay. At this, I noticed a flare of impatience. Then I was displeased at how quickly I had gone from excitement with technology to annoyance with inefficiency. I hovered my finger over the power button. Better to just turn off the whole mess.

But then the next channel loaded. It was an American music video: Taylor Swift singing, an old convertible sports car parking inside of a castle. Out steps a white male of cologne-ad grade. Inside the castle, he and Taylor exchange smoldering glances from across a long dining table. Then, a fight: Taylor defacing paintings, Taylor smashing the convertible with a golf club, Taylor whacking a tree with an axe. Cologne guy flees, and the song ends with a new guy, who looks almost the same in every way, stepping out of a new convertible.

The title popped up in the corner of the screen: "Blank Space." Stunned, I felt I had witnessed the abyss of samsara: the waste of desire, the spin cycle of dating, the unquenchable thirst of lust. I saw my own past, and I resolved then and there that it would not be my future. The song was catchy, which felt threatening, and I felt my commitment to celibacy tighten.

I wondered if this was a sign I was meant to see. I recalled the senior Dutch monk from the sauna who had disrobed, only to realize immediately that leaving had been a huge mistake. Maybe this was my chance to arrive at the same conclusion. For the second time, I reached for the remote to turn off the TV.

But then a voice in English said, "And at number two on the countdown . . ."

I set the remote back on the bedspread.

"It's Maroon 5, 'Sugar'!"

New video. Wedding reception. Anonymous stagehands erect curtains in the middle of a dining room. Curious parents crane their necks. An uncertain bride and groom furrow their brows. This wasn't planned. Then the curtains drop, and there's Maroon 5, the full band, in the flesh, surprising everyone with a live show. They crash more weddings this way. Dance parties commence at them all.

It wasn't until the second chorus that I realized I was rocking back and forth on the edge of the bed, all-out sobbing with joy. The surprise and the thrill and the public celebratory commitment of two people— all of it struck me as unspeakably beautiful. With each higher note and every new scene of an ecstatic couple, I cried even harder. I was vulnerable to this kind of curated content. After months away, I had been resensitized, so much so that when the next song played, number one on the charts, I completely lost it.

New video. Pink blazer. Dress shoes. Finger snaps. Horn section. Bruno Mars's "Uptown Funk"—an ode to life itself. By the first chorus, I had trouble hearing the music over the sound of my own weeping. "Hallelujah," they sang—a song of worship, a song of praise. By the time the second chorus ended, I was drenched in sweat. I'd been dancing and nodding and repeating the word *yes*.

When it was over, I turned off the TV and let the air hum. The songs echoed in the chambers of my body. I felt dizzy. Panting, wiping away tears and mucus, I climbed under the covers and wondered if I might always be this open to the world. Everything felt so intense.

On Saturday morning, I made my bed, meditated for a couple of hours, then checked out and continued in the direction of town. By noon, I was still walking. Given a full day to eat whenever, wherever, and however much I wanted, all I did was explore for six hours without a single sip or bite. Eventually I stopped at a restaurant and ordered a smoothie and some fish. From the table, I could see the Mekong River, flowing south, the direction I continued after lunch. I wanted a clear view of the river to feel tethered to something, but fences obstructed the scenery. One I passed was of familiar design: blue and red with decorative curls on top of the posts. An urban monastery.

As I peered in through the open entrance gate, my shoulders relaxed at the sight. There was a sala with a spear-tipped roof. Slippers piled outside of a doorway. Beyond a handful of structures was an unobstructed stretch of the grass-banked Mekong. I missed Poo Jom Gom and the vista from the cliff cave, and I stood resting my eyes on the river until I noticed a couple of young monks beside a hut staring back at me.

Embarrassed, I wheeled around to leave, but they waved.

I pointed at my chest. *Me?* I'd forgotten I was dressed like them.

They nodded and beckoned me in.

We sat together on a low wall overlooking the river. Both monks were eighteen years old and wanted to learn English. They took turns pointing to things around the monastery, which I'd name and they'd then repeat. We practiced the word *squirrel* until I forgot how to say it myself. We laughed, and after about an hour, they had to go and bid me farewell.

I left the monastery feeling refueled but uncertain of what to do next. Having meditated, eaten, and socialized with a few monks, I had done everything I did every day back at Poo Jom Gom. I wasn't in the habit of filling time with new activities, so I went with the first thing that came to mind and rented a moped from a roadside shop and drove to the outskirts of town, where I'd seen signs for an iodized salt factory.

A man with one tooth gave me a tour full of gesticulation and empty of English. He limped past pools covered in sheets of white crust and tubs of salt water bubbling over wood fires. Around a shack with a peeling metal roof and rusting equipment lay salt, everywhere, heaped in corners and crunching under every step. As we walked, the tour guide knelt and grabbed handfuls and tasted it, grinned, then motioned for me to try it myself.

As far as I could tell, no pinch tasted any different from the rest. The whole time I followed the man around and ate salt off the ground, my mind strained to translate the details of the experience into a metaphor. What did the salt represent? What about the man's single tooth? I didn't know, and I wondered—if it didn't mean anything, then what was the point? But a lighter part of me decided it was just something odd and fun, and that was enough.

The next morning, Sunday, I awoke in a new hostel well before dawn. I'd had an idea to offer food to the young monks I'd met, intending to greet them on their alms round, and had bought a sack of coconut cakes the evening before. The hostel was surrounded by a high fence with speared posts and a locked gate. Rather than finding an attendant and waking anyone up, I found a corner and scaled the fence with the sack of cakes slung over my shoulder.

Under the orange streetlights, I hurried to the monastery. I didn't know their alms route and didn't want to miss them. I parked myself right outside the blue-and-red fence at the entrance and watched the sky grow light. Within half an hour, I saw their procession of orange robes approaching. They were more than a dozen monks, all seemingly younger than me. The two I'd met recognized me and grinned from the middle of the line, then, as if remembering the etiquette of alms, dropped their heads again and stifled their smiles.

Barefoot, I knelt on my sandals to protect my knees from the asphalt and reached up to deposit one treat into each of the passing bowls. I bowed to each monk, as I had been bowed to myself on so many mornings. I felt woven back into the fabric of the global monastic community and coursed with pride. Right as I began to admire my own forethought and generosity, I realized I hadn't bought enough cakes.

The kids in the back of the line—no older than thirteen—smiled at me with unrestrained excitement, etiquette be damned, leaning sideways out of line and bumping into each other in their rush to get treats. But I was two cakes short. When they reached me, I raised the bag and my hands in useless apology, hoping these two children might bless me with forgiveness—or at least mask their disappointment for my sake. But when they saw I was empty-handed, their bodies sagged. I couldn't bear to look at them and hid my face in a deep bow as their small feet dragged past.

Next, I made my way to Savannakhet's central promenade, a picturesque strip of storefronts that ran perpendicular from the Mekong River to a small Catholic church. I meandered past benches and makeshift greenhouses with thin wood frames and plastic wrap sitting out in the sun, baking neat rows of peeled bananas inside. Most everything else was closed.

One doorway, though, was open. Inside, a TV was mounted high in the corner, airing what looked like a basketball game. I paused and looked closer. Sure enough, LeBron and the Cavs were playing my Atlanta Hawks. Beneath the TV was an empty table. I stepped back to check the facade of the building for a sign, but there was none. When I looked inside again, a man in a T-shirt had appeared from the back. He looked at me in surprise, and I raised my hands in apology and moved away, but then he pulled out a chair and beckoned me to sit.

There was no menu. On the wall were family photos and a shelf stacked with board games. The man and I exchanged no words, but he brought me a breakfast plate of fried rice from his kitchen, turned up the TV volume, and left me to relish the fourth quarter of live basketball at 7:00 a.m., uncertain of whether I was eating at a restaurant or the home of a kind stranger.

When I finished, I made some noise to catch the man's attention, coughing and clinking my glass to my plate and scooting my chair. But the man never returned, and I didn't want to intrude any farther into his house. I put double the cash I thought I owed on the table and left.

Back on the promenade, I felt compelled to visit the church. Christianity had never resonated with me, and it was a problematic export, but the hundred-year-old building of Saint Teresa's Catholic Church was lovely—beachy white with red accents and an octagonal bell tower. I meandered toward it out of a nostalgia for spiritual refuge.

In the courtyard, I heard a dog growl. From behind a planter stepped a massive German shepherd wearing a tattered pink sweater vest. Baring its teeth, it barked. I froze. Then it turned ninety degrees and continued barking, as if it had forgotten I was in front of it. I saw its eyes were cloudy and white, and I took a step to the side. Hearing this, the dog gnashed its teeth in my direction. But then it heard something else and barked that way, and I tiptoed quietly around it. From the safety of the church doorway, I watched the blind dog bark at nothing and wondered how often I did the same thing.

The church was open and empty. I sat alone in the pews and gazed up at the vaulted ceilings and stained glass, feeling reflective and suddenly sorrowful. I noticed a sculpture on the pulpit of an emaciated Jesus nailed to a cross, a rendition of Jesus in agony, and it put me in mind of suffering, the first noble truth. His neck was twisted, and I couldn't stop myself from thinking of the car accident, of the image I had concocted and hadn't been able to shake for over a year, that of buckled-up boys bent in the back seat of a crumpled SUV. That Jesus had been a son, a child, was something I'd never contemplated until this moment, and for the first time, I felt the tragedy of his death.

When I stepped out of the church and into the midmorning light, the dog was gone, and a tenderness remained. At the sight of a potted plant with pink flowers in the courtyard, I found a bench and wept. I felt raw from sadness and from two days of stimulation outside the monastery. After a while, the feeling subsided, and I rose and moved back toward the river. On the promenade, I noticed a white guy with a blond bowl cut sitting on the sidewalk in the sun. I hadn't seen a single tourist in Savannakhet. Judging from the way he stared back at me, he hadn't, either.

He raised a hand in greeting. I walked over. He was a social worker from London, traveling solo for a couple of weeks. He also didn't have a phone. He spoke slowly and seemed kind. When he proposed we meet up for dinner that night, I agreed and suggested a restaurant I'd noticed on my walk earlier that extended out into the Mekong River on a creaky floating dock.

We met at sundown, wearing the same outfits as before. He ordered a beer, and I asked for a meat dish. I had been surprised to learn that monks were not strictly vegetarian. Despite the precept against causing harm, monks were also expected to accept whatever food was offered to them, partly out of respect for the villagers of limited means but also because monks were beggars by design. They couldn't be choosers. Meat wasn't common, though. I wasn't a vegetarian then, and seeing as I was already eating dinner for the first time in months, I thought, *Why not?*

What arrived, however, was a plate of spicy gristle. To balance it, I requested a mango salad, but what came was a stack of unripe mango twigs that were even spicier than the meat. While the Brit sipped his beer and chatted about his travels, my stomach churned and my face burned.

He'd been doing a little writing, he said.

I nodded and exhaled and motioned for the waiter to bring a fourth glass of water.

Toward the end of the meal, the Brit invited me to come stay the night at his hostel. It had a second bed, he said. No one was using it. We could split the cost.

I shrugged. I'd been staying in different hostels and checking out each morning so that I could roam and land wherever I ended each day. I hadn't rented a room yet and was happy to save a little cash.

I followed the Brit back through the dark streets. I felt drunk and swollen from my first real dinner in five months, and my stomach gurgled as if in shock. I wondered if maybe it wasn't a good idea to sleep in the same room as someone I'd just met. He turned a corner in an alley and led me up a narrow staircase. I prepared a spiel about celibacy, just in case he made a move.

To my relief, there were indeed two separate beds. At a dresser by the door, the Brit placed his wallet and key and picked up a paperback book, which he tossed in my direction. It was a short read on Zen Buddhism.

He had finished it, he said, so I could have it. Then he climbed into his bed, said good night, and flipped off the light. I lay awake awhile longer, on guard, before drifting off.

I awoke in the dark. The clock on the dresser read 5:00 am. I felt hungover. The trial run had been fun, dinner was nice, and the Brit was charming enough, but I was past my limit and ready to get my passport and go home to my cave, my routine, my diary—I had much to record. While the Brit snored a few feet away, I snuck into my robes, grabbed the Zen book, and dashed off a thank-you note on the dresser. At the bathroom door, I hesitated, wanting to use it but not wanting to wake up my roommate and initiate a whole big goodbye. I decided against it, tiptoed out, and turned the door handle behind me so that it wouldn't click shut.

The streets were empty and blue with dawn. With a few hours yet before the visa office opened, I considered offering another round of coconut cakes, but my stomach had other plans. I felt full and fragile, like a paper bag holding a gallon of milk. I cursed myself for not using the Brit's bathroom and began searching for one in town with rising urgency. The church doors were bolted shut. Storefronts were yet to open. Soon I was tugging on random doorknobs along the central promenade, desperate, until I reached the end of the promenade and realized I only had one option.

I scrambled down a flight of stone stairs and into the tall grass of the riverbank. An orange film squelched from the mud and pooled in my footprints. The ground was littered with plastic bottles, wrappers, and bits of Styrofoam, which made me feel slightly better about what I was about to do. But then I did it. Right before I could lift my robe, I shat myself. Spicy mango and gristle flames. For two hours I hunkered in the tall grass until I was empty of fluid and thought. When the rays of morning sun turned the marsh muggy, I carefully removed my underwear, abandoned them in the grass, and gingerly made my way back up the stone stairs.

The visa office wasn't yet open when I arrived, so I found refuge in the air-conditioning of a café next door. I nibbled on a plain baguette, dabbed my clammy forehead with a napkin, and paged through the Zen book from the Brit.

In it, ink illustrations were paired with anecdotes of teachers whacking students into enlightenment. Its ethos combined the discipline of the Thai Forest Tradition with the slapstick of the Three Stooges. Losing interest, I fanned through toward the end, which dislodged a scrap piece of paper onto my lap.

It was the size of an index card and covered, front and back, in cursive phrases. The Brit seemed to have forgotten his bookmark. On it he had written a collection of epiphanies, reminders of wisdom, and urgent commitments to self-improvement. I pictured him biting his lip as he crafted each one, nodding to himself afterward, and thinking that he was really getting somewhere. I could see it because I had seen myself do the same thing.

But because the note wasn't mine, I could zoom out from its content and see the structure. The winding roads of introspection that seemed new and exciting were most likely nothing more than curves on a loop. The Brit would be no less wise for having lost his book of wise phrases. Suddenly I realized the same was true for my own diary. As if slapped in the face by a Zen teacher, I felt a release from my obsession with writing.

I was sick of laboring with a pen in the voice of a guru. For so many pages in my own diary, I had strained to be the spokesperson of the human psyche, writing the word *we* in my own diary 983 times. Finally, leaning back, I felt baptized in the blessed waters of boredom. I'd craved journaling the same way I'd craved food, until, by some lucky accident beyond the realm of willpower, the craving had been dislocated from me—the first time, in a hammock at a bus stop after pounding a six-pack of soy milk, and this time, in a Laotian café after reading a scrap of someone else's diary.

I crumpled and tossed the index card, wedged the Zen book between two others on a shelf in the café, and left empty-handed. The visa office was open.

VIPER

I was hobbled for a week after the food poisoning in Laos. For the next week, I limited intake at the meal to bananas, sticky rice, and capsules half as big as my finger that were filled with turmeric, prescribed by Ajahn Sukhito. Afterward, I shuffled slowly from the hermitage to my new dwelling, the tea cave.

My bowels remained unpredictable. One afternoon, I bolted up from meditation on the wooden platform in the cave, clenched to prevent another accident, and zipped across the cave and out the wooden gate. I scanned the ground for supplies—sticks to dig, leaves to wipe. I sought the high ground of the plateau to avoid contaminating a water source.

But the plateau was mostly rock. I couldn't dig a cat hole. I was running out of time. Panicking, I picked at a shallow divot of sand with a rock from a cairn, which reminded me—cats out here didn't dig cat holes. Ajahn Tira had said civet cats balanced their scat on the highest place they could, an alternative technique of waste disposal in dry climates—spread it on a rock in the sun, then let it dry and disperse. The bake-'n'-flake method.

Despite a month in a cave and five months in forest monasteries, I had yet to poop in the woods in Thailand. The predictability of intake extended to that of output—one in around 10:00 a.m., one out around 10:30 a.m., like clockwork. In fact, before Laos, I had gone so far as to perfect a meal ratio of sticky rice, a firming agent, to the rest of the fibrous offerings, which had the opposite effect, that had rendered wiping entirely superfluous. I'd written multiple triumphant entries in my diary about it: "the no-wipe shit."

This was important to me because monasteries didn't have toilet paper. I had not yet learned the hygienic or environmental advantages of a bidet, so I was repulsed by the spritz-and-bare-hand method customary in Thailand and much of the rest of the world. But food poisoning had upset my precious balance, and I made my first business on the bare expanse like a civet cat.

When I straightened, I noticed movement on the ground below. A squadron of thick black ants had marched over and surrounded the steaming intruder. They twitched as if angry and preparing for combat. One spread its pincers wide, reared back, and charged.

In disbelief, I watched the soldier hit its target head-on. Its entire front half sank in. Its back legs lifted into the air. For a moment, all was still.

Before his awakening, the Buddha had fallen face-first into feces. He'd fainted from extreme deprivation and dropped. When I'd first heard the legend, I'd marveled at the intensity and ached with jealousy. I wanted to have what it took to push myself that far.

But looking at the ant, I wasn't so sure. The ant also seemed to realize its error and began flailing, back legs scrambling for purchase on the ground to pull itself free of the mess it had dived into.

I howled with laughter. Over the previous months of isolation, the sound of my own laughter had scared me, and I had stifled it. But not this time. I felt a kinship with this ant. Here he was, this compulsive warrior, misinterpreting threats, charging in to solve problems that wouldn't have been problems if he hadn't charged in. Both of us seemed to glimpse in that moment the truth that plunging face-first into shit wasn't all that desirable.

The other ants seemed to intuitively grasp what I had not. Instead of lauding the bravery of their comrade and following his example, they retreated.

I ambled back to the cave with a reflective smile. Having witnessed the folly of some of my own extreme tendencies, I couldn't help but start to loosen my grasp on them. A measure of contentment had nestled into my routine, and I was surprised to find it characterized not by the presence of anything new but the absence of something old. Even though I remembered Ajahn Sumedho's lesson on release, I still expected growth by arrival—a new teaching, an original thought, a formation of words offering a new lens on life—but this nascent homeostasis felt more like growth by removal, a cleaning of gunk from my eyes.

This relief led me to reconsider the framing of monastic precepts. *Don't* do this, they said, *don't* do that, don't harm anything, don't eat after this time. At first, these all had struck me as dour directives intended to restrict. But perhaps they were more like guidelines that, once followed, enabled a kind of liberation: stay within these borders, and you'll be safe to move freely. Even the Four Noble Truths, I realized, followed a similar pattern. Rather than focusing on finding happiness, they pointed to the cessation of suffering.

I settled back into my seat on the wooden platform. I'd let my guard down, and a sudden sadness swept through me like a breeze across the mouth of the cave. This time, instead of steeling my spine against it, I let it roll through. I listened. And words followed. I liked it here. In a month, I was leaving.

And in swept something else. If I only had a month left, I'd better make the most of it. Or at least, I'd better not get hurt. The lapse in my strict demeanor ushered in a fresh awareness of just how isolated and unprotected I was way out in the middle of a foreign forest all by myself. Safety was a precarious thing. The sounds of snapping twigs and rustling leaves reminded me of the letter from my dad, the one with a Wikipedia printout of Southeast Asia's snakes. I clearly recalled that one, the Malayan pit viper, liked to hide in the brush.

I tromped through brush every day. Tira had left for another monastery while I was in Laos, but I remembered his instructions if I got bit by a snake. *Don't run.*

I scanned the rocky ground around the wooden platform. If I knew a somber attitude sometimes led me to underappreciate beauty, I hadn't realized it might also lead me to underestimate danger. For the first time, I couldn't close my eyes to meditate with my feet on the ground. I lifted them up onto the platform and tried sitting cross-legged for the rest of the evening.

The next day, I asked Ajahn Sukhito if the monastery had a snake identification book. I needed to cross-reference.

"Yes," he said, "we have one. But I will warn you: those who look at the book tend to encounter more snakes."

That gave me pause, but I looked anyway. Sure enough, the Malayan pit viper, a highly venomous snake whose brown-gray coloring camouflaged it under fallen leaves, was native to the area. For people who got bit, limbs were amputated, and death was a risk. I was crunching across two miles of viper territory every day. Twice a day, in fact, one of them in the dark.

I was officially on edge. First, I went to the corner of the kitchen pantry, where I stored my backpack, and retrieved a headlamp from the monastery plus the pair of wool socks I had yet to wear. The thick material would be hot on afternoon hikes, but I told myself they'd shield my ankles from fangs. With displeasure, I noted the ominous brand name of my knockoff rubber sandals: Mambaz.

I grabbed a broom from the shed and took to the trails on my hike back to the cave that afternoon. For hours, well into dusk, I swept two full miles of trail, clearing every leaf from each section of forested path between the sala and the plateau. If vipers waited under leaves, then I'd give them nowhere to hide.

The following morning, I rose from the wooden table, arms sore from the previous day, then grabbed my mesh bag and slung the broom over one shoulder. I was up on the plateau by 4:15 a.m. Even though there were no trees in this section, which meant no brush, which likely meant no vipers, I still scanned the ground for serpentine shapes.

A nearly full moon illuminated the plateau, good for visibility. But the forest canopy would plunge me back into darkness, and at the edge of the forest, I stepped on something that cracked. A couple of feet off the path, hidden in the shadow of the trees, I heard snorting and scrambling. Instantly, I knew I had surprised something heavy and hooved.

A wild boar. Before I could think, I crouched, whipped the broom across my chest like a bo staff, and bellowed a battle cry into the night. The animal crashed off through the brush, leaving me panting, sweating, and clutching the end of the broom.

It seemed my thinking about wildlife had called more of it into existence. Maybe Ajahn Sukhito had been right. I knew that was absurd on one level, but I couldn't help but wish for the blissful ignorance

I'd enjoyed for so long before looking at the ID book. I had been so enthralled with the grand optics of living in this environment that I hadn't ever stopped to really consider its hazards. Or else I'd loved the *idea* of danger because I had liked to imagine myself as a spiritual, special forces army of one.

I started hiking with more cautious steps in the forest. The one-way trip began to take longer than two hours. Sure, I'd grown accustomed to the beefy lizards that ate insects, but anxiety rose now about all sorts of creatures. The hordes of bats I had previously assumed were harmless, their daily blitz each dusk in the cave, their mucusy chirps. On multiple occasions, I had to duck when one flew inches from my face. I recalled with a sick stomach the only vaccine I had decided to skip during my appointment in Minneapolis—rabies.

In the ID book, I'd read about another snake that lived in the vicinity, the king cobra, whose venom could kill an elephant. Before I fell asleep, I considered another section I'd run through on spiders. The largest spider on earth, the giant huntsman, liked woody areas and lived, of course, in caves. Nowhere was safe. Rather than returning the broom to the shed, I kept it with me whenever I hiked, passing it over dark patches where I was about to step as if it were a white cane and I were blind, which, at night under the forest canopy, I almost was.

In daylight, cleaning set my mind at ease. After sweeping all the trails, I set to tidying the cave. A hulking stone slab formed the roof, and I started there. Wrapping my face in my robe, I reached up and brushed the cobwebs and dried guano. After the ceiling, I swept the dislodged debris from the table where I meditated and slept. The tiny, tar-filled porcelain saucers around each leg struck me as a trifling defense against all but the smallest insects. Still, I picked out every twig from the tar that could offer them a bridge.

I moved on to the far end, where a golden Buddha statue, three feet tall, perched in lotus on a natural rock ledge, as if supervising me. On either side of it were two orange candles the size of my arms, stunning when lit at night, casting a soft, warm glow and a thousand dancing reflections off the statue's complexion. But I rarely lit them. I hadn't wanted to deplete the resource at first. Now I didn't want to draw unwanted attention to my home.

On the end opposite the statue was a plastic bin. I had assumed that it, like the other bin at the cliff cave, was full of ratty towels and dry bars of soap, so I hadn't looked thoroughly. But now that I was deep cleaning, I wondered if it housed a nest of tarantulas. On high alert, I removed the top layer of towels, ready to jump back at the slightest move. At the bottom, I found two surprises.

First, there was a paperback book called *The Tao of Leadership*. I set it aside for later because the other item was a magazine, in full color, with a picture on its cover of a long-dead Thai monk. He had one of my favorite names, Ajahn Maha Bua, and was famous for his strictness. I decided to take a break and look inside.

It appeared to be dedicated to the contemplation of death. I could read none of the curly Thai text, but the pictures told enough of the story. Skeletons. Body parts. Photos of dead humans in various stages of decay. Each page presented unambiguous confirmation of the words from one of the chants I'd heard and muttered myself a hundred times at Nanachat: "I am of the nature to die. There is no way to escape death. All that is dear to me and everyone I love are of the nature to change." I flipped to a picture from a war that showed mangled bodies strewn across a dirt road. An image of actual dead bodies on the side of a road was too close to home. The *contemplation* of death, to me, suggested something more comfortably removed and analytical and based in *ideas*.

I rushed to another page, then paused. There was a doctored portrait of a woman. She was young and white and vaguely familiar, but it was hard to tell because a diagonal line cut across her face. Half the picture was superimposed with a skull, so one eye was a black, empty socket in a bald head of bone, and the other eye was alive and alert, decorated with mascara and twinkling beneath a coquettishly raised eyebrow and straight brown bangs.

I recognized this person. It was Mandy Moore.

Contemplating death was important, but it felt more so to contemplate how on earth the '90s pop music star Mandy Moore had made it into this small-print Thai magazine on mortality. I crossed one leg over the other and pictured some Ajahn, maybe Maha Bua himself, requesting editorial assistance from a volunteer who had an internet connection and Photoshop.

"Go find a picture of the most beautiful woman in the world," he might have said, "so that we may reveal the truth of what lies beneath even the most attractive surface."

It being roughly 1999, the volunteer might have gone home and typed "beautiful woman" into Google, and there, among the resulting rows of young, thin, white women with long hair, perhaps one had spoken to him.

The contemplation of death was supposed to help counteract laziness and lust. I'd heard monks suggest various thought exercises on the nature and decay of the physical form. "Picture the body as a sack of fluids"; "Imagine a beautiful corpse wrinkling into old age, then dying, then decomposing." Another mainstay chant concerned the thirty-two parts of the body. In our slow, detached monotone, we listed them aloud: "Urine, spleen, feces, sweat, brain . . ." To some extent, death had already forced such contemplations upon me. I'd awakened to a newfound sense of urgency, and my faith in lust had been shaken.

However, the image of half of Mandy Moore's face had the opposite of its intended effect. The lip gloss, the suggestively raised eyebrow, the hairstyle with that one loose strand that dangled coyly over her eye like a vine in the Garden of Eden—these were the elements of '90s allure I had absorbed as a boy. They triggered an ancient yearning. Frankly, I'd always been more of a Christina Aguilera "Genie in a Bottle" type, but it didn't matter. Desire had awoken.

I shifted to the edge of the platform and swallowed. I did not want to violate the precept on sexual activity, but now that I was thinking about *not* masturbating, that meant I was thinking about masturbating. I lay down. Tried to take a deep breath, all alone on the hard wooden table, hours away from anyone else. I recalled a quote from a senior Ajahn, calling masturbation "a serious blot on a monk's honor." *Not to mention on his robe,* I'd joked to myself at the time. Lust hadn't been a problem then.

In five months, I hadn't jerked off once, nor had I particularly wanted to. Not that I believed there was anything inherently wrong with it. More than anything, I wanted to show myself that I could go half a year without it. Then I remembered something Tira had said— hunger was more basic than lust. Now that my struggles around food and journaling had evaporated, I wondered if I'd become vulnerable to the next order of desire. Maybe, I thought, clenching my legs, maybe this was a sign of, like, progress? Like, I had been promoted? To the next level on the hierarchy of needs?

I caught myself. I knew exactly where this line of thinking led. If I had reached a new level, then I might convince myself that it was cause for some celebration. Hadn't Ajahn Sumedho said spiritual progress was characterized by release? Well, how about it? Why not treat myself to just one tiny little release?

While this predicament was new for my Thailand stay, it wasn't the only time lust had interrupted meditation. Years earlier, after my first monastic stint in New Zealand, I had come back to college as a twenty-year-old committed to deep meditation practice and to the discontinuation of all solitary sexual activity. But then I'd spend almost all twenty minutes I had set aside for meditation next to my laptop, thinking about what was off-limits. One day, I devised a strategy. I'd satisfy the urge first and *then* sit quietly in peace. And thus, a new approach was born. I'd even proselytized the technique to a few friends, half jokingly. Masturbate, then meditate. The 'bate-'n'-'tate method.

But I couldn't do that here. I mean, I could, but I didn't want to. Not at Poo Jom Gom. Not at the cave. Not when I could clearly remember how it felt to violate another precept—eating the Kinder Bueno in the tent months earlier at Nanachat. How unsatisfied I'd felt afterward. How I'd hated myself for giving in and then baselessly despised the other residents for "making" me hide it.

I had a hunch that whatever pleasure I felt from beating off in the woods would follow a similar sequence: a feeling of disgrace so unbearable I might try to offload it onto someone else. The shame-'n'-blame method. It wouldn't be *my* fault but Mandy Moore's, that treacherous temptress. It was idiocy. It was foolish misogyny. I knew it. But I also knew deep down that I was at risk of thinking it.

What didn't occur to me then was that such thinking was also a risk for the Thai Forest Tradition as a whole. Keeping women out, or always at a distance, made it easier to develop wrong views about them. I knew all too well what distances the mind could run when unchecked by reality.

For the moment, I couldn't bury the temptation, even if I buried the magazine back in the bottom of the plastic bin. Desire was like an itch. To ignore it was to enlarge it. I had to do something.

I had an idea. Maybe I could trick myself. Standing on the walking meditation path at the front of the cave, I faked masturbation. Gripping a shaft of air at my waist, I clenched every muscle and proceeded to unleash a burst of strokes as if I were doing the real thing. Then I feigned a climax, complete with an eye roll and a couple of grunts.

I couldn't believe it, but it worked. My heels returned to the ground, and I actually felt a measure of satisfaction. The desire had arisen and passed away, just like the Four Noble Truths said it would. Standing on the other side of the urge, I could look back and see how clearly it had arisen from boredom. How, had I really done it, I would've still been alone, still bored but also burdened with fresh regret. I called the new technique the pump stroke, based off the pump fake in sports, and I employed it multiple times over the following weeks.

By overdoing it with the clenching and grunting, I also made myself laugh, which, I realized, confirmed Ajahn Sukhito's warning that people can develop strange habits in solitude. I'd trusted that he knew what he was talking about at the time, but I couldn't imagine he had ever heard of someone who perched on their tippy-toes and faked beating off until they shouted, sighed, chuckled, and then returned to meditating. Living in a cave might make you wise, but it might also make you weird.

Over the next week, little red boils broke out around my waist and along the inside of my arms.

Theories for the rash abounded. An insect bite? Bat guano falling on me from the cave ceiling? Maybe cutting bamboo for fire breaks released some oil that irritated my skin? I stopped sweeping, cutting bamboo, and even taking the turmeric pills from Ajahn Sukhito.

Still, the rash spread. It reached my stomach by the second day. I couldn't help but consider more unlikely explanations. Like, what if the rash was a physical manifestation of a psychological disturbance?

Then it hit me: karma. In a bastardized, anxious conflation of Buddhist karma and Christian sin, I wondered if these boils were self-induced and I was to blame. I didn't think I was breaking the rule against solitary sexual activity, but perhaps I was flirting with it too much, and my internal lack of cleanliness was translating to the external? The more I turned this clunky theory over in the tumbler of my mind, the more it smoothed into something that felt reasonable.

Something else compounded my guilt. I'd expanded the pump-stroke technique to another prohibited activity: smoking weed. I mimed holding a joint between thumb and forefinger, taking a long drag, squinting, and exhaling a pretend column of smoke. I had actually felt a little stoned. But now I regretted all of it. I had to be violating some rule.

Then I realized I could check the actual rulebook. The Vinaya, the monastic code of conduct, outlined each and every precept. We had a copy in the library, so the following day, I looked.

I expected vague, commandment-style language but was surprised to find it clear, modern, and easy to read. An American monk had translated and updated the ancient Vinaya into a two-volume text. The line on sexual activity was crystal clear: intentional ejaculation was prohibited. Wet dreams, it explicitly stated, were unintentional and, therefore, OK. While the Vinaya didn't mention *hoping* for wet dreams or *faking* orgasms, I had to conclude that I was safe. Which meant I remained stumped on the origin of the rash.

One afternoon, instead of departing immediately for the cave after the work period, I hiked upstream from the kitchen with a packet of laundry detergent from the pantry, a bucket, and one of the blue plastic bins we used for storing offered sticky rice. Out of sight from the building, I stripped down and dunked my linens. The robes had absorbed a lot of sweat and dust over the last couple of weeks of traveling to Laos, sweeping, cutting bamboo, and beating down a couple of ground fires.

The water I twisted from the fabric was tinged brown. Scooping water into the bin, I sprinkled in some detergent and threw them in. With a fallen branch, I stirred, tossing in some loose sand to exfoliate the cotton. I dumped the dirty water on rocks away from the stream and repeated the cycle until the washing water stayed clear. Then I spread the robes, noticeably whiter, in a sunny spot to dry.

While I waited, I washed myself. With ample water and time, I let myself luxuriate, retrieving multiple buckets, tending to every nook and crevice. I normally scrubbed as if bathing were a task to be executed quickly, but now I treated it like a ceremony. I cradled my ears in each hand and let my soapy fingers explore the curls of cartilage and caress the soft lobes. I had never noticed the slight asymmetries between my left and right, and I marveled at the complexity of these seashell structures that lay on either side of my head, always out of sight, always at my service.

As much as I enjoyed the kind, intentional touch of a teammate or masseuse or lover, I realized it was rarely something I administered to myself. It felt foreign to touch my own body with gentle thankfulness, and I imagined it looked strange, too. I paused to open my eyes and check my surroundings. But no one was around. By the time the robes were dry, I felt as refreshed as if I'd spent a full day at the spa.

The next day, the rash was gone. For all my theories, I had neglected the most obvious: I and my robes were literally, physically filthy.

A few nights later, I awoke in the tea cave to the crack of thunder. Lightning flashed, illuminating a deluge in the forest outside. The storm had come out of nowhere. I shivered and pulled my sheet of robe up around my shoulders. Already, water was streaming down the overhanging rock above me. It would have trickled into the cave had it not been for a line of putty stuck across the ceiling; this upper lip forced the water to drip instead of running inside. Another lightning strike revealed a curtain of droplets descending from the edge of my shelter. For a moment, I appreciated the ingenuity. Clearly, someone else had lived here through the monsoon season.

But I wasn't totally dry. Squalls sent water blowing in. I lay on my side on the table, facing out, squinting as the storm intensified. I checked the digital watch I had brought out of retirement when grabbing wool socks from my backpack. It was only midnight.

Over the roar of the rain, I heard another sound, a shuffling and snapping, coming from the brush outside. Something alive. Something big, maybe looking for shelter.

I sat up. The sound was louder, closer. I grabbed the headlamp from the monastery and swept its beam across the mouth. Twenty yards away, through a break in the curtain of runoff, two pairs of eyes shone back at me.

My ears drew back. I could decipher the silhouettes—long bodies and tails—before their heads dropped and they disappeared in the dark.

Panthers? I thought. Fumbling with my sandals, I flipped the strap behind my heel and crouched in a defensive posture on the table. To the right, I heard another snap. I wheeled and saw them, ten yards away, close enough to clearly see the pair of animals. Both froze under my beam with a front paw lifted in midair.

They weren't panthers. More like oversize ferrets. And then I realized. Civet cats. I didn't care if they were harmless. I hissed and stomped on the table, and they turned and fled.

When my watch alarm beeped at 4:00 a.m., I hadn't slept, and the rain hadn't let up. I didn't want to hike. The ID book had said rain brought out frogs and lizards, which brought out snakes. I'd miss alms round if I waited, and Ajahn Sukhito might be upset. I wrapped myself tightly in my robe and stayed put for another hour.

At 5:00 a.m., the sun suggested its presence, and the rain abated. I set off at a fast clip. Out of the cave, over the plateau, down into the trees. If I booked it, I might get to alms on time. I knew the route inside and out and could move faster with some daylight. Water pooled in every divot in the rocks, and new streams trickled across the path.

The dawn light cast the path in shades of slate. On a straightaway, I noticed a smudge on the trail, a single fallen leaf. Without my broom, I thought to kick it clear. It had a spiraling pattern, and I suddenly realized it wasn't a leaf. Coiled in a tight circle in the middle of the path was a Malayan pit viper.

Skidding, unable to reverse, I leaped straight up into the air. Above it, I hovered for what felt like multiple seconds. For all my meditation, I was perhaps at my most purely attentive and thoughtless in this singular moment, regarding the snake below me. Like the sand, the snake's skin was a grayish beige, notched with thin black triangles that resembled streaks of soil. Its head bulged at the back and tapered like a bodhi leaf into a point. An upturned snout lifted its mouth into a permanent frown.

The moment my feet touched the sand, they were off again. I sprung back, splaying legs wide to preemptively dodge a strike. A couple of yards away, I caught my breath and gauged the snake's reaction. Motionless, it stared at me from unblinking vertical slits, its head wrapped in the center of its coil like a villain peering out from the raised collar of his cloak.

Some curious, young part of me wanted to touch it. Just a little. Maybe grab a stick and give it a nudge and see if there were different colors on the belly. I recalled the mnemonic I'd learned as a kid in the South for distinguishing the venomous coral snake's pattern from that of the nonvenomous king snake, "Red and yellow will kill a fellow. Red and black, venom lack." But I had since learned another saying, more useful in this circumstance: "Red and yellow will kill a fellow. Red and black . . . don't touch snakes."

I stepped into the leaves off the path to give it a wide berth. The viper stared back in the direction I'd come. On the other side of it, I continued on toward the monastery, pausing to double-check every twisted root and stray leaf.

My watch read 6:10 a.m. Already, I could feel Ajahn Sukhito's disappointment. I had failed to brave the storm undaunted, like a true warrior would, like past monks probably did during the monsoon season. I wondered if I'd lose my cave privileges for being late. I bristled at this possibility, partly because I felt the shame of falling short of my ideal but also because a small, competing voice in my head suggested the ideal was foolish. If I had left on time, I might not have spotted the snake in the dark. I'd rather be late than dead.

I heard shuffling on the path ahead and froze, ready for another animal. To my surprise, Pamutto charged up the path.

He was out of breath. "Are you all right?" he said.

"Yeah," I said and pointed back up the path. "It was raining, so I—I just saw a snake—I waited. It was a pit viper, a Malayan pit viper, like, *right* back there. What are you doing out here?"

I'd never seen anyone out here in the mornings. I must have really been in trouble.

"You hadn't arrived at your normal time is all. Ajahn Sukhito had a feeling about it and asked me to check on you."

"Really?" I said. For a flicker of a moment, this upset me—if I had not failed their rugged ideal, then, by not leaving me behind, they had all failed mine.

But the feeling melted when Pamutto touched my shoulder and smiled. The wick of my warrior flame was wearing to its nub.

No one had left for alms, he said, because everyone wanted to make sure I was safe.

LINKEDIN

Group meditation began every morning in the sala without a word. So it was a surprise when Ajahn Sukhito cleared his throat. He had an announcement.

"Do not be alarmed," he began, "but . . . there has been a sighting."

Bada caught my eye from the stage and shot me a dramatic and gleeful look.

Pamutto said, "A sighting of . . . ?"

"Drug smugglers," said Ajahn Sukhito. "Apparently, from time to time, they will come over the border from Laos and hide out in the national park." From behind his seat, he produced a printout, an 8"-by-11" black-and-white mug shot showing a skinny Laotian man with gaunt eyes who looked ready to fight.

It might've been scary had Ajahn Sukhito not been smirking.

"Oh my," said Pamutto.

"Ajahn," said Bada, pursing his lips, "what do you recommend in the case that we make . . . an encounter?"

I was smiling, too. As people committed to nonharm, we all seemed to understand that we wouldn't do anything if we made an encounter. Monks hurt no one, and in turn, we hoped, no one hurt monks.

"Well"—Ajahn Sukhito grinned—"send them . . . your *metta*."

Metta, "loving-kindness." That broke it. We all laughed.

"I have a second announcement," said Ajahn Sukhito. "I am going to spend the summer back in Israel, teaching. There will be an interim abbot who comes here in my absence. I'll depart in a week."

Our smiles dropped.

Bada raised a tentative hand. "Ajahn, are you sure you aren't leaving because of the smugglers?"

We laughed again, but this one sounded forced. Ajahn Sukhito couldn't leave Poo Jom Gom. He was Poo Jom Gom. The whole landscape felt like an extension of him. I thought I had two weeks left with him, and now I had one.

A couple of days before his departure, Ajahn Sukhito requested my assistance in counting money in the safe. That we had a safe was a surprise, though it turned out to be a metal box about as big and secure as a lunch pail. Monks, bound by the tenth precept, can't handle money, so Ajahn Sukhito watched over my shoulder at the kitchen island as I stacked the donated bills and coins—a mix of baht and US dollars. He recorded the totals himself on a notepad. As we finished, I pulled out an envelope of my own. I had stopped at a Western Union on the way back from Laos to withdraw a donation. I had decided on two thousand dollars.

Ajahn Sukhito seemed surprised. "It's a lot," he said.

It was. But in another sense, it hardly covered what I had received. Monasteries in the Thai Forest Tradition ran entirely on donations. Besides, I wasn't giving it all to Poo Jom Gom. I wanted half to go to Yupin. Without her, there was no monastery.

When I mentioned this, Ajahn Sukhito looked away in thought. He said it was generous and that others had donated to Yupin before, too, and that the funds went toward her kids' education. "But," he said, "half . . . it is too much."

This surprised me. "Why?" I said.

A gift of a thousand dollars, Ajahn Sukhito explained, in such a small town, would be considered enormous and potentially embarrassing. "Maybe," he said, "five hundred dollars instead of a thousand would be still . . . quite generous."

This felt strange. On the one hand, Ajahn Sukhito had lived in this community for two decades and surely knew better than I did what was culturally sensitive and appropriate. On the other, it sure seemed like Yupin was best suited to decide if the gift was too large herself.

Ajahn Sukhito had said *maybe*, but it hadn't sounded like a suggestion. I had been raised to avoid discussing money at all costs, I feared confrontation, and I also trusted Ajahn Sukhito.

I said OK. Five hundred for her. Fifteen hundred for the monastery.

Filing the cash in two separate parts of the safe, I felt hot. Later, I asked myself why I hadn't simply gone around Ajahn Sukhito and given Yupin a separate envelope. Surely *she* could decide herself if indeed the gift was too much. Perhaps I had wanted Ajahn Sukhito to *see* my gift to Yupin and be impressed with my generosity. For all my incremental growth toward self-possession and skepticism of male power in the Thai Forest Tradition, I had still subconsciously sought Ajahn Sukhito's blessing. And when he hadn't given it, I'd capitulated to stay in his good graces.

I had benefitted so much from learning to release and surrender, but I found myself wondering if I'd forgotten when it was important to hold on and fight. What was more, I knew the interaction would be one of my last with Ajahn Sukhito. It complicated our goodbye. The bad taste from holding my tongue lingered, which was an important insight, but still, one that had cost Yupin five hundred dollars.

Before we finished up, Ajahn Sukhito had me dump the coins from the bottom of the tin onto the kitchen island to finalize the count. One silver piece was a non-Thai currency, and Ajahn Sukhito said to leave it out because it was useless. With everything counted, I packed the notepad and the rest of the money away and returned the safe to the shed.

When I came back to the kitchen, I stopped in my tracks. At the island, Ajahn Sukhito was holding the extra silver coin between his thumb and forefinger, examining it in the light.

Throughout our meeting, I had already begun to reflect on the limits of the tenth precept. Monks were forbidden from handling money, but Ajahn Sukhito had essentially managed the bookkeeping as well as the direction of my donation. The precept had seemed so expansive, but now it struck me as narrow and easily circumvented.

Still, holding a coin seemed like a clear violation, even if physical contact with currency was clearly harmless. I sniffed to announce my presence.

Ajahn Sukhito jerked his arm as if the coin had burned his hand. The piece clattered across the tile.

I stood open-mouthed.

Ajahn Sukhito turned, and I saw he was smirking.

I blinked and cocked my head. We said nothing, and a slow smile spread over my face. If the joke was meant to be a teaching on dogma, I took it gladly. Still, after the donation talk, I was perplexed by the entire sequence. To a degree, Buddhist monks were still archetypes in my mind, so when they did anything that didn't fit my model, my eye twitched. I had expected to come to Thailand and become an archetype myself. Instead, I'd come and found the archetypes to be people. Which made them more impressive but also more complicated.

The following evening, he invited me to a final meeting. I made my way to his kuti, a sacred and off-limits place upstream from the kitchen in a dry rock clearing near the stream. The structure perched on the gentle stone slope. By monastic standards, the kutis of abbots and senior monks were often posh, and Ajahn Sukhito's was no exception. The floor was tile and the footprint around three hundred square feet, over half of which was a porch covered by a long, thin roof that extended past his room and was supported on the other end by a thick column with a sitting nook carved into it.

Ajahn Sukhito sat on the tile, leaning against the column, and I settled onto a cushion before him. A single candle flickered on the floor between us.

We bowed. Then a cell phone buzzed.

"What's this?" he said and fumbled around the cushion on the carved-out seat over his shoulder. He pulled out a phone, a first-generation Nokia brick. "Sorry," he said. "I generally turn this off after five."

I smiled and raised my hands in nonjudgment. I hoped I had developed a more forgiving attitude toward that which didn't fit my precious rustic ideal. "Doesn't look like you can surf the internet with that thing," I said.

"Yes, it's true. It only makes calls," he said. "It's the monastery's phone, really only to communicate with Nanachat."

It seemed a fitting introduction to our conversation. Although he was the one leaving the monastery the next day, I was leaving monastic life altogether the next week. I was about to reenter the world of, among other things, electronic devices and all the connection and distraction and stimulation they afforded. Before I left, I had some questions.

But I began by thanking him. I told him I had seen and experienced how difficult things could become less difficult. "Food was a big struggle until I finally got bored with struggling," I said, which made him smile, which emboldened me to ask if he had ever heard me swallowing during group meditation in the mornings. "I was certain for a few weeks that everyone could."

He shook his head. "It's always intriguing to see what places we think other people's minds have gone."

"You know," I said, "being self-conscious about swallowing actually helped, in a way, because it led to more focus on body awareness. Like, if I was really distracted and maybe getting angry, and I realized that was happening, I might pause and ask myself, 'Are my *legs* angry?' and bring awareness down into them, and the answer was always no, because the experience of anger was in my head or chest or arms, and that made the anger feel smaller, just knowing that it didn't exist everywhere."

"Yes," Ajahn Sukhito said. "Body scanning. That is"—he searched for the word—"a classic. To meditate with the body can be especially helpful for *heady* people, for Westerners, because it brings us away from the brain. Gives respite. It's a staple of my own practice." He paused and looked away as if listening to the dark around us. "Thai teachers were historically tough, but that was largely because of the Thai cultural context. Thai is *sabai*, 'relaxed,' so teachers would tend toward toughness. But toughness is easy to overdo for Westerners, who tend toward overexertion already. That's also why we have a more holistic lifestyle. It's not just 'eat the meal, go meditate.' We plant things, meditate together, work together."

I felt a quick sadness at how long it had taken me to see the truth of what he said. For months, I missed the pleasantness of doing anything together because I thought I needed to be a hermit. I thought more toughness was the answer when in fact it was the obstacle.

"A lot of times," I said, "I noticed how my desire for intense periods of perfect concentration often got in the way of actually concentrating."

Then I told him about the word I had made up to remind myself of the balance I found so hard to strike.

"Diligentle," he repeated aloud, tilting his head back, feeling it out for himself. He nodded in approval, and my heart quietly leaped. "It implies consistency . . . more than work or effort or toughness, which all have a kind of *force* and intensity to them that isn't totally suitable for *long-term* success in the practice . . . I also like the word *persever-ance.* There is the story of Ananda, the Buddha's assistant, who needed to become fully enlightened before a meeting of only arahants," he said, referring to followers who were fully enlightened. "Ananda tries, tries, tries, doesn't get it, and finally decides to rest. The moment his head hits the pillow"—Ajahn Sukhito's hand turned in the air—"he becomes an arahant."

He waited a few moments and said, "The warrior can be helpful. But it can also be narrow."

He looked away. The night around us had grown darker and the flame between us brighter. I'd learned to love these spaces in our conversation. I could listen to the ripples of what he said. I could wait until the water was calm and clear enough for me to see what I wanted to say next. I found a rising curiosity about how monastic life had changed for Ajahn Sukhito since he had ordained. So I asked.

"Over my twenty years of practice," he said, "I've dropped many . . . ideas and ideals, which had made things difficult for me."

I was surprised he could sum up two decades of practice in that one sentence, but then again, he had just described my experience, too. He looked out into the space of night and seemed to speak kindly to his younger self. "Now, monastic life . . . it's a dream come true."

I studied him. I might've been suspicious of the cliché, but hyperbole was so rare from him, and he seemed to believe exactly what he had said, that I believed him, too. Sometimes, I supposed, it could be that simple.

Which led me to ask about simplicity. I knew he had a special reverence for it. Weeks earlier, I had heard him give an offhanded framing of romantic relationships, not in terms of good and evil—as some monks and even old Buddhist texts did—but in terms of simplicity. "Many partners," he'd said, "not so simple. One partner, more simple. Zero partners, the most simple." I'd tucked this and other nuggets away as I prepared to leave the monastery, perhaps in an effort to stockpile wisdom as a defense against the onslaught of the outside world.

I had found another nugget in the tea cave, beside the magazine about death with half a portrait of Mandy Moore, in the tattered paperback book, *The Tao of Leadership*. It said, "If you want to be free, learn to live simply." I had brought the book to Ajahn Sukhito and asked what he thought.

"*Simplicity* is a key word for me," he said. "For myself, even though on a worldly scale I have nothing, it takes *time* when I accumulate things." He gestured behind me to the enclosed room of his kuti, where I'd gotten a glimpse inside before we had sat down and noticed the windowsills and the single shelf were dotted with slim dhamma books, pretty stones, and small gnarled pieces of wood, natural sculptures collected from the forest.

He motioned to the bag of his belongings a few feet away on the tile floor: a single reusable grocery bag that I knew contained all he would take on his three-month trip. "For laypeople in Israel," he said, "it is so *obvious* that simplifying would improve their lives."

He spoke not with resentment but sympathy, as if he were truly pained by the unintentional suffering he saw people gather for themselves. He returned his gaze to me then and said, "I have a poem that I often read that perhaps I can show you. But anyway," he said, "it's beautiful, the Tao book, and that line, 'If you want to be free . . .' But . . . it can be a bit . . . slogan-y. The word *diligentle*, too. These things must be practiced."

I was afraid he might say something like that. I'd spent so long hunched over so many diary pages with white knuckles from gripping my tool, trying to build my way to wisdom, but in the end, I never constructed catchy, airtight phrases that contained real answers. Maybe it hurt to hear Ajahn Sukhito imply my diary wouldn't shatter the earth. But because I sensed that already, he could say what I had not yet admitted, and hearing it also felt like a small relief.

I would never have asked what I did next if I hadn't been leaving. This was my last opportunity, so I plowed ahead.

"I have a specific question about wee—er, marijuana," I said. "Sometimes, I feel like I can have a tiny little bit and can relax, like—"

"No." He cut me off. "That's delusion."

I should've known I wouldn't persuade a monk from the Thai Forest Tradition, someone who'd sworn off intoxicants for twenty years, to endorse getting stoned, but for some reason, I pressed. "I don't drink alcohol anymore. I haven't really since the car accident. But with . . . marijuana, sometimes I feel like I actually have, like, *better* dhamma discussions with people when I'm slightly . . . when I've used a little bit."

"It clouds the mind," he said. "It isn't clarity. Any insight you think you've gained from it probably won't last, or it will be wrong thinking."

I swallowed. He hadn't chastised me like this before. I knew I wouldn't get any traction, so I moved to the other topic about which I felt compelled to seek his counsel. Sports.

I had a feeling I'd run into another wall, but I had to plead my case. For me, participating in sports was bigger than entertainment. "It's taught me so much about discipline," I said. "How to do things that are good for me that I don't always want to do. General health. Calmness under pressure. How to be a good teammate. How to respond to mistakes. A foundation for body awareness. Training sometimes feels like moving meditation . . ." I trailed off.

A small breeze ruffled his orange robes. He inhaled and looked away in deliberation.

I tensed. I missed running. High fives. Teammates. Most of my friends were past and present teammates. I wasn't going to quit, but if Ajahn Sukhito said this, too, was delusion, then I would leave Thailand feeling more lost than ever. Again, I sought his blessing. Although I was twenty-five years old, I still felt at my core like a child, wanting answers from the outside, even if they were answers I didn't like—it was easier to rebel against an authority than to shoulder the weight of being one for myself.

Ajahn Sukhito turned back to me. Despite months of practice cultivating my breath, I held it.

"You know, I had never thought about sports that way," he said. "I can see it."

I waited for the caveat, but that was it. My mouth dropped open, and I scrambled for another question before he could change his mind. I asked if he had any general feedback for me.

Immediately, I regretted asking. Ajahn Sukhito shifted. "Feedback is generally more . . . indirect in monastic life," he said.

This was awkward. My corporate American was showing. What had I been expecting, a bulleted list of constructive criticism, or perhaps an assurance he would act as a reference for future employers?

He continued, "Maybe also it's Thai culture. Confrontation is generally avoided. Monks in the Forest Tradition are not really into the *interviews* that many other retreat teachers do. People being their own teachers is a kind of motto. But, of course, if people have questions, they can ask."

He paused.

I nodded and waited, hoping that my silence would encourage him to tell me something more about myself.

"Back in lay life," he finally said, "it is natural to experiment—wisely—for a period of time." I had once described my life after college to him as a series of experiments. "Your . . . loss . . . of your friend. Reflecting on this can be incredibly important for adding urgency to how you decide to spend your time."

Before I knew it, I had raced up a tree of thought: urgency—he was right. Maybe I shouldn't leave, but I had to, but maybe I'd come back someday, or maybe I'd ordain somewhere else, closer to home, or . . .

As if he read my mind, Ajahn Sukhito offered me the feedback I needed most. "We don't need to get too far ahead thinking about the future, though. If you return to a monastery again, think about it as another six months to one year. No need to go further, *commit your whole life*," he said with pseudo-dramatic flair. "It can't do you any harm. Family is often a tough point for people who consider going forth, but it sounds like yours understand to some degree what you've been doing."

They did. My parents and grandmother had started meditating since I left.

"That's invaluable for them," he said. "Your actions can be quite inspiring for others, rather than only being . . . a good talker."

Or writer, I thought, of the diary.

"It's important to enjoy this monastic lifestyle, too," he said. "Not just grit and grind toward some future happiness."

I felt the same quick stab of sadness—or was it truth?—from earlier in the conversation. I wished I'd heard that guidance earlier. But then again, I *had* heard it earlier. I'd preached it to sports teams—"Enjoy the process"—and to kids in the mountains: "Happiness is the journey, not the destination." I just kept forgetting or refusing to practice it myself.

There seemed to be nothing left to say. I thanked him.

"You've done well," he said. "It takes maturity not to get lost in the afternoons here. You seem to have a reflective ability that . . . can point to the thinking mind being a tool, rather than something to beat down."

Darkness held us close in the orange glow. We looked at each other with smiling eyes, then rose to our knees. Ajahn Sukhito turned to the Buddha statue atop the seat behind him, and we both bowed to it. When he turned back to me, I knew it was my turn to bow to him, and I did, gladly, even though I felt we had become sort of friends, and even though I felt conflicted about the strict hierarchy and about how he had redirected my donation. I loved him, and on the third and final bow, I let my forehead kiss the tile floor and rest there for an extra beat.

Amid his unceremonious departure the following day, Ajahn Sukhito handed me a small scroll the size of a twig, bound by a paper clasp. Once he had left, and the first afternoon without him stretched on, I unrolled the paper and found a poem, written in his clean ink script:

> Simple mind
> Knowing task, knowing duty
> Patient heart
> Nothing to complain
>
> Simple mind
> Knowing now, knowing nature
> Patient heart
> Growing little by little

I wasn't sure what to make of most of it. But once I'd gotten to the end, after the reminders on simplicity and patience, the last line made some sense. Which wasn't unlike the last five and a half months. I'd been hunting epiphany since day one, searching for a turtle with a mustache. Meanwhile, my heart had become a little more ready, and some peace had slowly crept up on me.

While growth might happen little by little, change might not. A lot happened at Poo Jom Gom in very little time.

First, we welcomed an interim abbot—Ajahn Sukhito's replacement. A Norwegian monk who, despite his pronounced hunch, approached seven feet tall. A bulbous forehead shaded shifty eyes and a curious smile. In look, manner, and even his low speech, he resembled the scheming Mr. Burns of *The Simpsons*. Except the Norwegian was also young—only nine rains retreats, so he wasn't an Ajahn but, all of a sudden, was our most senior monk. The older monks from Michigan and China had returned to Nanachat when Ajahn Sukhito left.

Which left us juniors alone with the creepy new guy. During the first work period under his supervision, he joined me, Bada, and Giorgio and casually remarked while sweeping, "You know, when you're out in the world, and you've had this training . . . women, they're really attracted to you. Like, really. Yes. It's true. You'll be riding the train, and you can pick up on it. They really want you."

Bada shifted and smiled. Giorgio turned away. I channeled my inner Ajahn Sukhito and stared back at him blankly.

I happened to meet Pamutto in the sala before hiking out to the tea cave in the afternoon, and I told him what the Norwegian had said over a cup of tea.

Pamutto said, "He said that to you, too? He told me monks really have to watch out if they disrobe because so many women will want them that a monk will find himself getting married and having a family in no time and then never be able to come back and ordain."

"He's odd, right?"

"Yeah, the way he kinda stares at you for too long?"

"He must have some stuff going on."

"Seriously," Pamutto said. "I never thought I'd say this, but I really miss Ajahn Sukhito."

The Norwegian wasn't the only new arrival. The next day, a woman moved into the guest kuti where I had first lived. She was Thai, in her fifties, and wore white robes like mine. Her name was Dtong, and she carried herself with a quiet, unmistakable dignity. She wore glasses, had short dark hair, and spoke excellent English. She could translate between Yupin and me.

Shortly after she arrived, she asked if I could help with the cooking during group meditation. Had Ajahn Sukhito been present, I might've thought to ask his permission, but he was gone, and our rigid customs seemed to have left with him. While the other monks meditated, I began staying in the kitchen to help.

Dtong approached one morning with her hands in prayer and asked if I could help make berry toast.

"Because you are American," she said.

"Sure, that sounds great. We have bread?"

"Oh, do you need bread?" she said.

"For toast?" I said.

"No, berry toast," she said.

"Right. Toast with berries, like a spread."

"Am I saying it incorrectly? Berry toast. Berrytos."

"Oh! Burritos?" I said.

She threw up her hands. "Ah, whatever."

When she found out that I was leaving in a week, she offered me her phone after the meal so that I could coordinate my plans. She pulled out a brand-new iPhone and I held out my hand, but she placed it directly on the kitchen island, then retracted hers to avoid physical touch, the same way a monk would with the opposite sex.

Over the next couple of days, I learned through Pamutto that Dtong was a *maechi*, a laywoman who had dedicated her life to the practice and committed to following all eight precepts whether or not she was in a monastery. Strict lay Buddhists follow the first five precepts—no killing, stealing, lying, illicit sex, or intoxicants. Maechis dial up the precept on illicit sex to full-on celibacy, plus add the next three—no eating after noon, no entertainment or beautification, and no sleeping in a luxurious place. Maechis follow these monastic precepts, but they live, by and large, out in the world. They have to, because women can't ordain in Thailand. So when Dtong visited a monastery, even if she had more years of practice than our interim abbot, she was treated as a visiting layperson, and a female at that—not only did she eat last, but she was also automatically tasked with cooking the meal and cleaning up afterward.

I made a batch of pitiful bean burritos and, after eating the meal and cleaning up, carried Dtong's phone to the kitchen table. I unlocked the screen. Logged out of her Gmail account and into mine. Waited for my inbox to load. Meanwhile, I tried very hard to marvel at the device—*my, how technology has advanced during my long absence from the outside world!*—but in fact, I got used to it pretty quickly, and within a few minutes, I was showing Dtong how to close all the open apps that were draining her battery.

There was a message from MJ with the address of an Airbnb she'd reserved for us in Bangkok. I thumbed a reply: See you soon, I might be strange, I won't have eyebrows, and would you mind bringing some cream for rashes.

There were many more unread messages. The bold font demanded attention, but I didn't want to look. It was overwhelming enough to plan the first day outside the monastery. I couldn't think any further than that. I got up and handed the phone back to Dtong, or tried to. She nodded toward the kitchen table. I said, "Oh, sorry," and placed it there for her to pick up.

Imagining myself on the outside made me wonder how Dtong balanced her own practice. She didn't listen to music. She didn't eat after noon. She was doing what Pamutto and I could only dream of: maintaining a deep and committed practice no matter where she was. She followed the path without the support of prestige. Without hardly any support. Maechis often needed financial backing from their own families. No one bowed to her. No one offered her room and board in a beautiful forest designated for her practice. No one asked her to give a dhamma talk. I didn't trust the impulse to simply marvel at her humble labor. I felt annoyed she didn't get formal respect.

In Ajahn Sukhito's absence, and in the puerile presence of our new interim abbot, I felt Dtong had become Poo Jom Gom's spiritual anchor. I found myself checking my posture around her. While the new guy crept around the edges, Dtong's kind stability set the standard.

Then Bada disrobed.

Bada—the last person I would've predicted. He seemed as content as anyone in monastic life. He approached me in the afternoon.

"Is it true?" I said.

He closed his eyes, lowered his head, and said gravely, "It is true." Then he looked up and grinned.

"May I ask where you'll go?"

"Missouri," he said.

"What?"

"Apparently there is a teacher there who can guarantee the stages of jhana."

I searched his face for traces of doubt or guilt. But his eyes only shone.

"Well," I said, "I hope it's everything you want it to be."

He thanked me and stuck out his right hand, and for the first time, we shook. Not a bow—just like that, it seemed he wasn't a monk anymore.

"Might you be willing to write me a recommendation?" he said.

"For the Missouri monastery place?"

"Yes," he said. "You will also be outside when I am outside. You could attest to my suitability."

I shrugged. "Yeah, why not? Happy to."

He handed me a scrap of paper with an email address and a name—his real name, Mohammed—and then said he would find me on LinkedIn.

The next afternoon, I met Pamutto in the kitchen to take tea together. Without Ajahn Sukhito and with so much going on, we needed to talk.

"I'm kind of embarrassed to say this because it's so obvious now," I said, "but senior monks are all so *different*. I kind of expected them all to be one type of way, but then you get Ajahn Sukhito on one end of the spectrum, like, super introverted and deliberate and solemn—"

"No, you're right," said Pamutto, "and then on the other side, you get someone like Ajahn Tira, who's this happy-go-lucky, everyday kinda guy. It reminds me, you know, I heard a senior Ajahn say once that some elements of personality carry over into enlightenment. That makes some sense to me. Not that we know who's enlightened or anything."

Senior monks, I had learned, could confide in each other about whether they had achieved nirvana, but none had shared such information with the likes of me or Pamutto. Monks were discouraged from divulging their spiritual standing, which had been disappointing at first, because I was curious and because I imagined wanting to announce my own enlightenment the moment I got there. But the more I'd thought about it, the more I understood the wisdom of withholding. It had to do with language. I had used the words *enlightenment* and *nirvana* interchangeably, but their meanings, in fact, were opposite. While *enlightenment* suggested becoming luminous, the Pali word *Nibbana* (*nirvana* in Sanskrit) literally translated to "blowing out" or "extinguishing." Our goal, then, was not to become a light around which others might congregate. Instead, it was to extinguish the flame of our own craving. Advertising my status was antithetical to the process of release.

"And then there's this new guy," I said, nodding in the direction of the interim abbot's kuti.

"Right," said Pamutto. "He makes me nervous."

"Me too. Did I tell you that thing Ajahn Tira said, 'If you're struggling with lust, just fast'? Somebody should tell him that."

The interim abbot's line about being desirable on the outside had stuck with us. What I didn't realize was that it had awoken something in me that I preferred would lie dormant: that I still wanted to be desirable, and I wasn't wholly committed to celibacy.

"Yeah," Pamutto said. "It won't be me, though. I've just been steering clear of him, to be honest."

"Same," I said and gazed at the bamboo beyond the kitchen. "Makes leaving easier, in a way."

"I know. For me, too, actually," said Pamutto, who was heading back to Nanachat soon. He hadn't sent the letter to his parents. He hadn't decided to ordain, but he hadn't decided to disrobe, either. "I've been kind of dreading going back to Nanachat, but now, I'm like, that wouldn't be so bad, really."

I agreed. Ajahn Sukhito's demeanor had cast an almost omniscient presence over Poo Jom Gom—strict but secure. Sensing our lack of supervision, we poured a third cup of tea.

I repeated my flimsy commitment to celibacy. "I mean, I'm definitely going to try it on the outside. Probably."

As if to toast the unusual, likely discouraged, length of our conversation, we clinked cups and said cheers.

"Oh," said Pamutto, "I've got something we can look at."

He popped up and over to the tiny library in the back of the kitchen, returning with a large hardcover book. He spread it on the table—a comprehensively illustrated textbook on human anatomy. We studied pages of skeletons and various organs and told ourselves that when you really thought about it, the human body wasn't all that attractive. Celibacy, we agreed, just made sense.

On a cross section of the human head in profile, we examined the components of the face. From this scientific angle, we felt we could see the truth of human lips. Behind their sensual allure, lips were nothing more than flaps of skin! Their superficial red coloration, called the vermilion zone, was just that, a zone—nothing inherently attractive about it.

We nodded and shrugged. We told each other how strange it was that people smooshed vermilion zones onto other people's vermilion zones and called it kissing and actually liked it. This was our version of contemplating *asubha*, the Pali term for the inherent unattractiveness of the human body. In the moment, it worked. It was hard to feel lust when looking at a diagram of a large intestine. Partly, I held tightly to the practices that had given me purpose for the last half year. Partly, it also felt unkind to inform Pamutto that the friend I would meet in Bangkok in less than a week was an intelligent, creative, beautiful woman to whom I had professed my love six months earlier.

We poured a fourth cup of tea. Tonight, we were brothers in celibacy. When we ran out of hot water, Pamutto scampered off to his kuti, brought back his thermos, and poured us a fifth cup. Then a sixth. We talked of astrology and Nietzsche and our diverging futures. A free-ranging chat over drinks was rare and especially precious because we both knew we'd probably never see each other again.

Finally, one of us checked the time. We'd been talking for seven hours.

"Whoa," we said. Suddenly the night seemed quieter. Our friendship had allowed us to inch one foot further into the other's world.

And now we had to separate. To lessen the blow, we hatched a plan for me to write to him after I had spent six months out in the world. He gave me his email address and his real name: Scott.

The following day, a crate arrived from Italy. After the work period, we gathered around it.

Giorgio beamed. "From my mother," he said.

He slid a panel from the top. The package carried a distinctly rustic beauty—not cardboard and Styrofoam but blond wood and packing straw, which Giorgio gently lifted like an archeologist at a holy site. He peered inside, then straightened, pinched the air, and named each item as he lifted it from the crate.

A slender glass bottle of red sauce. "Ah, the marinara."

Another sleek bottle with a thin neck. "Ah, the olio d'oliva." Giorgio held it in two hands as if he'd delivered a newborn child. Then he passed it to Pamutto, who was placing everything in a display arrangement on the kitchen island.

Giorgio pulled out a sheaf of brown paper and said, "Ah, Mama."

"What is it?" I said.

"This is the same word in English, Grant." He passed it to me and smiled. "The spaghetti."

I reflected on how I had hoarded the KIND bars my father had sent months earlier. How I had glowered when I saw Giorgio pluck small treats and stash them in his robe pocket. And now how Giorgio opened his box in public and stored his goods in the common pantry. Sure, it would've been difficult for him to hide a crate, but now, I gave him the benefit of the doubt. He was sharing. This was a celebration.

Unable to eat outside the meal, we were happy to admire the bottles and jars with labels in Italian cursive. Eventually, we nestled them in the pantry beside the cans and boxes covered in Thai.

Meanwhile, Giorgio finished unpacking. From the bottom, he pulled a pair of white Kappa boxer briefs. He shook his head. "Ah, Mama."

"Those are nice!" I said. Then I added, "They match the pakao white."

"You can have them," Gorgio said.

"What? No. They're from your mom."

"Grant"—he lowered his voice—"I do not wear them. Please. They're yours."

I grinned and thanked him. Having thrown out the soiled pair in Laos, I was back to even.

Pamutto said, "We're really gonna have a feast tomorrow."

"Ah, no," said Giorgio, "this is the tragedy. Unfortunately, I have bad news. You see, Yupin does not know how to cook these things. The last package that arrived, with the ingredients from my mother, they sit in the pantry. Still, they are there. Sit, sit, sit."

I perked up. "I can do it." I was the only one who was allowed to miss the pre-meal meditation to help cook. I had made burritos. I could make pasta.

The next morning, while Yupin zipped between her multiple complex preparations, she took breaks to watch me cook with the new ingredients. With a furrowed brow and a studious, hands-on-hips posture, she stood beside me while I boiled a pot of water, dropped the noodles in, and waited. In a separate pan, I warmed the marinara, added olive oil and salt and pepper, and asked Dtong to communicate that what Yupin made every day was much harder than what I was doing.

Yupin shook her head.

I nodded mine.

Dtong hadn't made pasta before, either. She said something to Yupin, laughed, and then said to me, "Agree to disagree."

I served the pasta on an oval plate. Yupin rang the bell. The monks came and filled their bowls, and then we all ate quietly in our separate places before various Buddha statues. After the meal, Giorgio marched down from the sala, into the kitchen, and gave me a hug.

He held me close, then straightened his arms, with his hands resting on my shoulders, and said, "Just like my mother makes it."

U-TURN

The tea cave was the pinnacle of solitude I sought in coming to Thailand. Hidden in the woods, off-trail, two hours' hike from the hermitage, which, as far as I knew, was the nearest civilization in any direction—the distance from humanity offered a chance to learn to listen to myself. The extreme also offered a badge of honor, the pursuit of which seemed harmless enough, until one night, when I awoke in the dark on the platform and realized I wasn't alone.

Across the ravine, forty yards away, the beam of a flashlight swept across the mouth of the cave. I heard twigs crack under boots. Before I could think, I had rolled off the platform and ducked behind it.

My knee had knocked the corner on my way down, and whoever was out there must have heard it. The flashlight darted back overhead and began sweeping back and forth. The steps came closer, thirty yards away now. Then the flashlight turned off.

I lay still, listening over my frantic breath, peering out into the dark. I smelled tar from the porcelain cup nearest my face, the moat under each platform leg meant to keep out trespassers. I knew in my bones who was out there. Ajahn Sukhito had shown us his mug shot.

Had I paused to listen to myself, I would've easily identified mortal fear as the emotion coursing through my body. Had I taken another moment to assess the badge of honor I was supposedly earning by living in a remote cave, I would've struggled to see the value of isolating myself in the crosshairs of a criminal in the woods in the middle of the night. The risk of extreme solitude, which I had largely neglected, was that if shit went wrong, I was on my own.

Training my ears to the outside for footsteps, I reached up onto the platform and located the wool socks I had folded under my elbows for padding as I slept. I slipped them on, followed by my rubber sandals, whose heel straps I flipped back. I was going to run.

There were two possible escape routes. The path I normally took out of the cave led directly away from the intruder, but it funneled between two boulders that collected dry leaves. The exit would be heard.

Another path ran in a gradual descent along the ravine for a couple hundred yards before curving left and climbing back onto the plateau. There were fewer leaves, but it was exposed and meant closing the gap between me and where I had last seen the flashlight. It was the long way, and I had never taken it at night, but I didn't want to risk a chase. I crept out.

Lighter patches of sand promised silent steps under the speckled moonlight. After twenty paces, I glanced up, took one wrong step, and directly crunched a leaf.

I heard a shout. Aggressive. The flashlight clicked on. Its beam swung wildly around the cave. A few footsteps crashed through the brush, then abruptly stopped.

I bounded behind a shrub and curled into a ball. I couldn't hear over my own panting and so stuffed a handful of robe into my mouth to muffle the sound. The forest in this section was not dense, nor was I camouflaged—a white man wearing white robes with a bald head that was pouring sweat and glistening like the full moon. I tried to slow my breathing. Maybe they hadn't seen—

Deet deet! Deet deet! Deet deet—my watch alarm. It was 4:00 a.m. I smashed my hand over it. Too late. The man shouted. He sounded angry. The flashlight veered back up the path and hit my robes, and I sprang from my crouch as if I'd heard a gunshot.

I sprinted down the ravine. Rounding the turn at the bottom, I leaned sideways and pumped my fists and knees and climbed through a clearing of tall grass until I hit the plateau. On the open rock, I leaped and skidded and didn't look back. I knew the path by heart. For at least a mile, I ran for my life.

Eventually, I reached the far edge of the forest on the other side of the plateau, found the trail, and downshifted to a jog. I hadn't heard anything. Feeling out of immediate danger, I found myself loosening. I shook my arms and began laughing uncontrollably. I kept my eyes trained to the ground for snakelike shapes but felt crazed and alive and sped up on straightaways and jumped over logs. In the back of my mind, I knew I would never return to the tea cave. There was nothing I needed to retrieve or prove. I resolved to spend my final nights on the floor of the kitchen by the bookshelf. I'd take safety over honor. I had two days left, and I intended to survive them.

Dtong and Yupin helped form a plan for my departure. The following morning, I would hop in a car with some women from the village who were going to run errands in Ubon. They would drop me at Nanachat, where I'd spend the afternoon. In the evening, the guest monk could call a cab from Nanachat to the train station, where I could board a red-eye trip to Bangkok.

My bag was already packed. It had never really been unpacked, and since I'd moved out to the caves, it had sat untouched in a cranny of the library. Still, I checked the contents: flattened sneakers, rolled hiking pants, wrinkled T-shirts—all unworn. From the top pocket, I slipped out my phone and brought it to the kitchen to charge. Dtong had explained to me that there was indeed electricity at the monastery—the single kitchen outlet only worked from 6:00 a.m. to noon.

I was wary of my phone. I half expected a deluge of notifications when I returned to it fully charged after the work period, but of course, none came. Without Wi-Fi, and in spite of the fluke text from Punch Pizza months earlier, the phone was useless.

Except for the camera. I stood up, stepped off the kitchen ledge, and carried it out to the stream. Water carried soundlessly along the rock bed from one pool to the next. Still but flowing. I recalled a quote from Ajahn Chah that the mind at peace was like still, flowing water, a contradiction that, looking at the stream, I wondered if I was any closer to understanding. I had soaked my feet at this spot, aborted countless meditations, grappled with hunger, and sobbed with gratitude. I held my phone at arm's length, angled the tree and the pool and the rock into the frame, and took a picture.

The next morning, Yupin hopped down from her three-wheeled moto and waved me over.

"OK!"

I stepped out from under the kitchen roof where I'd been waiting. Pamutto and Giorgio swept the paths like it was any other morning. We'd already said our goodbyes. I lifted my backpack into the bed of Yupin's trike and climbed aboard behind her, and we sped off down the driveway. Through the village, we accelerated over potholes, past roosters, and by small fires villagers set in their front yards to burn trash. For most every alms round, I had kept my head down, and now I felt permission to let my eyes linger with curiosity and thanks on the homes that had nourished us, their cinder-block walls, tile floors, and open front doors.

We pulled up to the main road that bisected town. Our tires purred along the fresh, dark asphalt and wound to a stop. A truck was waiting: a gleaming, green, four-door Nissan, brand new. A young woman—my age, braces, wearing a sundress and wedge heels—stepped down from the driver's seat and motioned for me to throw my backpack in the bed. The back-seat window rolled down, and two more women in their fifties smiled and bowed and greeted Yupin. I stood smiling and waiting to be told what to do. The young driver knew some English and reiterated the plan to drop me at Nanachat on their way to Ubon.

Yupin checked in with me, saying, "OK?" And I realized she might not be asking if I was OK with the plan but simply if I was OK. My face must have shown what I had realized: this would be the hardest goodbye. I'd shared more time with Yupin than anyone else in the last six months. I nodded, and my eyes welled, and hers did, too, and after a couple of seconds of this, she scoffed at convention and spread her arms wide for a hug. I wasn't a monk anymore. I never really had been. We embraced, and I said, "Kop khun ka, kop khun ka"—*thank you, thank you*—but I wished I could express something stronger and so bowed to her like I would an Ajahn and pressed my palms to my chest, and she hugged me once more and said, "OK."

I climbed into the front seat, turning back and waving. Yupin waved, too, then spun her trike around and headed back toward Poo Jom Gom, back to prepare another day's meal.

On the road, the driver told me in broken English that she was a student at nursing school. Each time she smiled, she grew self-conscious and closed her mouth over her braces. The two in the back seat chuckled back and forth and asked me what I thought of Thai people, and I said *jai dee*, "kind," and that was about all we could say to each other, so they laughed and returned to chatting between themselves. The driver hummed along to a CD she had slid into the dashboard. KIDZ BOP, covers of '90s American boy-band hits sung by a chorus of children. I might've considered the soundtrack to be a torture on par with the never-ending loop of a commercial from the bus trip across Thailand six months earlier, but now I couldn't help but chuckle at the futility of my fight for the fantasy of rustic purity. I'd been outside Poo Jom Gom for hardly five minutes, and already I was enveloped in the modern, globalized world, speeding in a Japanese car down a straightaway that had been cut through high forest, reclining in a heated seat.

The driver grabbed her phone from the console, unlocked it, and began swiping with her thumb. I leaned back farther and glanced at the speedometer: sixty-five kilometers per hour. Then up to seventy, then seventy-five. She kept looking down. I straightened. My hand crept over to the door handle and gripped it. When she finally looked up, she let her foot off the gas, and I let out a long exhale.

She asked for my full name. I told her, then immediately wished I hadn't because she looked back down at her phone, and I saw she was on Facebook, searching for me.

She had spelled it wrong and asked for it again.

I winced and took a deep breath. As I spelled my last name, she dropped her other hand from the wheel so that she could type with both thumbs.

I couldn't handle it. I reached out to offer to take the phone and do the typing myself, but she turned the screen toward me.

"You?" she said.

I'd forgotten what my profile picture was, and for a moment, I didn't recognize myself: a portrait in front of an ivy-covered wall with animations overlaid from the time a friend had hacked my account and doctored the photo as a prank, but then I'd never cared to change it. Cartoon sunglasses covered my eyes. Bubblegum-pink block letters ran across my forehead, saying, "Smooch!" There was an emoji of a turd with eyelashes and a pink bow.

"Yeah," I said. "That's me."

She friend-requested me.

"Great," I said. The task was done.

But then she asked if I could accept the request on my phone. Right now.

"I don't have service," I said.

She turned toward me, hurt, and kept her gaze on me, off the road.

"No service." I held out my hands in helplessness. "I will, though. I will. Later. Later," I promised and pointed her attention back to the road.

Soon the county highway expanded into six unmarked lanes. A familiar sight. I recognized the visa office where I'd gotten my first renewal stamps. So when we passed it, I also knew we had missed the turn for Nanachat. After a minute, the women in back were leaning forward, speaking to the driver, and pointing backward. They knew we'd missed the turn, too.

The driver said, "Ah," pulled onto the shoulder of the highway, and stopped. I thought we might pause here to discuss directions, but she kept the car in drive, then accelerated into a sweeping arc, whipping a U-turn across all six lanes of two-way traffic.

In the distance, I heard screeching. The sound continued for so long that I had time to consciously wonder, before we got hit, whether we were about to get in an accident. The truck jolted and spun. The seat belt turned to stone around my shoulder and hips, and my head bounced forward off the seat. The rubber tires grabbed the asphalt when we landed, halting our rotation and setting the rest of the truck rocking back and forth.

We were sitting in the middle of the highway. *Don't unbuckle,* I thought, and turned back to see if there was more oncoming traffic. Through the back window I saw a mess of automobiles, stopped, parked at diagonals, some people already standing outside with the doors open, all looking in our direction. Then I saw the two women in the back seat covered in blood. One was unconscious, and her neck was limp and her mouth made gurgling sounds. The other groaned like she was waking up from a bad dream, reached to her forehead, and touched a lump that was already the size of a grapefruit. No seat belts.

The driver was crying. I opened the door and stepped out into the sun, holding out my hands for balance in case shock had so far concealed some injury. I found the back door to help the unconscious woman. Her limp body was bent sideways. Her head, when I touched it, was burning hot and drenched in sweat. I held it steady. *Immobilize the spine,* I had learned in wilderness medicine. But I had no idea if I was helping. I wasn't in the wilderness anymore.

A white minivan with red crosses on all sides appeared, an ambulance. People in white rushed over to the back seat. I stepped back and saw the truck's new shape. Its rectangular bed had been smooshed into a triangle. The driver tiptoed out from the other side, moving without a purpose, her hands upturned as if they were wet and she was looking for a place to dry them.

We locked eyes. She squared herself to me, pointed, and yelled, "Go!"

"What?" I said. "No. We need to—"

She stomped her wedge heel and threw her finger to the wind and screamed it again.

I held my hands up and backed away. Then I realized my backpack wasn't in the truck bed. I weaved through the crowd of cars and motos and bystanders to where the gravel shoulder shrugged into dry grass. There, thirty yards away, was my pack, dusty, scuffed, but fine. Hoisting it up, I made my way back toward the truck, hoping the driver had cooled off, but when she saw me returning, she started yelling and pointing away again.

It felt wrong to leave, but with her shouting at me, it felt more wrong to stay. A tuk-tuk had pulled over nearby, a three-wheeled trike like Yupin's except covered by a metal cage. The operator leaned against the side. I figured he would refuse me a ride because I'd been involved. Maybe I was supposed to stay and give someone a report. But when I approached, he motioned me into the back. I said, "Wat Pah Nanachat," and he nodded as if it were obvious.

All of a sudden, I was back on the highway. Leaving the scene. Alive. In shock. We made a three-point turn on the shoulder, and I gripped the metal roll bars as he headed the wrong way up the highway, weaving through the crowd of stopped vehicles.

He eased the tuk-tuk over into the left lanes, past the visa office, and onto the road toward Nanachat. I was acutely aware that tuk-tuks lack seat belts, and at every noise, I jerked to locate its source, as if seeing something coming would prevent it from happening. With each turn of my head, a stiffness spread down my neck. By the time we approached Nanachat, I couldn't turn without rotating my entire torso.

Before I knew it, he had pulled up to the monastery gate, I'd paid, and he'd left. For a few minutes, I stood breathing at the entrance with my backpack on the ground, feeling myself again on the knife edge between monastic life and the outside world. Now unable to swing the pack up onto my knotted shoulders, I cradled it to my chest like a baby and entered Nanachat for the last time.

As usual, no one welcomed me at the end of the winding driveway. But it didn't matter. I welcomed the place. I dropped the pack in the kitchen dorm and made a beeline for the woods. I first thought of going to the forest sala, to the skeleton and the small glass case with the child preserved in formaldehyde, but when I got there, I found I needed to stay in motion. If I stopped, I might fall apart.

The stillness of midday had descended. There was no holiday, no crowd, no breeze. The meal had come and gone. After the open highway and the sun and the dust and the engines and the crash, I felt at home again among quiet shades of green. It was amazing, when I thought about it, that I hadn't already died in a car accident at some point. Moving cars were always inches away from death, and I blasted music and texted at stoplights. And that was when I was alone. I remembered the road trips the Frisbee team would take in college, a caravan of borrowed cars packed to the brim with boys and snacks and duffel bags, weed hidden in a box of Triscuits between the cardboard and the plastic. Once a year, the whole team drove straight through the night from Minnesota to Texas, where we squeezed thirty boys into a rental house that slept ten, covering every square foot with sleeping pads. Spring break. We practiced at whatever fields we could find and partied before the weekend competition, a tournament against teams from all over the country whose members spent the week doing the same thing as us.

We drove a thousand miles down I-35, a drive that symbolized the thaw of spring. We took turns behind the wheel, told stories, played hot seat. The tournament was our time to don the white tees from Target we'd bought in bulk, spray-painted with stencils derived from inside jokes, and ripped the sleeves off in feverish anticipation of grass and sun and dirt. The drive south was our winter migration from trudging in down coats through zero-degree darkness to Sunday-night track workouts and 6:00 a.m. indoor practices.

Before winter finally broke in Minnesota, tournaments gave windows of relief. Another was in California in February, and we persuaded friends to shuttle us up to the Minneapolis airport, cramming again into those cars, pressing our knees against one another in the back seat. We knew each other's ailments and inquired after sore calves and twisted ankles. We gave each other massages because we weren't the kind of sport that had funding to hire someone but also because we liked doing it ourselves, knowing each other in this physical way. We trained our bodies, threw them, admired them, ignored and disrespected them, assumed in our youth that they would do whatever we asked of them, and we were usually right. To compete was to inhabit the space between head and earth. We loved it, and we loved each other, hugged each other, and sometimes, in drunk moments, kissed each other, often for laughs at a party, or else on a dare in a messy, aggressive way, like warriors showing how far we were willing to go for one another. We shouted that we didn't give a *fuck*, and of course, the opposite was true.

Our language consisted of distilled phrases that were meaningless to outsiders: ribbings, well-known tales that were passed down from one generation to the next that half the team could and would interrupt in the retelling to add their own color and flourish. Maybe James and the guys were telling a story when they pulled out of campus and onto Highway 52 the night of the accident. Maybe they were laughing and turning up the music when the 4Runner hit ice and slid into an eighteen-wheeler and three of them died.

Two lived: a young player and the driver, one of those friends who had offered to drop them at the airport. The next day, I had visited those two in the ICU of Hennepin County Medical Center. I brought flowers and talked in the hallway with the parents of the driver. He was sleeping, they said, sitting in chairs they had brought outside his room, almost like they were guarding the entrance, and I could see in their red, crumpled foreheads shock and fear and something like anger. Their son had been driving, and he had lived. I knelt at their feet, so I wasn't above them, and handed them the flowers and told them I loved them even though I'd never met them and that there was nothing but love for them from us all, and that I was so, so, so sorry. Or something like that. I blacked out parts and only remember next walking outside toward my own car on the salt-crusted sidewalk, calling my mom, and making noises I had never made before in public.

I had taken a few days off work, but then, too soon, I'd donned my suit and tie again and flown to another hospital, this one in Indiana. They were all the same. The hotel lobbies and airport bathrooms and ICUs were indistinguishable in every city, and I knew then that I couldn't keep looking at spreadsheets and trying to convince people I knew what I was talking about. So one night I drove back to my hotel at fifteen under the speed limit and sat alone with the lights out and bought a one-way flight to Thailand.

And now I was done. My six months were up.

Word spread around Nanachat about the accident. An Ajahn I remembered from my early days at Poo Jom Gom—the jolly old monk from Michigan—invited me into the office. He was the interim abbot while the others were traveling. Josh was also away, living with a senior monk in another hermitage.

He asked how my neck was and told me they'd arrange for a taxi to take me to the train station that evening. Then he trailed off and took me in.

"That accident," he said, "good reminder of the transience of all things, huh?"

"Shyea, Jesus," I said.

"I spoke with Yupin," he said. "They were worried about you. They took the one woman to the hospital. She's stable."

"Good," I said.

"It *will* be an adjustment out there," he said. "Keep your balance. Keep practicing. And remember!" He wagged a finger at me. "Don't go falling in love! Falling in love is suffering. *Young* people do that."

He laughed. I grinned but made no promises.

Outside the office, a friend was waiting. Yanissaro, the young American monk, smiled at me from behind his thick-frame glasses.

"You're back," he said.

"Yeah."

"And you're leaving," he said.

"Also yeah."

"And you got in a wreck? Talk about a rude awakening." He held out a small glass cylinder with a tin lid. "Here," he said. "It's like Tiger Balm. Come with me."

I followed behind him, grateful for someone to be with. We curled behind the office, down a familiar path, then turned off onto a thin trail I hadn't seen before. Behind a dense section of trees was a small building with a screened-in porch. Yanissaro propped the screen door open and gestured to the two front steps with a kind smile and a tilt of his head.

"Sit," he said.

I sat on the lower stair, with him behind me on the higher one. He spread the menthol balm across my neck and set his thumbs to pressing and sliding. He asked no questions, made no suggestions, let me simply breathe under his hands.

After a while, he patted my shoulder once and said, "Break."

I raised my head and thanked him, and we sat on the porch steps facing the woods and talked about a dream he'd recently had about being visited in his kuti by an alien on a Harley. He had drawn a cartoon of it, actually, he said, and pulled a comic strip from his mesh bag. I studied the panels, feeling amused and confused and touched that he would show me something so personal.

"I used to have grand aspirations for this," he said. "Before I ordained, at least. I don't really show these to anybody. Not exactly what we're supposed to be doing here . . . drawing . . . but . . . seems harmless enough."

I tried to shrug and winced. "I hope so," I said. "I've put a lot of dreams on paper, too."

"Anyway," he said, twisting open the tin of balm. "Round two."

"You sure?" I said.

"Yeah, man. Your neck got rocked. Besides"—he turned his hands upward—"my schedule's free."

I faced the forest and paused for a moment to take it in. I let my eyes climb the columns of trunks and the branches shaped like buttresses until they rested on the leafy vault overhead. Then I shut them as my friend spread the pungent balm and began rolling his thumbs down my spine. I slipped out of my sandals, nestled my bare feet into the cool pebbles of the path, and rocked gently to the undulations of his hands. Then I bowed forward, head toward heart, exhaling whispered prayers, inhaling the cold, burning scent.

EPILOGUE

Before I left for Thailand, the craving for a rite of passage was as vague as it was intense. Surely, I assumed, *some* light would shine at the end of the tunnel. What I didn't understand was that I'd really only wanted a tunnel—the privacy of darkness, the comfort of direction. To emerge, then, was to lose my bearing. When I left monastic life, I encountered a whole new world that demanded as much adjusting as entering had in the first place.

I folded my robes and left them above the Nanachat kitchen in a bin, where they waited for the next man. I put on my hiking pants and tennis shoes and took a cab to the Ubon train station, where I hunkered in an empty waiting room with pink walls and paintings of the king. I felt shy. Rather than exploring the station, I meditated for three hours until the overnight train arrived. On my way to board, I did indulge in one treat, a pack of twenty dried bananas, all of which I ate in my top bunk on the sleeper train, marveling at the layers of luxury: a real mattress, clean sheets, a temperature-controlled car gliding on steel rails through the night.

Early on at Nanachat, I had been pleased to learn it was customary for young Thai men to spend a few months in a monastery to be considered fit for marriage. The notion jibed with my aspirations for a life-altering journey, suggesting that afterward, somehow, I would be officially, unequivocally different. Not fit for marriage—that part I interpreted as a symbolic placeholder, merely representing growth.

Never did I imagine that monastic training would, in fact, prepare me for exactly that. It took spurring myself to the ideal of supreme self-sufficiency for me to see that such a thing was a mirage and that, in the end, I didn't really want it.

I met MJ in the outskirts of Bangkok at sunrise the next morning. In the doorway of her Airbnb, we hugged for a full minute, finally separating so that we could see each other and say something. But we could only take turns inhaling, shrug as we found no words, and fall into laughter. That afternoon, I suggested we visit the mega-monastery where Pamutto had first ordained, which was called Dhammakaya and was a world away from the last six months. It felt bigger and busier than the international airport beside it. We stopped at a grocery store, and I pulled over in the produce aisle and sobbed at the luxury and burden of so much choice. On the cab ride back that evening, we touched vermilion zones for the first time.

We took a train north to a town called Pai, ate street food, and got violently ill. For a week, we baked inside a thatched-roof hut the size of a kuti, rotating between the toilet and the bed, spewing out of both ends and falling deeper in love by the minute.

We flew south and scuba dived. Underwater, we breathed slowly and communicated with our hands, skills that happened to prepare us for our third week together, a seven-day silent meditation retreat. During breaks, we went off by ourselves to a bench on a hillside overlooking the ocean, beckoning to each other with our eyes, refusing to break our oaths of silence. Outside the meditation hall, I left little notes and wildflowers in MJ's sandals for her to later discover. One day I found a note from her in my sandal that I will cherish forever, which read, "If we don't get some bug spray, I'm gonna fucking lose it."

Ajahn Sukhito had once said, "Many partners, not so simple. One partner, more simple. Zero partners, the most simple." In my head I had swung, as I often did, from one extreme to the other, from the ideal of everything to that of nothing, neglecting the richness of the middle.

For our last remaining days in Thailand, MJ and I retired to a quiet beach on the island Koh Phangan. We lay in the shade of palm trees and agreed then and there that, while crazy, we were going to move in together. We had only been traveling for three weeks, but we knew we were going to get married.

And a few years later, we would. In addition to having a family ceremony, MJ would spend a week at an all-female monastery and ask the head nun to give us a marriage blessing when I picked her up. The nun, Ayya Anandabodhi, would sit before us in the small sala, backed by a statue not of the Buddha but his aunt, Mahapajapati Gotami, the first female monastic, who had been refused ordination by the Buddha but had gone ahead and ordained herself anyway. Gotami's image would feel like an appropriate audience for the blessing of our union. Anandabodhi, too, would be a fitting officiant, a model of severity and softness. She would tie yellow bracelets around my and MJ's wrists, telling us that celibacy wasn't the only sacred way of living, and in so doing, point me toward integrating my past with my future.

But for the time being, MJ and I reclined on the beach of Koh Phangan and tentatively settled on moving to California. I'd read my rejection message from the Foreign Service, and it dawned on me that if I wasn't a monk, I'd have to find a job.

I wondered aloud if the Bay Area might be the perfect place to bridge our spiritual and professional lives. I wanted something enlightened. It being 2015, I thought of a place like Google. They offered seminars on meditation, and their motto was "Don't Be Evil," which sounded to me a lot like the Buddhist precept of nonharm. A job there might offer passion and prestige, a salary and salvation. I wanted it all, a desire that, somehow, didn't strike me as familiar. But that trap would be another story. MJ and I fell silent and listened to the waves lap the sand, content to imagine our present bliss extending into the future in a line as clean and far-reaching as the ocean horizon before us.

ACKNOWLEDGMENTS

I imagined that writing a book, like living in a monastery, would be a solitary endeavor. I was wrong. While both involved periods of solitude, neither would've been possible without a long list of venerable people.

To MJ, you took this book to a level I never could have alone. For three years, I toiled without reading you a single word, knowing that when I did, you'd bring the same narrative intelligence that allows you to fast-forward ten seconds during all but the best TV shows, a practice that irked me until I began to understand your uncanny eye for spotting lags in a story. Thank you for your generous attention and creative heart. Thank you for giving so much of your time and body for us to raise our sweet child, Reggie. Thank you for encouraging me toward art. Your bravery to speak up and dig deep inspires me to try the same. I love you and can't wait to read your book.

Mom, thank you for your love of language and of me. Dad, thank you for your encouragement to nourish my spirit and explore masculinity. Camille, thank you for your companionship and nuanced balance of validation and challenge.

Thank you to all those who have supported my monastic sojourns. The Carleton College Career Center, in particular Brent Nystrom and Jess Mueller, encouraged and funded my first foray into monastic life in 2011 as well as the first piece of writing I published in the *Voice* about exploring monastic life. Ajahn Chandako received me as a college senior at Vimutti Monastery in New Zealand and planted seeds that continue to grow; Ajahns Amaro and Pasano allowed me to stay at Abhayagiri in Northern California; Ajahns Sirripañño and Kevali let me stay at Wat Pah Nanachat, and Ajahn Sukhito took me in at Wat Pah Poo Jom Gom; Ayya Anandabodhi allowed me to visit Aloka Vihara, where she blessed my marriage. To these elders and all the other practitioners in and beyond the Thai Forest Tradition who have shared their wisdom, humor, and presence—Ajahn Sumedho, Ajahn Jayasaro, Yupin, Pamutto, Bada, Giorgio, Barry, Alexi, Steven, Josh, and every villager and layperson surrounding each of the aforementioned monasteries who keep them running with constant generosity, or *dana*—thank you.

The Pacific University Master of Fine Arts in Writing program provided invaluable support and community. Mike Magnuson was a stalwart, offering navigation away from the whirlpools of perfectionism that could've stalled progress on the first draft. Joe Millar helped me understand the importance of balancing thought with feeling and image. Ellen Bass modeled power, logic, and syntax, as well as how to set a container for effective feedback. Claire Dederer gave timely praise and ruthless insight on the importance of cutting writing that's mere "throat-clearing." Jill Deasy and Emmi Greer continue to be the kind of writing companions one dreams of befriending—honest, unflinching, and playful. Roxan McDonald gave critical feedback on the first draft. To the exquisite crew of Sorcerers and Sewers—Andy Cole, Will Long, Kathryn Herron, Brock Hummel, Samantha Kimmey—thank you, and let's keep the game alive. To Scott Korb, Chris Abani, Debra Gwartney, Kwame Dawes, Sanjiv Bhattacharya, Pete Fromm, Cate Kennedy, Valerie Laken, Dorriane Laux, Shara McCallum, and every faculty member and student who read their raw work aloud, thank you for modeling the courage and generosity it takes to share the writing process.

I'm grateful to the Ultimate Frisbee community, which, among so many other things, continues to provide friendships that I've not experienced anywhere else. Thank you to Evan Padget for the line about feeling like a pack of ham in a VCR and for showing me time and again how to tell a good story in so few words. Thank you to Isaac Saul for the impressive example of writing output, the sunrise throwing sessions and discussions at McCarren Park, and the critiques of my proposal and title. Thank you to all the following Ultimate programs I've been so fortunate to represent: Paideia School, Carleton College, Atlanta Chain Lightning, Minneapolis Sub Zero, San Francisco Revolver, and New York PoNY, as well as the national teams and those from the American Ultimate Disc League.

To the team at Girl Friday Books—Karen Upson, Kristin Mehus-Roe, Sara Addicott, Elayne Becker, Paul Barrett, Katherine Richards, and Georgie Hockett—thank you for believing in this project and making this dream of mine come true. Your counsel and collaboration have been superb. Thank you to Clete Barrett Smith for providing extensive feedback on a late draft as well as generous personal reflection on the manuscript that made me realize why I had wanted to publish this in the first place.

Finally, thank you to all those who have helped make this happen in direct and indirect ways: Pablo Rochat, Kylee Gubler, Bernie Schein, Bonnie Sparling, John Capute, Jane Pepperdene, Kasia Urbaniak, George Saunders, John Randolph, Tara Love, and Mellie Logan.

ABOUT THE AUTHOR

Photo © Kylee Gubler

Grant Lindsley is a writer in Brooklyn, New York. He encountered his first Buddhist monk as an undergraduate at Carleton College, where he majored in psychology and minored in neuroscience, because he was majorly interested in himself and minorly interested in himself on drugs. He subsequently spent months training as a monk with the Thai Forest Tradition, a sect of Theravada Buddhism that seeks to follow the exact rules of the historical Buddha from over 2,500 years ago. Lindsley has worked at NOLS and briefly worked at Google until publishing his resignation letter in the *Washington Post*. An accomplished Ultimate Frisbee player, he has won multiple national championships and two gold medals for Team USA at the World Games. He received his master of fine arts in creative nonfiction from Pacific University and his master of business administration from Cornell Tech. He enjoys pranks and being outside with his family.

CPSIA information can be obtained
at www.ICGtesting.com
Printed in the USA
JSHW081452090423
40058JS00007B/7

9 781954 854987